European Perspectives on Men and

European Perspectives on Men and Masculinities

National and Transnational Approaches

Jeff Hearn
Helsinki University, Finland

and

Keith Pringle
Aalborg Universitet, Denmark

with members of Critical Research on Men in Europe (CROME)

palgrave
macmillan

First published in hardback 2006

First published in paperback 2009 by
PALGRAVE MACMILLAN

Palgrave Macmillan in the UK is an imprint of Macmillan Publishers Limited, registered in England, company number 785998, of Houndmills, Basingstoke, Hampshire RG21 6XS.

Palgrave Macmillan in the US is a division of St Martin's Press LLC, 175 Fifth Avenue, New York, NY 10010.

Palgrave Macmillan is the global academic imprint of the above companies and has companies and representatives throughout the world.

ISBN-13: 978–1–4039–1813–0 hardback
ISBN-10: 1–4039–1813–9 hardback
ISBN-13: 978–0–230–59447–0 paperback
ISBN-10: 0–230–59447–6 paperback

This book is printed on paper suitable for recycling and made from fully managed and sustained forest sources. Logging, pulping and manufacturing processes are expected to conform to the environmental regulations of the country of origin.

A catalogue record for this book is available from the British Library.

A catalog record for this book is available from the Library of Congress.

10 9 8 7 6 5 4 3 2 1
18 17 16 15 14 13 12 11 10 09

Printed and bound in Great Britain by
CPI Antony Rowe, Chippenham and Eastbourne

Contents

List of Figure and Tables

Figure

Tables

Preface and Acknowledgements

This book has a history going back to at least 1997. It was then that it was realised that there was a need for a number of women and men researchers who had worked largely within their own national context to work with each other in a comparative, European and transnational way.

This led to the forming of the Research Network on Men in Europe in 1999, and in turn the funding of the Thematic Network on 'The Social Problem of Men: the Social Problem and Societal Problematisation of Men and Masculinities' from 2000 to 2003. The Thematic Network initially comprised researchers in ten countries (Estonia, Finland, Germany, Ireland, Italy, Latvia, Norway, Poland, Russian Federation, the UK), which in due course were augmented by four more affiliated members (Bulgaria, Czech Republic, Denmark, Sweden). This initiative was and remains part of the umbrella collective, Critical Research on Men in Europe (CROME) (www.cromenet.org).

The Network has been co-ordinated by a steering group of four principal contractors (Keith Pringle [Network Co-ordinator], Jeff Hearn, Ursula Müller, Elżbieta H. Oleksy) with an additional seven participating members (Janna Chernova, Harry Ferguson, Øystein Gullvåg Holter, Eivind Olsvik, Voldemar Kolga, Irina Novikova, Carmine Ventimiglia). We would particularly like to acknowledge the important contributions made by Janna, Øystein and Carmine in the work of the Network.

The main research assistant for the Network was Emmi Lattu, with additional part-funded research assistance by Teemu Tallberg. Eszter Belinszki, Astrid Jacobsen and Joanna Rydzewska were research assistants in Germany and Poland. Satu Liimakka carried out copy-editing work, and Hertta Niemi was a research assistant in the final stages of the project. The affiliated members of the Network have been Dimitar Kambourov, Steen Baagoe Nielsen, Marie Nordberg and Iva Šmídová.

The Network Administrator position was occupied for most of the period of the Network by Jackie Millett. She provided invaluable expert administrative support to the Network, particularly in setting up the Network's administrative and financial systems. This position has been occupied for the last part of the Network's funding by Diane McIlroy, who also provided invaluable administrative assistance.

We would also like to acknowledge a number of organisations and people whose contribution was invaluable in the processes that led to the production of this book. We are grateful to the Research Directorate of the European Commission who funded the Thematic Network (contract number HPSE-CT-1999-0008), the findings of which form the basis of the book. We are particularly grateful to Virginia Vitorino, who was the Scientific Officer for our project at the European Commission throughout the life of the Network (2000–2003); her continuous support was most valuable.

Others who have participated in the research and support work of the Network include Beata Duchnowicz, Agnieszka Dziedziczak-Foltyn, Elina Hatakka, Maj-Britt Hedvall, Joanna Kazik, Simon Kerridge, Jason Levine, Claire Mackinnon, Marczuk Magdalena, Martin Moore, Alex Raynor and Tamar Pitch. We are extremely grateful for this work. We would like to thank the many other researchers, policy-makers and practitioners who have commented on the work of the Network, and particularly Dawn Lyon and Jouni Varanka for their detailed comments. We also wish to acknowledge the valuable feedback provided to the Network by the participants who attended its two Interface Workshops in Cologne and Łódź, and the Final Conference in Helsinki. We are grateful for all these contributions. For assistance with graphics we thank Arttu Paarlahti and Paul Fogelberg.

This long, co-operative process has led to collaborative writing and publication by the members of the Network. Jeff Hearn and Keith Pringle have been the main authors of this book with additional co-writing by Harry Ferguson, Dimitar Kambourov, Joanna Kazik, Voldemar Kolga, Emmi Lattu, Ursula Müller, Hertta Niemi, Marie Nordberg, Irina Novikova, Elżbieta H. Oleksy, Iva Šmídová and Teemu Tallberg.

We have valued and continue to value all these transnational researches, networking, writing and friendships immensely.

***

Jeff Hearn would like to thank colleagues in the Swedish School of Economics (Helsinki) and Huddersfield for creating such a good working atmosphere. Significant progress on writing the book was made while at Växjö University in May–June 2004, and he would like to thank Ulla Johansson and Monika Hjeds in particular for their hospitality and discussions there. He also thanks Hans Wessels, June Butt, Trevor Butt and John Davis, for friendship and support, and especially Liisa Husu.

***

Keith Pringle would like to thank Mia Eriksson for ongoing discussions about intersectionality and men's violences. He is also grateful to colleagues and ex-colleagues at the Centre for Gender Studies, Stockholm University, Mälardalen University College and Aalborg University.

Jeff Hearn and Keith Pringle
August 2005, Helsinki and Aalborg

Members of Critical Research on Men in Europe (CROME)

Harry Ferguson is Professor of Social Work at the University of the West of England, Bristol, UK. He was previously Professor of Social Policy and Social Work at University College, Dublin. He has taught, researched and published widely on gender, men and masculinities, domestic violence and child abuse/protection and on the application of critical social theory to social policy and social work. His most recent book is *Protecting Children in Time: Child Abuse, Child Protection and the Consequences of Modernity*. He has published seven books and numerous articles and is a regular contributor to the media on issues of child and woman abuse and gender/men's issues. He has produced the first large-scale research study of gender and identity in the lives of Irish men. Other recent publications include *Keeping Children Safe: Child Abuse, Child Protection and the Promotion of Welfare*; *Changing Fathers? Fatherhood and Family Life in Modern Ireland*; 'Working with men and masculinities', *Feedback: Journal of the Family Therapy Association of Ireland*, 1998; *Protecting Irish Children: Investigation, Protection and Welfare*; *Understanding Men and Masculinities*, *Men & Intimacy*.

Jeff Hearn is Professor, Swedish School of Economics, Helsinki, Finland, Linköping University, Sweden and the University of Huddersfield, UK. He was previously Research Professor, University of Manchester, and Co-convenor of the Research Unit on Violence, Abuse and Gender Relations, University of Bradford. His current research focus is 'Men, Gender Relations and Transnational Organising, Organisations and Management'. He was Principal Contractor of the EU Framework 5 Thematic Network 'The Social Problem of Men: the Social Problem and Societal Problematisation of Men and Masculinities'. His publications include: *The Gender of Oppression*; *Men in the Public Eye*; *'Sex' at 'Work'* (with W. Parkin); *The Violences of Men*; *Gender, Sexuality and Violence in Organizations* (with W. Parkin); co-edited *The Sexuality of Organization*; *Men, Masculinities and Social Theory*; *Violence and Gender Relations*; *Men as Managers, Managers as Men*; *Men, Gender Divisions and Welfare*; *Hard Work in the Academy*; *Information Society and the Workplace*, and *Handbook of Studies on Men and Masculinities*. Other research initiatives include: co-leader, Academy of Finland-funded Sexualised Violence Research Consortium; lead partner, NorFA Nordic Research Network 'Violences, Agency Practices and Social Change'; and the EU Framework 6 Concerted Action on Human Rights Violations.

Dimitar Kambourov was born in Varna, Bulgaria. He has an MA in Bulgarian, an MA in Cultural Studies, and a Ph.D. in Literary Theory. His teaching focuses on literary theory, postmodern culture and literature, and gender at Sofia University, and literature, culture and media at the New Bulgarian University. He is an Associate Professor of Literary Theory and Programme Director of the MA in Literary Studies, at Slavic Studies, Sofia University, and part-time lecturing Professor of Literature, Culture and Media and Programme Director of the MA in Cultural and Literary Studies at New Bulgarian Studies at the New Bulgarian University. His spheres of interest are Literary Theory, Critical Theory, Modern and Postmodern Literature and Culture, Gender, Cultural Regionalism and Globalisation. His books include *Yavori i Kloni* [Sycamores and Branches]; *Bulgarska Poeticheska Classica* [Bulgarian Poetic Classics], and *Men in the Global World. Integrating Post-Socialist Perspectives* (co-editor with Irina Novikova).

Joanna Kazik is a graduate of the University of Łódź, Poland, and the University of Glasgow, UK. She is Senior Lecturer in the Department of Studies in English Drama and Poetry at the University of Łódź. Her research interests and numerous publications focus on Middle English literature, gender studies and contemporary drama. Currently, she is working on pre-modern and early modern carols.

Voldemar Kolga is Professor of Personality and Developmental Psychology, and Chair and Head of the Women's Studies Centre, Tallinn University; the Centre was founded in 1995. He is also a board member of the Estonian Women's Studies and Resource Centre (NGO). He gained a Ph.D. from St Petersburg University, Russia, 1976. His early research was on cognitive styles. His twenty years' experience of teaching has been on psychology: introductory psychology, life-span psychology, personality psychology, social psychology, critical thinking in society, history and modern psychology, Internet psychology, and aspects of introduction to women's studies (men's studies). His current research interests include: social representations of human rights, including gender issues; educational influences and infant IQ; and corporate philanthropy. His publications are mainly in Russian, Estonian and English. He is active in the media; project expert in the Soros Foundation, and the Tiger Leap Foundation infotechnology project. His books include: *Me and Human Rights; We, the World and Human Rights*; 'To be a woman and a man in Estonia at the turn of the millennium', *Towards a Balanced Society: Women and Men in Estonia*, (http://www.undp.ee/gender/); *Psychology of Personality: Western and Eastern Approaches* (with A. Kidron).

Emmi Lattu has a Masters degree in Sociology and is a doctoral student at the University of Tampere, Finland. Her research topic is women's use of physical violence in Finland. During 2000–2003 she worked as the main research assistant for the EU FP 5 Thematic Network 'The Social Problem of Men: the Social Problem and Societal Problematisation of Men and Masculinities' in the Department of Management and Organisation, Swedish School of Economics,

Helsinki, Finland. She has co-authored many articles and reports on this material in Finnish, Nordic and international journals, and co-edited in 2002 a special issue of *NORA: the Nordic Journal of Women's Studies* Vol. 10(1) on gender, men and masculinities.

Ursula Müller is Full Professor of Sociology, Women's Studies, Department of Sociology; Director of the Interdisciplinary Women's and Gender Studies Centre, University of Bielefeld, Germany. She has completed various empirical investigations on gender relations, such as *Sexuelle Belaestigung am Arbeitsplatz* (Sexual Harassment in the Workplace), 1991 (with project group) (representative survey for Germany and case studies); survey and in-depth interviews on the impact of the women's movement on German men (1986, together with Sigrid Metz-Göckel); asymmetrical gender culture in organisations (for instance, institutions of higher education, 1999); further publications on feminist methodology, psychogenetical and sociogenetical explanations on men's violence against women, gender segregation on the labour market, and other issues. She is a former Dean of the Department of Sociology, a member of Senate, University of Bielefeld; a member of the concilium of the German Sociological Association. She has Guest Professorships in Vienna (Institute for Advanced Studies) and St Petersburg State University, and is German Co-ordinator of the Socrates Women's Studies Network NOISE. She was German editor of R.W. Connell's *Masculinities* (*Der Gemachte Mann*, 1999); and Research Director of a project on organisation, professionalisation and gender within the police, and another one on diversity in German organisations. Her most recent research activity has been project director for the first large-scale German representative survey on violence against women. She is also the European co-ordinator of a Tempus-Tacis programme on Gender Studies in Higher Education which led to the institutionalisation of the first MA in Gender Studies in Russia (State University St Petersburg).

Hertta Niemi has Masters degrees in both Social Science and International Politics, and studied in Estonia and Scotland. She is a research assistant and a doctoral student, Department of Management and Organisation, Swedish School of Economics and Business Administration, Helsinki, Finland. Her work as a research assistant has entailed interviewing men and women informants on men's changing organisational practices in six European countries. Her own research area concerns political organisations, including parliament, as a gendered workplace. She has been involved in the editorial work in the collective book *Organisations in Flux?* (edited by P. Eriksson et al.), and is a co-author of *Men and Masculinities in Europe* (K. Pringle et al.).

Marie Nordberg has a doctorate in Ethnology, Göteborg University. She has contributed to several research reports and anthologies on men and masculinity and teaches at the Centre for Gender Studies, Karlstad University. Her thesis deals with men in non-traditional occupations. Marie is also involved in a Nordic project called 'Men, Welfare and Social Innovation' and in a transnational project on men, fashion and power, 'The Decorated Male'. She is an affiliated member in the Critical Research on Men in Europe (CROME) Network and has been involved in organising three Nordic research conferences on Men and Masculinities.

Irina Novikova is Professor of the Department of Culture and Literature, University of Latvia. Since 1998 she has been Director of the Centre for Gender Studies, University of Latvia. Her research and teaching interests are contemporary American women's literature; gender in urban and visual cultures; gender and genre – autobiographical forms; gender, ethnicity and citizenship. She has around 40 publications in these research areas. She is editor of the first major international Latvian-language collection on gender studies, *The Anthology of Contemporary Feminist Theories*; editor of *Too Early? Too Late? Feminist Discourses, Ideas, Languages in Latvian*; co-editor of the volume *Men in the Global World: Integrating Post-socialist Perspectives*, and author of *Gender and Genre: Women's Autobiography and Bildungsroman*. She has also translated the book by Nira Yuval-Davis *Gender and Nation* into Russian.

Elżbieta H. Oleksy is Full Professor of Humanities at the University of Łódź and the University of Warsaw, Poland. She is Dean of the Faculty of International and Political Studies and Founding Director of the Women's Studies Centre, both at the University of Łódź. She has authored, co-authored as well as edited and co-edited 17 books, for example, *Gender – Film – Media. East–West Dialogues*; *Mass Media in Civil Society. Equal Rights in Media Reporting*; *Women in Dixie's Land*; *Women's Studies around the World*; Special Issue of *Women's Studies International Forum*, and over 70 articles and book chapters on cultural studies and feminism published in Europe, the USA and Australia. She is the President of the Council of the Association of Institutions for Feminist Education and Research in Europe (AOIFE), and Polish representative of the Women's International Studies Europe (WISE). She is Expert of the European Commission for Women in Science in the countries of East Central Europe and the Baltic States. She has co-ordinated a number of international projects funded by TEMPUS-PHARE, the United Nations Development Programme and the British Council. She is Polish representative of the Socrates Women's Studies Network NOISE and the Socrates Thematic Network ATHENA II. She chairs the University of Łódź Accreditation and Quality Assurance Committee. Her research interests concentrate on issues of gender in cultural studies, especially film and television.

Keith Pringle is Professor in Social Work at Aalborg University, Denmark; Honorary Professor at Warwick University, UK, and Guest Professor in Social Research at Mälardalen University College, Sweden. He was Co-ordinator of the EU Framework 5 Thematic Network 'The Social Problem of Men: the Social Problem and Societal Problematisation of Men and Masculinities', a managing partner in a EU-funded comparative research project entitled 'Hearing the Voices Of Refugees in Policy and Practice in the European Union', and is currently involved in two Nordic Council of Ministers-funded research networks. He has co-ordinated a sub-network on men's practices within the EU-funded Framework 6 Co-ordinated Actions on Human Rights. He has previously held Guest Professorships at Uppsala University, Stockholm University and the Baltic and East European Graduate School at Södertörns University College. His research areas include: comparative welfare, gender, child welfare, racism. His most recent major publications include: (co-editor) *A Man's World? Changing Men's Practices in a Globalised World*; (co-author) *Through Two Pairs of Eyes: a Comparative Study of Danish Social Policy and Child Welfare*; (author) *Children and Social Welfare in Europe*; (co-editor) *Protecting Children in Europe: Towards a New Millennium*; (author) *Men, Masculinities and Social Welfare*. He is co-editor of *Tackling Men's Violence in Families – Nordic Issues and Dilemmas*, and is currently co-editing the *Routledge International Encyclopaedia of Men and Masculinities*.

Iva Šmídová has focused on the topic of Men's Studies from the early 1990s. In her MA thesis and later in her Ph.D. studies in Sociology (completed in 2004) she worked on a qualitative research project on Different Men in the Czech Republic (Alternative Lifestyles connected to environment protection). On her visiting fellowship at the New School for Social Research, New York (1997–8) she developed curricula for gender courses that she has taught since then. She co-ordinated a series of seminars on gender for teachers, was a grant co-ordinator of a research project on equal opportunities of women and men in employment (1999–2002, Open Society Fund), and co-founder of the Gender Centre at the School (www.fss.muni.cz/gender). Since September 2001 she has worked full-time at the Department of Sociology, Faculty of Social Studies, Masaryk University in Brno, Czech Republic. In January 2005 she was appointed Head of the Gender Studies Programme there.

Teemu Tallberg has a Masters degree in Social Science and is a Ph.D. student at the Department of Management and Organisation, Swedish School of Economics, Helsinki, Finland. He has previously worked there as a research assistant on two projects: the EU FP 5 Thematic Network 'The Social Problem of Men: the Social Problem and Societal Problematisation of Men and Masculinities', and 'Men, Gender Relations and Transnational Organising, Organisations and Managements'. The latter led to co-authored publications including *Gender Divisions and Gender Policies in Top Finnish Corporations*. He has also co-authored a report on property crime, and has a publication on representations of men in educational films used by the Finnish Defence Forces in the training of conscripts (STAKES, 2003). He is currently studying men's networks and gendered power in organisations.

1
Studying Men in Europe

Jeff Hearn and Keith Pringle

Introduction

Men have long dominated public, and indeed also private, agendas. Much of what is called politics, research and public discourse more generally has been centrally about men, often overwhelmingly so – an unnamed, obvious but strangely invisible, process – an absent presence.[1] Men, masculinity and men's powers and practices have typically been taken-for-granted. Gender has largely been seen as a matter of and for women; men were generally seen as ungendered, natural or naturalised.

This state of affairs is now changing to some extent; it is much less the case than the recent past. There has been the gradually growing realisation that men and masculinities are just as gendered as are women and femininities. Over the last twenty years or so men, that is, both the embodied collectivity of men and the topic of 'men', have become more explicit subjects within growing political, media, academic and policy debates throughout most countries of Europe. Recent years have seen the *naming of men as men* (Hanmer, 1990; Collinson and Hearn, 1994). Now, in many European countries hardly a day goes by without aspect of men's position or experience or life figuring in the mass media. In some respects this process of making men explicit is *not* totally new, as there have indeed been previous historical periods of public discussion and debate on men and masculinity, particularly at times of rapid social change and gender challenge from women.[2]

What is newer, however, is that these debates, particularly academic debates, are now more explicit, more gendered, more diverse, and sometimes more critical. The growth of interest in the study of men and masculinities, both in Europe and beyond, derives from several directions and traditions. This gendering of men is both a matter of changing academic and political analyses of men in society, and contemporary changes in the form of men's own lives, experiences and perceptions, often developing counter to their earlier expectations and earlier generations of men. In particular there has been a substantial development of critical studies on men and masculinities in Europe.

This chapter introduces recent developments in studying men, and the social, political and academic contexts that inform them. It describes the work of the 14-nation Research Network on Men in Europe, from whose collaborative research this book arises, and the comparative and transnational analytical frames of reference for studying men in Europe.

Social change – or no change?

These various focused debates and studies on men can be seen very much as part of more general social changes in gender relations in society. Throughout much of Europe contemporary gender relations can be characterised by relatively rapid change in certain respects, for example, rates of separation and divorce, and changing employment patterns, alongside the persistence of long-term historical structures and practices, such as men's domination of top management, men's propensity to use violence and commit crime, and so on. This can thus be understood as a combination of contradictory social processes of change and no change (Hearn, 1999a).

The social transformations, restructuring and change within Europe have many facets. They include men's relations to:

- economy and technology: with transformations away from primary and secondary employment towards tertiary and quaternary employment;
- nation, race and ethnicity: with the growth of multiculturalism, new nationalisms, new racisms, and cultural and religious backlashes;
- demography, health and the life course: with the ageing of the male population;
- family, households, children, fatherhood: with changing forms of living arrangements away from the nuclear family;
- education: with the recognition of some boys' and young men's relative lack of educational achievement;
- personal life: with the changing forms of men's patterns of consumption;
- sexuality: with the gradually increasing recognition of gay rights, increasing public debate on sexuality, and also growing sexualisation in mainstream culture;
- violences: with gradually increasing recognition of men's violences to women, children and other men, even though such violences seem remarkably resistant to change.

A number of social changes now seem to be in place whereby men and masculinities can be talked about as problematic. We can now, at least, ask such questions as: What is a man? How do men maintain power? Is there a crisis of masculinity? Or is there a crisis of *men* in a more fundamental way? Do we know what the future of men looks like or should be? What policy and practice implications follow both in relation to men and boys, and for men and boys?

The making of men more gendered, in both theory and practice, has meant that previously taken-for-granted powers and authority of men, social practices of men, and ways of being men can now be considered to be much more problematic. They may not yet be much more negotiable, but they are at least now recognised as more open to debate. The paradox is that men and masculinities are now more talked about than ever before when it is much less clear what and how they are or should become.

Social and political contexts

Among the several influences that have brought this focus on men and masculinities, first and foremost is the impact of Second, and now Third Wave Feminisms. Questions have been asked by feminists and feminisms about all aspects of men and men's actions. Men have always been on feminist agendas. For example, Hanmer (1990, 39–41) lists 56 feminist publications 'providing the ideas, the changed consciousness of women's lives and their relationship to men – all available by 1975'. In the 1980s there were further feminist empirical studies of men (for example, Cockburn, 1983, 1991; Metz-Göckel and Müller, 1986), theoretical consolidations regarding men (for example, O'Brien, 1981; hooks, 1984) and feminist (for example, Friedman and Sarah, 1982) or mixed (for example, Jardine and Smith, 1987; Chapman and Rutherford, 1988; Hearn and Morgan, 1990) conference debates on men.

Different feminist initiatives have focused on different aspects of men and suggested different analyses of men and different ways forward for men. This has been well represented in feminist debates (for example, Hanmer, 1990; Segal, 1990; Schacht and Ewing, 1998; Adams and Savran, 2002; Gardiner, 2002). The form that feminism has taken in Europe is more diverse, in terms of different national contexts, but overall there has been a closer relation between feminist movements and the state and state reform than has been the case in the US. More generally, feminism has also demonstrated many theoretical and practical lessons for men, though men seem to keep ignoring or forgetting most of them. One of the most fundamental is that the understanding of gender relations, women and men has to involve attention to questions of power. Another is that to transform gender relations, and specifically men's continued dominance of many social arenas, means not only changes in what women do and what women are but also that men will have to change too. This lesson is hard for many men to hear, even harder to act on. These insights have led to what might be called the power perspective on men, masculinities and men's practices, with vital implications for politics, policy development and personal practice.

A second factor focusing attention on men and masculinities has been some men's specific and explicit relations and responses to feminism (for example, Brod, 1987; Connell, 1987, 1995; Hearn, 1987, 1992; Kimmel, 1987; Brittan, 1989; Holter, 1997; Messner, 1997; Digby, 1998). These include those that are specifically profeminist or anti-sexist; there is also work that is ambiguous in relation to feminism or even anti-feminist in perspective. Western men's responses to feminism have been various, and also uneven throughout Europe. Since the early 1970s there have been, in various Western countries, 'anti-sexist men' and 'profeminist men', followed in the 1980s by the media creation of 'new men' and by 'wild men' or 'mythopoetic men'. The last two categorisations, imported from the US, have had an uneven presence, with, for example, greater relative impact in parts of the Nordic region than the more urbanised UK. The 1990s brought 'newish man', 'new lads', 'men's rightists', and even 'post new men'. In many different ways and in many different countries and contexts, other more composite groups and categories of men have identified as men, such as, 'older anti-sexist men' and 'black gay men'.

Third, other forces for change include gay movements, queer politics, other 'new sexual movements', and the proliferation of sexual discourses (for example, Weeks, 1977/1997; Plummer, 1981, 1992). These have been especially important in the larger urban centres, such as Amsterdam, Berlin, London and Manchester, and less so in the rural regions of Europe. While it is difficult to generalise about these critiques, they emphasise the desirability of (some) men to each other, the more public recognition of men through same-sex desire, and the associated or implied critique of heterosexual men's practices. They thus both complement and sometimes conflict with some feminist analyses (Edwards, 1990).

There is also a range of other critical, more or less gendered, perspectives that have directly or indirectly problematised understandings of men and masculinities. These include postcolonialism, studies on race and racism, poststructuralism, postmodernism, and globalisation studies.

Critical approaches to men's practices

The variety of disciplinary and methodological frameworks available for the study of men, masculinities and men's practices include approaches from: biology, stressing sex differences; essentialism searching for the 'real' masculine; sex/gender role theory; gender-specific socialisation and identity formation; history; anthropology and cross-cultural studies; the range of feminist theories; patriarchy theory; conceptualisations of multiple masculinities and hegemonic masculinity; focus on habitus; gay theory; queer theory; social constructionism and discourse theory; deconstruction; postmodernism; postcolonialism; and transnational globalised conceptualisations; as well as a host of perspectives in cultural, literary, visual and aesthetic theory within the humanities.

There are tensions between approaches that stress gender dichotomy and inevitability to gender adversities, as against those that emphasise change, processuality, flexibility and self-reflection for different genders. There are also variations in the extent to which these studies take a critical stance towards men and masculinities, between the development of feminist/pro-feminist Critical Studies on Men (Hearn, 1997), as opposed to the much more ambiguous and sometimes even anti-feminist activities of 'Men's Studies', which can become defined in a much less critical way as 'by men, on men, for men'. In this sense Critical Studies on Men are part of the broader project of Women's Studies and Gender Research, rather than competitive with them.

Having said that, there are, in some senses, as many ways of studying men as there are approaches to social science. They range from analysis of masculine psychology and psychodynamics (Craib, 1987) to broad societal, structural and collective analyses of men (Walby, 1986, 1990; Hearn, 1987, 1992; Hanmer, 1990). Increasingly, they have interrogated different masculinities in the plural, not the singular – hegemonic, complicit, subordinated, marginalised, resistant (Cockburn, 1983, 1991; Carrigan et al., 1985; Westwood, 1990; Connell, 1987, 1995; Pringle 1995) – and the interrelations of unities and differences between men (Hearn and Collinson, 1994). They have included, on the one hand, detailed ethnographic descriptions of particular men's activity and the construction of specific masculinities in specific discourses (Edley and Wetherell, 1995; Wetherell and Edley, 1999), and, on the other, analyses of men and masculinities within a global context (Connell, 1993, 1998; Hearn, 1996a; Pease and Pringle, 2001).

The approach adopted in this book argues for international, transnational (rather than national or regional), interdisciplinary Critical Studies on Men (CSM) (Hearn, 1997, 2004a): that is, *historical, cultural, relational, materialist, deconstructive, anti-essentialist* studies on men (see, for example, Connell et al., 2005). CSM examine men as part of historical gender relations, through a wide variety of analytical and methodological tools and approaches. The notion of men is social and not to be essentialised and reified, as in some versions of the equivocal term 'men's studies'. Men are understood as historical, cultural and changeable, both as a social category and in particular constructions.

CSM are: on men; explicitly gendered; critical; by women and men, separately or together. They seek to present critical, explicitly gendered accounts, descriptions and explanations of men in their social contexts and contextualisations. These kinds of debates have been studied in different disciplinary contexts and traditions – sociology, social psychology, social policy, political science, literature, cultural studies, and so on. While much of the initial initiatives has come from the those scholars studying social institutions in society, more recently there has also been a major growth of attention in similar questions within cultural studies, literature, and the arts, with an emphasis on semiotic and poststructuralist approaches.

Internationally, CSM has been something of a relative 'success story' in the 1990s though work has been growing since at least the 1970s. There are now various established academic journals, such as *Men and Masculinities*, and various book series. The study of men and masculinities is no longer considered so esoteric, as it was, say, twenty years ago. It is established, if often rather tentatively, for teaching and research in different localities of Europe. While it has examined boys' and men's lives in schools, social welfare institutions, families, management, the military and elsewhere, many aspects remain relatively unexplored. As research has progressed, it has become more complex, and concerned less with one 'level' of analysis, and more with linking previously separated fields and approaches.

There has been a particularly strong emphasis within CSM on the *interconnections* of gender with other social divisions, such as age, class, disability, ethnicity, racialisation and sexuality. The idea that the gender of men is derived from any kind of fixed, inner trait or core is especially antagonistic to CSM. There are also well-established arguments within CSM that men's gendered relations of and to power are complex, and even contradictory (see, for example, several chapters in Brod and Kaufman, 1994). For example, the collective, historical power of men may be understood as maintained by the dispensability of some men, for example, as soldiers in war (Hearn, 1987), even with the violence to, and killing of, women and children, usually as non-combatants.

Critical Studies on Men have brought the theorising of men and masculinities into sharper relief, making men and masculinities *explicit objects* of theory and critique. Among the many areas of current debate, we would draw attention to three particular sets of questions that have preoccupied researchers: the concept of patriarchy; similarities and differences between men and between masculinities; and men's, or male, sexualities and subjectivities (Collinson and Hearn, 1994). In each case, there are tensions between generalisations about men and masculinity and specificities of men and masculinities.

More specifically, the notion of hegemonic masculinity was developed in the late 1970s and early 1980s, as part of the critique of sex role theory (Eichler, 1980). In a key 1985 article Carrigan, Connell and Lee wrote:

> What emerges from this line of argument [on the heterosexual-homosexual ranking of masculinity] is the very important concept of *hegemonic masculinity*, not as 'the male role', but as a particular variety of masculinity to which others – among them young and effeminate as well as homosexual men – are subordinated. It is particular groups of men, not men in general, who are oppressed within patriarchal sexual relations, and whose situations are related in different ways to the overall logic of the subordination of women to men. A consideration of homosexuality thus provides the beginnings of a dynamic conception of masculinity as a structure of social relations. (p. 586: emphasis in original)

In the book *Masculinities*, Connell (1995) discusses and applies the notion of hegemonic masculinity in more depth. He reaffirms earlier discussions of the link with Gramsci's analysis of economic class relations through the operation of cultural dynamics, and also notes that hegemonic masculinity is always open to challenge and possible change. Hegemonic masculinity is now defined slightly differently as follows as:

> . . . the configuration of gender practice which embodies the currently accepted answer to the problem of legitimacy of patriarchy, which guarantees (or is taken to guarantee) the dominant position of men and the subordination of women. (p. 77)

Masculinities operate in the context of patriarchy or patriarchal relations. The notion of patriarchy is understood in this context not simply in its literal sense of rule of the father or fathers, but more generally as men's structural dominance in society. The development of a dynamic conception of masculinities can itself be understood as part of the feminist and gendered critique of any monolithic conception of patriarchy, that was developing around the same time in the mid 1970s and early 1980s (for example, Rowbotham, 1979). Thus the notion of masculinities fits with a more diversified understanding of patriarchy (Walby, 1986, 1990; Hearn, 1987) or patriarchies (Hearn, 1992). In reviewing the field, Connell (1998) has summarised the major themes in contemporary studies on men as: plural masculinities; hierarchy and hegemony; collective masculinities; bodies as arenas; active construction; contradiction; dynamics.

There is also a growing lively debate on the limitations of the very idea of 'masculinities', including around the confusions of different current usages in the term (for example, Donaldson, 1993; Nordberg, 2000; Whitehead, 2002). The very concept of 'masculinity/masculinities' has been critiqued for its ethnocentrism, historical specificity, false causality, possible psychologism and conceptual vagueness (McMahon, 1993; Hearn, 1996b, 2004a). Cross-cultural research has used the concept of 'manhood' (Gilmore, 1991) and historical research the notions of 'manliness' and 'unmanliness', in the UK (Mangan and Walvin, 1987) and Sweden (Andersson, 2003; Tjeder, 2003).

We generally prefer to talk rather more precisely of men's individual and collective practices – or men's identities or discourses on or of men – rather than the gloss 'masculinities'. However, the latter term is still used at some points in this book, as it remains the shortest way to refer to how men act, think, believe and appear, or are made apparent. The concept has been very important, even though commentators use the term very differently, in serving several definite academic and political purposes. Perhaps above all, more recent studies have foregrounded questions of power.

Men's relation to social power is closely interlinked with men's relations to social problems, that is, in both the creation and experiencing of problems, and the broader issue of the societal problematisation of men and masculinities (see, for example, Holter and Aarseth, 1993; Popay et al., 1998). Not only are men now increasingly recognised as gendered, but they, or rather some men, are increasingly recognised as a gendered social problem to which welfare systems may, or for a variety of reasons may not, respond. These processes of problematisation of men and construction of men as gendered social problems apply in academic and political analysis, and in men's own lives and experiences; they exist at the societal level, and very importantly in quite different ways in different societies. Thus while it may be expected that some kind of problematisation of men and masculinities may now be observable in most, perhaps all, European societies, the form that it takes is different from society to society.

Social problems exist in terms of men's violence, crime, drug and alcohol abuse, buying of sex, accidents, driving and so on, and indeed the denial of such problems as sexual violence (for example, Ventimiglia, 1987). These are all activities that are social in nature, and have both immediate and long-term negative effects on others, friends, family and strangers. Some men suffer from adversity, as with ill-health, violence and poverty. The vulnerabilities of some men and masculinities are perhaps more graphically illustrated by relatively large numbers of men across Europe taking their own lives.

More general societal problematisation may appear in public concern around young men, crime, relatively low educational attainments in schools; in others, it may take the form of anxieties around the family, fatherhood and relations with children. Elsewhere, links between boyhood, fathering and men may be emphasised; or men's ill-health, alcohol use, depression, loneliness and low life expectancy; or the problem of reconciling home and work, with pressures towards long working hours; or men's violence to and control of women and children; or men's participation in and continued domination of political and economic institutions; or changing forms of men's sexuality.

These and other forms of gendered problematisation of men and masculinities and constructions of men and masculinities as gendered social problems have been examined in their European national contexts. In these problematisations, there is great national and societal variation in how men and masculinities interact with other major social divisions and inequalities, in particular, class, 'race', xenophobia and racism, ethnicity, nationalism and religion. The intersection of 'race', ethnicity, nationalism and nationality appear to be especially and increasingly important for the construction of both dominant and subordinated forms of men and masculinities. This entails investigation of the complex interrelations between these varying genderings and problematisations and the socio-economic, political, state structures and processes within and between the countries.

There is also growing concern with more precise specifications of men's individual and collective practices within gendered globalisations, or glocalisations. Indeed one of the most important trends of recent critical research on men has been towards more international, transnational and global perspectives. This is to be seen in a wide range of publications that seek to move attention away from the Western world and individual nations as the focus, and towards the South and transnational and postcolonial studies on men (for example, Connell, 1998; Ouzgane and Coleman, 1998; Morrell, 2001; Pease and Pringle, 2001; Cleaver, 2002; Morrell and Swart, 2005; Ouzgane and Morrell, 2005).

There is an increasing focus on global transactions in processes of masculinity formation and transnational categories of men and masculinities, as in 'global business masculinity' (Connell, 1998), 'men of the world' (Hearn, 1996a) or the central place of men and masculinity in the collective violence of war (Enloe 1990; Higate 2002), with the apparent increased use of rape and sexual violence in war. This seeks to locate such considerations within recent debates about globalisation and men's practices, throwing some doubt on the more ambitious claims of globalisation theses. Despite these recent developments, there remains a massive deficit in critical transnational studies of men's practices and in the sources available for such study. This book seeks to contribute to reducing that deficit by focusing on national and transnational perspectives on critical studies on men in Europe.

Comparative welfare systems

The second major analytical background to these studies on men in Europe has been provided by the field of comparative perspectives on welfare responses to social problems and inequalities. Reviewing studies on men has aimed to facilitate greater understanding of changing social processes of gender relations and gender construction in the context of welfare responses to associated social problems. This has necessitated attention to the challenges and difficulties of comparative research. In recent years a comparative perspective has been applied to various studies within sociology, social policy and other disciplines. There are many reasons for this tendency. One of the most convincing reasons is the potential offered for deconstructing the assumptions that underpin social practices and policies in different countries. In turn, such a process of deconstruction facilitates a reconstruction of more effective policies and practices. There is also an awareness that such practices and policies increasingly interact transnationally, at both European and indeed global levels: consequently research may seek to explore the processes and outcomes of those interactions and connections.

In many cases where specific social issues have been studied transnationally, attempts have been made to apply various general theoretical categorisations to particular issues. In the case of differential welfare regimes, the most common model applied in this specific fashion is that devised by Esping-Andersen (1990, 1996). Contrasts can be drawn between Liberal or Neo-liberal (including the UK), Social Democratic or Scandinavian (including Denmark, Finland, Norway and Sweden), and Conservative Corporatist (including Germany and Italy) welfare regimes in Western Europe. This framework has been critiqued and expanded to include Southern European countries, within the so-called Rudimentary, Latin Rim or Catholic Corporatist model (including Italy, either as a whole or only the south, and Ireland) of welfare (Leibfried, 1993), There has also been an extensive critique of such models in terms of their insufficient attention to gender relations (Lewis and Ostner,

1991; Leira, 1992; Lewis, 1992; Orloff, 1993; O'Connor, 1993; Sainsbury, 1994, 1996, 1999; Duncan, 1995; Tyyskä, 1995; Walby, 1997; Duncan and Pfau-Effinger, 2001; Hobson, 2002). In his later work, Esping-Andersen (1999, 2002) has sought to absorb at least some of the insights from these critiques. There has been a considerable development of further research on gender relations and welfare issues in Europe (Dominelli, 1991; Rai et al., 1992; Aslanbeigu et al.; 1994; Leira, 1994; Duncan, 1995; Walby, 1997).

Commentators have taken various positions regarding the analytic value of these applications from the general to the particular (Alber, 1995; Anttonen and Sipilä, 1996; Harder and Pringle, 1997; Pringle, 1998a; Pringle and Harder, 1999), partly depending on the issue studied. There has been a strong tendency to focus on Western, Northern and Southern Europe in these debates rather than the full range of European nations including those of Central and Eastern Europe.

A variety of categorisations of comparative welfare systems have now been produced; such as: Distinctions between Anglo-Saxon, Scandinavian (Langan and Ostner, 1991); Strong, Modified, Weak Breadwinner States (Lewis 1992; Ostner 1994; Duncan 1995, 2001); Private Patriarchy with High Subordination of Women, Public Patriarchy with High Subordination of Women, Private Patriarchy with Lower Subordination of Women, Public Patriarchy with Lower Subordination of Women (Walby 1986, 1990; Waters 1990; Hearn 1992). Transitional from Private Patriarchy, Housewife Contract, Dual Role Contract, Equality Contract (Hirdman 1988, 1990). These are all very useful as broad guides to social arrangements. They, however, need to be developed in two ways: the specification of differences with and amongst the gender welfare policy regimes of former Soviet bloc nations; and the specification of differences amongst men and men's practices. There is also a need for considerable open-mindedness in the assumptions that are brought to bear in such analyses. For example, Trifiletti (1999), through a feminist perspective on the relations of gender and welfare system dynamics, has provided detailed arguments that Southern European welfare regimes may not in fact (contrary to some opinion) be more sexist than those in Northern and Western Europe.

There is also a wide range of further broad feminist and gender-sensitive work that examines global and transnational change through a gendered lens (for example, Mies, 1986; Anthias and Yuval-Davis, 1992; Peterson and Runyan, 1999), which also have direct and indirect implications for the re-analysis of men and masculinities in the context of transnational and global relations. The critical study of men's practices has, until very recently, largely escaped specific comparative scrutiny, although it has received important attention within broader and relatively established transnational feminist surveys of gender relations (for instance, Dominelli 1991; Rai et al., 1992). Yet the limited amount of work devoted specifically to men's practices transnationally suggests there is immense scope for extending critical analysis in that respect, through the national and cultural contextualisation of men, men's practices and masculinities, and their problematisation.

While there is much talk of global economic convergence, the extent of this is far from clear and needs to be counterposed by the impacts of national and local/glocal pressures, national boundaries and organised labour at the national level (Edwards and Elger, 1999; Gibson-Graham, 1999; Waddington, 1999; Kite, 2004). In the field of social welfare there appear to be complex and contradictory patterns of convergence and divergence between men's practices internationally which await further interrogation (Pringle, 1998d, Pringle and Harder, 1999). Attempts have been made to push forward the boundaries in the comparative field using profeminist perspectives to consider men's practices in Asia, Southern Africa, the Americas (South, Central and North), Australasia and Europe (Pease and Pringle, 2001).

More generally, there are growing moves towards a more transnational focus in policy development in relation to men. There are now many transnational organisations and groupings, for example, the Council of Europe, the UN and UNICEF, which now see the importance of the place of men in moving towards gender equality. These initiatives need to be understood in relation to the growing academic and policy literature on men in development studies, which also examines the impact of globalisation processes on men and gender relations (Sweetman, 1997; Cornwall and White, 2000; Greig et al., 2000; Chant and Gutmann, 2000; *the network newsletter*, 2000; Harcourt, 2001; Sweetman, 2001; Ruxton, 2004).

European contexts

Given recent advances in both the critical studies on men and comparative welfare analysis, the time is ripe for the application of such perspectives to studies on men in Europe. The context for studying men represented in this book is the geographical area of Europe, European forms of society and government (and the EU in particular), and the pervasive traditions of European social science. These are clearly very difficult to characterise, but it is important to do so to some extent. This is especially so as the greatest volume of studies on men, critical or otherwise, have been produced from the US, with its own traditions and geopolitics. Thus it is necessary to locate European studies in relation to that body of work, and global debates more generally. We not do seek to suggest that there is a 'European' way of studying men, less still to essentialise Europe and European-ness.[3] Such 'occidentalism' would be just as foolish as advancing orientalism (Said, 1979). However, there are several broad trends and tendencies that can be briefly noted:

- The historical and cultural diversity amongst and within European countries, and thus among both men and studies on men in those localities.

- European studies on men are part of European social science and humanities traditions.
- Variations in the forms of feminism in Europe, both from other parts of the world and between European countries. State policy reform has been a key part of feminist theory and practice in many parts of Europe, thus in turn influencing studies and policies on men.
- Governmental, policy and indeed research agendas in Europe are increasingly influenced by the existence of the European Union.

The historical legacy inherited by the EU includes the attempts to develop broad social democracy and stop fascism happening again. The EU itself can be understood in part as a project of positive possibilities largely led and negotiated by men politicians after the Second World War in contradiction to short-term nationalistic interests, and devised to reduce men's historical tendencies to nationalistic conflict and war, and so achieve relative stability in Europe. At the same time, the dominant features of the gendered social order that privilege men and men's agendas also apply to governments, both national and transnational, as in the case of the EU. Thus governments, national and transnational, EU and other, can be seen as both part of the problem of men's dominance and part of the solution.

The EU promotes a single institutional framework, parliamentary government, the rule of law, single and free market economy, along with the principle of subsidiarity and a relatively high degree, albeit contested, of social and economic policy harmonisation and state intervention.[4] In May 2004 the Union expanded from fifteen to twenty-five member countries, including eight from the former Soviet bloc.[5] There are other important European regional groupings, such as the European Economic Area and the 'Schengen' Treaty area, which was originally signed in 1985 by seven EU countries, to end internal border checkpoints and controls.[6] There is no one Europe (Böröcz and Sarkar, 2005).

The European Research Network

This book arises primarily from the work of the Research Network on Men in Europe, a 14-nation network of feminist and profeminist researchers researching collaboratively on the study of men's practices. The Network has in turn led to the creation of the collective – Critical Research on Men in Europe (CROME) (www.cromenet.org). Though the planning began much earlier, the Network formally began in March 2000, under the title 'The Social Problem and Societal Problematisation of Men and Masculinities', and was funded until 2003 by the Research Directorate of the European Commission under its Framework 5 Programme (Hearn et al., 2004a). So the life of the Network now spans over seven years. It continues as part of the Concerted Action on Human Rights Violation within the EU Framework 6 Programme (http://www.cahrv.uni-osnabrueck.de/).

Figure 1.1 The fourteen countries

The Network comprises researchers with backgrounds in a range of academic disciplines – sociology, social policy, social work, psychology, literature, media and cultural studies, ethnology, as well as women's studies and gender studies – and from a number of European countries, initially Estonia, Finland, Germany, Ireland, Italy, Latvia, Norway, Poland, Russian Federation and the UK, and subsequently also Bulgaria, Czech Republic, Denmark and Sweden.

Of the fourteen countries in this study, eleven are member states, one is likely to join in 2007, and the other two are in partnership agreements. Seven of these countries are from Western Europe and were EU-15 members (*Denmark, Finland, Germany, Ireland, Italy, Sweden, the UK*); one, *Norway*, is from Western Europe but outside the EU; four are from the former Soviet bloc of Central and Eastern Europe and since May 2004 EU-25 members (*Czech Republic, Estonia, Latvia, Poland*); *Bulgaria*, which applied for EU membership in December 1995 according to the current timetable is due to be part of the next phase of enlargement by 2007–2008; and the *Russian Federation* lies outside the current EU process.

In addition to the four countries above that joined the EU in 2004, six other countries acceded at that time: Cyprus, Hungary, Lithuania, Malta, Slovakia and Slovenia. Romania applied for membership at the same time as Bulgaria and is due to be part of the next phase of enlargement. Turkey was recognised as a candidate country in 1999.[7] The Commission recommended at the end of 2004 the preparation of a framework for negotiations, and membership negotiations were opened in October 2005. Although some broad differences can be identified between Central and Eastern European countries and Western European countries, by virtue of their different political and economic histories, there are also commonalities, overlaps and anomalies. This is perhaps clearest with the case of Germany, spanning the former 'Iron Curtain'.

Aim

The overall *aim* of the Research Network is to develop empirical, theoretical and policy outcomes on the gendering of men and masculinities. Initially, the Research Network has focused on two closely related questions: the specific, gendered *social problem* of men and certain masculinities; and the more general, gendered *societal problematisation* of men and certain masculinities. The association of the gendered problematisation of men and masculinities, and the gendered social problem of men and masculinities is complex, as indeed are the differential responses of welfare systems. But at the very least it is necessary to acknowledge the various ways in which the more general gendered problematisations of men and masculinities both facilitate and derive from more particular recognitions of certain men and masculinities as social problems. Such recognition can apply through the use of measurable information, such as official statistics, as well as through less exact discursive constructions in politics, policy, law, media and opinion-formation.

The social problem aspects of this project refer to both the problems that men create, for example, men's violence to women and children, and the problems that men experience, for example, the social exclusion of some men. These social problem perspectives interlink with the processes of problematisation of men; gendered social problems apply both in academic and political analysis, and in men's own lives and experiences; they also exist at the more general societal level, in quite different ways in different societies.

Objectives

The specific *objectives* designed to achieve that overall aim have been:

(i) To analyse and understand more fully across the European Union and its potential members and associated states the differential associations of men's practices with a variety of social problems including: *men's relations to home and work; men's relations to social exclusion; men's violences;* and *men's health.*

(ii) To formulate provisional strategies to address some of those social problems in terms of national and EU responses on equal opportunities and other policy areas.

(iii) To identify areas for further enquiry so as to further develop such strategies.

(iv) In the context of European Union enlargement, to anticipate some of the national and transnational social problems relating to the impact of men's practices upon social cohesion and inclusion in established, recent and potential new member states of the EU.

(v) To gain a more adequate understanding of contemporary and changing representations of men, and negotiations around such representations in governmental and other official, media and research contexts.

Specific questions

Within this broad framework, the Network has investigated a wide range of more *specific questions*:

(1) In what ways is the problematisation of men and their practices conceptualised both within and between the countries in the network?

(2) To what extent and how may these conceptualisations intersect with the cultural/social/economic/ideological contexts within which they occur?

(3) To what extent does this analysis relate to existing comparative analytic paradigms?

(4) Are there domains of influence linking conceptualisations about men's practices across Europe? How might these be understood?

(5) Are there indications of interaction between domains of influence operating in these countries specifically or more generally across Europe and cultural/social/economic/ideological domains beyond Europe? If so, how are these to be understood?

(6) What is the relationship between the social problems of men's practices, and the societal problematisation of men's practices, as constructed through dominant discourses in different national contexts and the EU, both as presently constituted and in the context of its eastward expansion?

(7) What social policy responses should address the problem of men as constituted in specific countries and of concern in the developing EU?

(8) What do the preceding research questions tell us more broadly about the processes constructing gender, gender relations – and the means of changing those processes?

Methodology

The methodological perspectives of the Network are characterised as:

- *comparative orientation*;
- *gendered approach to both research content and research process*;
- *use of multiple methods*; and
- *ethical sensitivity*.

Gender collaboration

The Network brings together women and men researchers who research men and masculinities in *an explicitly gendered way*. Such a meeting point for women researchers and men researchers is necessary and timely in the development of good quality European research on men in Europe. This work has offered many, varied opportunities for collaboration and learning across countries and between colleagues. As part of the development of our collaborative research practice, we decided at the beginning of the project that publications relating to the whole project, rather than researchers' own individual countries, would normally be collectively authored for the three years of the project *per se* and one subsequent year, unless individuals wished otherwise.

Research on men that draws only on the work of men is likely to neglect the very important research contribution that has been and is being made by women to research on men. Research and networking based only on men researchers is likely to reproduce some of the existing gender inequalities of research and policy development. Gender-collaborative research is necessary in the pursuit of gender equality, the combating of gender discrimination, achievement of equality and anti-discrimination work more generally.

Themes and methods

Initially, four main themes have been addressed and four main methods have been used to gather information on critical research on men, and develop that research in the countries. This has involved reviews on:

- men's relations to home and work (see Chapter 6);
- men's relations to social exclusion (see Chapter 7);
- men's violences (see Chapter 8); and
- men's health (see Chapter 9).

Of these themes, the first, third and fourth are clear and familiar, although some choices had to be made as to where to discuss a number of overlapping issues. For example, suicide could be understood in relation to both violence and health, but was included here within the latter category because of the links with mental health.

Social exclusion is a more complex concept. It has become more popular in recent years in both academic and policy circles, not least from the influence of the EU itself.[8] The concept of social exclusion has, in some quarters, become preferred to such concepts as poverty, deprivation or marginalisation, arguably because it offers a more open and wide-ranging platform for analysis and intervention.[9]

These reviews were completed in each country in terms of:

(i) relevant academic and analytical literature within each country (see Chapter 2);
(ii) statistical sources (see Chapter 3);
(iii) governmental and quasi-governmental legal and policy statements that explicitly address men (see Chapter 4); and
(iv) media representations, in particular selected national press output in order to examine explicit and implicit analyses on men and masculinities, and their problematisation (see Chapter 5).

In each case, during the course of the project national reports (making a total of 40 reports, each addressing the four main themes), as well as transnational summary reports, were produced. The Research Network has also acted as an information resource for other researchers, policy-makers and practitioners for the future. Currently, it has sought to achieve this in several ways, including, from towards the end of 2000, the web-based European Database and Documentation Centre on Men (www.cromenet.org).

Comparative and transnational challenges

There is now a developing theoretical and conceptual infrastructure, and conceptual language, for addressing men, masculinities and men's practices at a transnational level. The research focus is conceptualised here around the notion of 'men in Europe', rather than, say, the 'European man' or 'European men'. This first perspective highlights the social construction and historical mutability of men, both within the welfare contexts of individual nations, and within the context of the developing form of the EU. This involves the examination of the relationship of men and masculinities to European nations and European institutions and welfare configurations in a number of ways:

(a) in terms of national, societal and cultural variation amongst men and masculinities;
(b) in terms of the historical place and legacy of specific forms of men and masculinities in European nations and nation-building;
(c) within the EU and its transnational administrative and democratic institutions, as presently constituted – particularly the differential intersection of men's practices with European and, in the case of the EU, pan-European welfare configurations;
(d) with regard to the implications of the new and potential member states of the EU;

(e) in terms of examining the implications of both globalisation for Europe, and the Europeanisation of globalisation processes and debates;
(f) with regard to the formation of new and changing forms of gendered political power in Europe, for example, regionalised, federalised, decentralised powers, as derived by subsidiarity and transnationalism.

Such questions around the changing configurations of Europe are addressed in Chapter 10. However, in undertaking transnational comparison, the problematic aspects of the enterprise have to be acknowledged. In many fields of transnational studies there are major difficulties posed by differing meanings attached to apparently common concepts. Moreover, this specific difficulty signals a broader problem: for diversity in meaning itself arises from complex variations in cultural context at national and sub-national levels – cultural differences which will permeate all aspects of the research process itself. There are several possible practical responses to such dilemmas. On the one hand, as some transnational commentators suggest (for example, Munday, 1996), it is perhaps possible to become over-concerned about the issue of variable meaning: a level of acceptance regarding such diversity may be one valid response. Another response is for researchers to constantly check out with one another the assumptions each brings to the research process. Furthermore, the impact of cultural contexts on the process and content of research itself is a central part of transnational working.

The configuration of countries in the Network presents several specific opportunities for comparative study. First, in terms of 'testing' general welfare regime typologies in relation to the issue of men's practices, these countries include 'representatives' of all three of the welfare regime typologies identified by Esping-Andersen (1990, 1996): Liberal or Neo-liberal; Social Democratic or Scandinavian; and Conservative Corporatist. The spread of the countries – in Southern, Northern, Western, and Eastern Europe – presents a broad cultural, geographical and political range within Europe.

Second, these and other considerations also have to be framed within developing notions of what 'being European' constitutes. This clearly has salience in relation to the recent expansion of the EU eastwards. Moreover, the issues of social marginalisation consequent upon the development of an alleged 'Fortress Europe' are also highly relevant to the lived experience of many men, both those who are excluded and/or those who are actively involved in processes of exclusion.

Third, it is possible to explore the extent of differential social patterns and welfare responses between countries that are often grouped together on alleged grounds of historical and/or social and/or cultural proximity, for instance, Norway and Finland; and, to a lesser extent, Ireland and the UK.

Fourth, the inclusion of countries from Central and Eastern Europe allows exploration of the way recent huge economic, social and cultural changes there have impacted upon attitudes and practices relating to men. This allows investigation of the various constellations of practices and beliefs between the countries in the context of their different historical and cultural trajectories. Added saliency is provided by the extent of 'cultural exchange' (often relatively one-way) that has occurred between those countries and Western and Northern Europe.

Transnational research practice

Finally, in this chapter let us turn to questions of research practice. While it is important not to diminish the importance of specific national and cultural contextualisations of the problematisation of men and masculinities, there is a sense in which Europe, or at least parts of it, is becoming a research site, arena or even laboratory itself. This is not to suggest any false homogeneity, but rather that the extent of cultural and other linkages is increasing to the extent that discussion of one part easily invokes other parts.

As noted earlier, the Network brings together women and men researchers who are researching on men and masculinities in an explicitly gendered way. Matters of politics and practice apply throughout this work – in the forms of organising and collaboration between women and men across national borders and languages; in the attempt to develop ethically-sensitive research practice; in relations to other researchers, funders and policy-makers; and moreover, in relation to the gradually developing and very different national and transnational political forces that there are of and around men, on the issue of men, and around different men and different men's interests. In this last sense at least, the study of men nationally and transnationally is likely to become of growing political, policy-related, media and practical interest in the future.

Transnational projects of these kinds raise many questions of politics and practice – in forms of organising and collaboration between women and men across national borders and languages; in the attempt to develop ethically-sensitive research practice; in relations to other researchers, funders and policy-makers; and in the gradually developing and very different national and transnational political forces that there are on the issue of men, and around different men and different men's interests. In this last sense at least, the study of men nationally and transnationally is likely to become of growing political, policy-related, media and practical interest in the future. This is an initiative that carries both huge potential for transforming gender relations, as well as some dangers of it being used by some men to reassert their demands for yet more resources, both academically and in policy and practice, whether through governments, business, other organisations or in the home and other personal spaces.

Part 1

Overviews

2
Academic Research

Jeff Hearn and Keith Pringle, with Ursula Müller, Elżbieta H. Oleksy, Harry Ferguson, Voldemar Kolga, Emmi Lattu and Irina Novikova

This chapter reviews academic research on men's practices in the fourteen European countries of the Network: Bulgaria, Czech Republic, Denmark, Estonia, Finland, Germany, Ireland, Italy, Latvia, Norway, Poland, Russian Federation, Sweden and the UK. Separate national reports were prepared for ten of the nations on the four themes of home and work, social exclusion, violences and health, and these were supplemented by national reviews in four countries. The time framework of the national reports is generally the 1990s, though some information is provided on the 1980s in some cases in order to track changes over time. This is especially important in the transitional nations.[1]

This chapter reviews two interconnected aspects: the state of *substantive findings* of studies, in this case on men in Europe; and the state of the *disciplinary and sub-disciplinary development* of those studies on men. We begin with discussion of some of the broad features of European studies on men, and of the national contexts within which academic research on men and men's practices is carried out. This is followed by a focus on the four main themes of home and work, social exclusion, violences and health. Finally, we present some conclusions from this review.

European studies on men

It is clearly difficult to summarise the state of research on men in the fourteen countries, even though our focus here is mainly on only four broad themes: home and work, social exclusion, violences and health. There are of course broad patterns, but it should be strongly emphasised that the social and cultural contexts of the state of research in the different countries are very varied indeed. With this caveat strongly in mind, we seek to describe some of the main contours of critical research on men in Europe, without essentialising them or creating some mythical notion of 'Europeanness'.

As noted in Chapter 1, it may be useful to locate European studies on men in relation to studies elsewhere, including those in the US, which has provided the largest concentration of studies, but also global debates more generally. US, European and indeed wider global research on men has to be understood in relation to the general features of society, politics and academia.[2] We focus here on four dimensions:

- Nation, nationalism and ethnicities;
- Feminism, the market and the state;
- Academia;
- Geopolitics and transnationalism.

Nation, nationalism and ethnicities

While the US is a very large multi-state nation, Europe is a multi-nation continent. Although most of Europe is a contiguous landmass, there is a great amount of historical, cultural and linguistic diversity amongst and within European countries, and thus among both men and studies on men in those localities. The US has one national language – English – as well as a large and growing Hispanic minority, ethnic diversity and multiple local languages; in Europe most nations have a different distinctive language, though some have two or more national languages. With some notable exceptions, language does indeed appear as a key basis of nationhood in the European context. One does not usually talk of Floridian or New Jersey studies on men, but one might speak reasonably of Norwegian or Czech studies. The national and local contexts need to be understood to make sense of the different orientations of the national research.

Linked to this, specific national context is a very important and often taken-for-granted aspect of studies on men in both Europe and the US. These national contexts often bring their own national ethnocentrisms and over-emphases on an assumed, taken-for-granted or overstated homogeneity. This is, however, being challenged, especially in the 'centres' of the former European empires, with their increasingly confident postcolonial, black and minority ethnic populations. Despite the emphasis on ethnic and other diversities, ethnocentrism, or US-centrism, is common, in that the US, like most 'central' powers, is not usually contextualised, as is often necessary in studies in and of smaller, 'more marginal' countries.

Feminism, the market and the state

The roots of studies on men lie with feminism and men's responses to feminism, but the form of feminism varies, both in comparison with other parts of the world and between European countries. In the US case, feminism is a very varied and complex development, with relatively strong strands of, for example, radical, liberal and black feminisms. The intersections with the civil rights, gay and black movements are also very important.

In Europe, feminism, and men's responses to it, has in many national contexts been relatively closely aligned to the state rather than the market. This would seem to follow from the greater development of state intervention and the welfare state in particular in many European countries, as compared with the privileging of the market in the US. This former development is most clearly seen in the Nordic countries, as in the phenomenon of state feminism, and, in a very different way, in the countries of the former Soviet bloc. Yet, at the same time, feminists have often been active against the state, and this has been an important feature in, for example, Germany, Ireland and the UK. This is seen in the notion of the autonomous women's movements and in feminist organising against men's violence in those parts of the women's shelter movement operating outside the state, or against state control of reproductive rights. Thus state policy reform has been a key part of feminist theory and practice in many parts of Europe. These matters provide key political contexts for studies of men, which are thereby relatively closely aligned to state policy, especially social policy, reform. This is again clearest in the Nordic case, where there has been a close relation to equality politics (rather than feminism *per se*), a number of broad societal surveys, as well as attention to the more positive aspects and potentials of men for change, and to the diversity of men's positions and practices, such as on fatherhood.

These features are in keeping with differing structures and ideologies in relation to the state, market and civil society. The US is a low tax capitalist economy, even with the huge power of the state, the military and other apparatuses. Critical studies on men there have not been strongly directed to the state, but rather focus much more on the power of individuals and groups of individuals to change in families, communities and, to an extent, workplaces. In Europe, even with the very large variations noted, there is a much closer engagement with the state, state reform, social policy and welfare issues. This is even though in some of the former Soviet bloc countries there is now a clear distrust in the state and faith in the market to solve social problems, thus highlighting again the complexity of gender politics.

Academia

There are definite contrasts to be made between the academic contexts of studies on men in Europe and the US. In many ways most critical studies on men are working against the academic mainstream. However, even at the more critical edge of US studies on men, there has been a dominance of studies based in positivism, psychological and social psychological understandings of masculinity, psychoanalysis, role theory and various forms of culturalist theory. Studies are often very good on description, less good on theoretical analysis. Some of these features appear to follow or reproduce the cultural faith in the individual and the market, with lesser attention to structural analysis, political economy, and less faith in change through state, socialist, social democratic or even 'third way' programmes. With some notable exceptions, most US research on men is not framed in relation to neo-marxism or Critical Theory.

European studies on men are part of European social science and humanities traditions. While positivism is still extremely important as an approach in all European countries, and is perhaps being revived in various new technocratic, 'third way' and 'evidence-based' guises 'beyond ideology', European studies on men are also relatively strongly influenced by European critical social theory. This applies, whether this is Critical Theory from Germany, poststructuralism from France, humanistic discourses in the Nordic countries, or cultural studies from the UK. Within many of these various strands, it is difficult to understand European social theory and their related studies on men without some reference to neo-marxism, structural analysis, critiques of positivism, and indeed left and social democratic politics.

Geopolitics and transnationalism

Though both are part of the North, the geopolitical situation of US and Europe is very different. The US is often considered the world's only super-power; Europe is a mix of the EU and its members, both established and recent, including some newly independent nations, some other nation-states which seek to join the EU and some which do not, and the Russian Federation spanning Europe and Asia. The Council of Europe currently has 45 member states and one applicant country, Monaco. At the time of writing, some European countries, or rather their governments, most obviously the UK, but also including Denmark, Italy and Poland, are strong supporters of the US government; others are not. Some EU governments favour much closer political unity in developing, say, European foreign and military policy; others do not. In the US the analysis of men and the new forms of US imperialism is rarely a subject of critical study. In Europe the analysis of men in relation to these complex forms of transnationalism and international relations is beginning, in the light of the differential (post)imperial and (post)colonial histories of European nations.

Governmental, policy and research agendas in Europe are increasingly influenced by the existence of the EU, even for those countries that are not members. With the expansion of the union in May 2004 to twenty-five member countries, of the fourteen countries in this study, eleven are member states, one is likely to join in 2007, and two are in partnership agreements. Contemporary studies on men in Europe cannot operate outside consideration of this EU context, itself a unique transgovernmental arrangement. This applies almost regardless of the social arena under consideration, whether it is, for example, law, social policy, employment, education, violence or social exclusion. This presents a distinct site for research, policy and action, or set of sites, compared to other parts of the world.

National contexts

The state of studies on men in the national contexts varies greatly in terms of the volume and detail of research, the ways in which research has been framed, as well as substantive differences in men's societal position and social practices. The range of interests, concerns and frameworks underlines both the variable state of critical studies on men and the variable national contexts. The framing of research refers to the extent to which research on men has been conducted directly and in an explicitly gendered way in relation to, first, feminist scholarship, Women's Studies and Gender Research; second, gay and queer theory; and third, a focus on and presentations of the 'voices' of men (as against those affected by men).[3] Other differences stem from different theoretical, methodological and disciplinary emphases, assumptions and decisions (Hearn, 2003a; Connell et al., 2005), and more substantively from men's power relations with women, children and each other in the countries.

In all the countries the state of research on men is uneven and far from well developed. In most countries research on men is still relatively new and in process of gradual development. The overall extent of national research resources seems to be a factor affecting the extent of research on men. In some countries, especially in Germany, Norway, Sweden and the UK, but also to an extent elsewhere, it can be said that there is now some form of relatively established tradition of research on men that can be identified, albeit with different methodological orientations.

While the greatest quantitative development of studies on men has been in Germany and the UK, there have been important developments in all countries. This applies especially to Norway and Sweden, to an extent in Denmark, Finland, Ireland and Italy, and rather less so in the transitional nations of Bulgaria, Czech Republic, Estonia, Latvia, Poland and the Russian Federation. In most countries, though there may not be a very large body of focused research on men, a considerable amount of analysis of men is still possible, drawing on secondary and other sources that do not have an intended or explicit focus on men.

There are also some striking contrasts between the types of topics that have been researched across these and other countries. For example, the problem of men's violence has gained greater research attention in Germany and the UK than has been the case in the Nordic countries. In the latter, questions of men and childcare, fatherhood and home–work relations have been more centre stage. Such differences seem to be connected to differing political traditions and ideologies, rather than the relative size of the problem of violence *per se* in the countries concerned.

Studies in each country operate in different political and academic traditions in studying men, as well as distinct historical conjunctions for the lives of men. In some cases these social changes are profound, for example, the German unification process, post-socialist transition in Bulgaria, Czech Republic, Estonia, Latvia and Poland, and in Ireland rapid social changes from a predominantly rural society through a booming economy, as well as the political conflicts, challenges and changes in Northern Ireland. Somewhat similarly since the 1950s Finland has experienced change when people moved from rural to suburban areas in search of work. This has been reflected in 'lifestyle studies' and 'misery studies' of class-based structural change (Kortteinen, 1982; Alasuutari and Siltari, 1983). These address men, patriarchal structures and changes in lifestyle, though they do not identify as research on men.

An interesting, paradoxical issue is that the more that focused gendered research on men is done the more that there is a realisation of gaps that exist, both in specific fields and at general methodological levels. In many countries the situation is made complex by a difference between the amount of research that is relevant to the analysis of men, and the extent to which that research is specifically focused on men. For example, in Finland there is a considerable amount of relevant research but most of it has not been constructed specifically in terms of a tradition of focused, gendered explicit research on men (see Hearn and Lattu, 2002; Hearn, Lattu and Tallberg, 2003a). One might also see certain contrasts between the UK and Ireland, even though they share some geographical, historical, social and linguistic features, or between Denmark, Finland, Norway and Sweden, even though historically they have shared some features of broadly similar social democratic, relatively gender-egalitarian systems, a feature that is now undergoing some change, especially in the Danish case. This way of understanding variations between and within countries is more accurate than crude typologies of nations (see pp. 9–11).

While overall, relatively many studies have been conducted on some research topics, there is much variation in the relation of research on men with feminist research. Research on men can also be contextualised in relation to the historical timing and extent of development of the women's movement, and the extent of identification of 'men' as a public political issue, for example, as objects and/or subjects of change. This may be clear in the UK, where feminist and profeminist research has been influential in producing a relatively large amount of studies (Pringle, 2000). In Norway there is a growth of equal status policy development that is not necessarily directly feminist-related (Holter and Olsvik, 2000). In Sweden the gender equality project has had a clear impact on studies on men that might assist policy development in that direction (Nordberg, 2006). In Germany, as in most countries, both non-feminist and feminist traditions, or at least influences, can be seen (Müller, 2000). Parts of the newly emerging German studies on men refer in a distorting way to feminist research, with sometimes overt, sometimes more or less subtle, contempt for their results and theses. This is a challenge that has had to be dealt with by feminist and profeminist researchers in their own national contexts.

This parallels Nordberg's (2000, 2001) comments on the Nordic situation that it is not unusual in Sweden and the Nordic region more generally that men doing men's studies neglect feminist research and often underplay the power relations between men and women. She suggests that 'this neglect can also be explained by the earlier lack of gender studies focusing on men's own experiences and because many male (and some female) researchers appear to consider that men are often stereotyped in feminist research.' (Nordberg, 2006). While in most countries there is evidence of the positive, if sometimes indirect, impact of feminist scholarship on research on men, there is a frequent neglect of the findings and insights of feminist research in much of that research.

At the same time, there is the question of to what extent critical perspectives are embedded in social science in national contexts. For example, class has been addressed much more critically in Sweden, than have racism, ethnicity, age, disability or gay and lesbian issues. The close connections of class and ethnicity are still resisted in much Swedish social science. In Nordic countries, social science and public discourse more generally is often not culturally attuned to critical or conflict-based studies or approaches. Thus the ways in which men and masculinities are addressed, critically or not, are also affected by the broad cultural contexts. These include tendencies towards consensus in social institutions associated with the long-term social democratic welfare project, fundamentalist forms of Lutheranism, incorporation of radicalism within the state, self-satisfaction in society, and identification of Swedish social science as an arm of the social democratic state from the 1930s onwards (Pringle, 2003).

There are also very different, sometimes antagonistic approaches within the same country, for example, between non-gendered, non-feminist or even anti-feminist approaches and gendered and feminist approaches. These differences sometimes connect with different research topics and themes, for example, research on men's violences, or even on non-violence, may, understandably, be more critical towards men, while research on men's health may be more sympathetic and less critical. They to some extent represent and reflect disciplinary and indeed methodological differences in the analysis of men, which in turn sometimes are differentially influential in different research areas.

The large amount of existing research material is also often scattered within a wide variety of different traditions and disciplinary locations, or without an explicit gendering of men and masculinities. There is great need for comprehensive secondary analyses of the large amounts of existing research results on 'men' in a gendered perspective. A lot of studies have produced interesting, but broadly spread data which could well be used to contribute to a fuller picture of men in society in a gendered perspective, but this work is still to be done. The picture research provides often consists of fragmented details, lacking an integrating gendered perspective.

Key points in national studies

Having discussed some of the general features of research in men across Europe, we now turn to consider some of the features of the various national studies in their national context (see Tables 2.1 and 2.2). In recent years there has been a relatively large amount of research activity in the *UK* devoted to men,

Table 2.1 Demographic and political information on the fourteen countries

	Bulgaria	Czech Republic	Denmark	Estonia
Population[1]	8.0	10.2	5.4	1.3
Relation to the EU	Possible member 2007–08	Joined May 2004	Joined 1973	Joined May 2004
Membership of Eurozone	No	No	No	No
Male life expectancy[2]	67.4	72.0	74.1	66.3
Male:female life expectancy[3]	90.3	91.5	93.8	86.1
Homicides[4]	3.87	2.52	1.02	10.61
Male suicides[5]	25.6	26.0	21.4	47.7

	Latvia	Norway	Poland	Russian Fed
Population[1]	2.3	4.5	38.6	144.1
Relation to the EU	Joined May 2004	Member of European Economic Area 1994	Joined May 2004	Partnership and Cooperation Agreement 1997
Membership of Eurozone	No	No	No	No
Male life expectancy[2]	65.4	75.9	69.7	60.7
Male:female life expectancy[3]	85.8	92.8	89.2	83.1
Homicides[4]	6.47	0.95	2.05	22.05
Male suicides[5]	48.4	18.4	26.7	69.3

[1] In millions, 2002
[2] At birth, 2002
[3] Ratio of male to female life expectancy at birth, 2002
Source: UNDP *Human Development Report* (2004). Tables available at: http://hdr.undp.org/reports/global/2004/pdf/hdr04_HDI.pdf
[4] Per 100,000, 2002
Source: G. Barclay and C. Tavares with S. Kenny, A. Siddique and E. Wilby (2003) *International Comparisons of Criminal Justice Statistics 2001*. Research Development & Statistics Bulletin, Home Office, London, Issue 12/03
Available at: http://www.homeoffice.gov.uk/rds/pdfs2/hosb1203.pdf
[5] Per 100,000, most recent year available, as of June 2004 (figures from 1999–2002).
Source: World Health Organisation.
Available at: http://www.who.int/mental_health/prevention/suicide/en/Figures_web0604_table.pdf
* European Coal and Steel Community
** European Economic Community

Finland	Germany	Ireland	Italy
5.2	82.4	3.9	57.5
Joined 1995	FDR founded ECSC* 1952, EEC** 1958, Unification of FDR and GDR 1990	Joined 1973	Founded ECSC* 1952, EEC** 1958
Yes	Yes	Yes	Yes
74.3	75.1	74.3	75.5
91.1	92.5	93.3	92.2
2.86	1.15	1.42	1.50
32.3	20.4	20.3	10.9
Sweden	**UK**	**USA**	
8.9	59.1	291.0	
Joined 1995	Joined 1973	Not in Europe	
No	No	No	
77.5	75.6	74.2	
93.9	93.8	92.8	
1.11	1.68	5.56	
18.9	11.8	17.1	

Table 2.2 Economic and social information on the fourteen countries

	Bulgaria	Czech Republic
GDP per capita[1]	7,130	15,780
Growth rate[2]	−0.6*	1.4
Rich:poor ratio[3]	9.9	5.2
Male:female earned income[4]	152	179
Male:female economic activity rate[5]	116	120
Men in parliament[6]	73.7	84.3
Men as managers[7]	—	74
Public expend. health and education[8]	6.4	11.1

	Latvia	Norway
GDP per capita[1]	9,210	36,600
Growth rate[2]	0.2	3.0
Rich:poor ratio[3]	8.9	6.1
Male:female earned income[4]	145	135
Male:female economic activity rate[5]	125	118
Men in parliament[6]	79.0	63.6
Men as managers[7]	63	72
Public expend. health and education[8]	9.3	13.6

[1] PPP (purchasing power parity) US $, 2002
[2] GDP per capita annual growth rate % 1990–2002
[3] Richest 10% to poorest 10%, 2002
[4] Ratio of male to female earned income, 2002
[5] Ratio of male economic activity rate to female economic activity rate 2002
[6] Men as proportion of members of parliament, 2002 or previous
[7] Men as proportion of legislators, senior officials and managers, 2002 or previous
[8] Public expenditure on education as percent of GDP 1999–2001 plus public expenditure on health as percent of GDP 2001
Source: UNDP *Human Development Report* (2004). Tables available at: http://hdr.undp.org/reports/global/2004/pdf/hdr04_HDI.pdf
* GDP per capita annual growth rate % 1990–2001 UNDP *Human Development Report* (2003). http://hdr.undp.org/reports/global/2003/pdf/hdr03_HDI.pdf
** Note: major change from previous year, with ratio of 14.2 UNDP *Human Development Report* (2003). http://hdr.undp.org/reports/global/2003/pdf/hdr03_HDI.pdf
*** Data based on the International Standard Classification of Occupations (ISCO-68) as defined by ILO 2002

Denmark	Estonia	Finland	Germany	Ireland	Italy
30,940	12,260	26,190	27,100	36,360	24,430
2.1	2.3	2.5	1.3	6.1	1.5
8.1	14.9	5.6	6.9**	9.7	11.6
139	159	143	192	255	222
119	122	115	143	189	169
62.0	81.2	62.5	68.6	85.8	89.7
78	63	72	66	72	79
15.3	11.7	11.6	12.7	9.2	11.3

Poland	Russian Fed	Sweden	UK	USA
10,560	8,230	26,050	26,150	35,750
4.2	−2.4	2.0	2.4	2.0
9.3	20.3	6.2	13.8	15.9
161	156	141	167	161
125	122	112	133	122
79.3	92.0	54.7	82.7	86.0
66	63	69	69	54***
10.0	6.8	15.0	10.9	11.8

particularly in the fields of home and family, work and organisations and men's violences. The last mentioned represents a massive social problem and permeates all other issues related to men's practices in society. From a European perspective, the body of work on violences represents one of the most distinctive and valuable contributions made by British researchers. Much, but by no means all, of this work has been broadly informed by feminist research. There is also a considerable amount of work on gay studies and queer studies, and a growing body of research on men's relations with 'race', racism and ethnicity (Hearn, 1999a; Pringle, 2000, 2006).

The situation in *Germany* has some similarities but also some differences. There, problems formerly addressed as 'women's problems' have at least in part been successfully redefined as gender conflicts. Various examples have been brought into public and scholarly attention, and are best seen in the context of growing attention of gender politics as a whole. The distribution of housework and conflicts between men and women about this distribution, debates about men as fathers, a widespread awareness of male violence against women, and a tendency to destigmatise homosexuality are relevant here, as well as the challenge German men feel from women's demands for more and more effective affirmative action policies. New emerging fields of research are gender and organisations, subtle discrimination, and new structural and cultural challenges in the reconciliation of work and home for both genders. Recent studies on men have often been concerned to show how men too are affected by health risks, by violence and so on, without connecting them more systematically to societal context. Indeed in some studies, men now appear as the neglected gender. Societal change in favour of women, placing men at risk of becoming the disadvantaged gender, has been the underlying theme of some non-profeminist writing.

In this context, the increasing recognition of a plurality of masculinities that has occurred in recent studies in Germany and indeed elsewhere may serve the purpose of referring to the interrelations of those various 'types' only, without relating them to femininities and gender (power) relations. The insight that masculinities are interrelated with each other attracts strong analytical attention; a common reproach against feminist research is it being falsely accused of ignoring the plurality of men by treating them theoretically as a homogenous block. One characteristic of German research on men and masculinities is that even the normal scientific procedures of giving a 'state of the art' report as a context of research are rather frequently violated. In a way, this corresponds to the myth that Women's Studies has neglected gender as a social structure. However, in giving attention to the neglected and hidden realities of women in society, Women's Studies have always pointed to gender relations. In most cases, in recent German studies on men, the notion of gender as structure is not theoretically and empirically located in society, its economy, institutions and culture, but reduced to a rather simple role concept. For these reasons there is a need for more awareness of feminist research and for placing the study of men within a broad gendered socio-economic context (Müller, 2000, 2006).

There has been some relatively well-developed research on men in *Norway*, especially on men in families and as fathers. This includes national surveys of practices and attitudes (for example, the *Men in Norway 1988* survey; see Holter 1989, 1997; Holter and Aarseth, 1993). Several important questions have been identified by Holter and Olsvik (2000) in recent Norwegian research debates. First, it is often said that Norway is a 'relatively egalitarian' country in gender terms. Traditionally, gender segregation in everyday life has been somewhat relatively less marked, even with the strong gender segregation in the labour market. Masculinities have been somewhat more heterosocial and less homosocial, compared, for example, to parts of continental Europe. A pattern of 'masculine normalcy' or a 'male norm' may have been more important. A second question is what are the possibilities for extending men's role as caregivers, especially as fathers, and how can the barriers against this development be identified and removed? Third, can men be targets of gender discrimination, for example, men in caring roles in working life, or as sex objects in the media; how does this relate to discrimination of women? Fourth, what are the main causes of male violence against women, including authoritarian social contexts, patriarchal privilege, structural violence and violence between men? And fifth, how can an active gender policy be renewed and improved, especially in terms of men's participation?

While relatively much effort has gone into analysing some aspects of gender in Norway, 'equal status' or 'worth' are less well mapped. For example, what are men's interests? How do they vary? References to gender still often mean 'women'. Men's reports on their practices regarding equal status issues, for example, household time-use, are often lacking. Holter and Olsvik (2000) suggest that several feminist researchers have pointed to the problem of men being defined around gender notions developed by and for women, or deduced from women's needs and circumstances (as a so-called 'derived subject'). They argue that that this can lead to a renewal of stereotypes on both sides: a tradition of blaming men, linked to 'competitive' feminism or ideas of the woman-friendly state, that often works together with older traditions of blaming women.

Critical studies on men and masculinity were not a separate research area in *Sweden* from the 1970s to the 1990s. The research concerning men was done mainly by women from a feminist perspective and was integrated into Women's Studies. In the 1980s two books, building on Anglophone research and theory, were published by the government: Jalmert's (1984) *Den svenske mannen* [The Swedish Male], and Bengtsson and Frykman's (1987) *Om Maskulinitet. Mannen som forskningsobjekt* [On Masculinity. The man as an object of research]. The psychologist, Lars Jalmert, declared that the Swedish man was an 'in-principle man': positive to gender equality in principle but not in practice. In the 1980s a 'Workgroup for the male-role' was established by the government to change men's traditional roles. Hearings were held, reports published, and research was connected to and implemented in state-funded projects directed at changing the sex-segregated labour market (Nordberg, 2005, 2006).

Nordberg (2006) has noted how much of research on men has been closely connected to the gender equality project. This applies in studies of fatherhood, men in non-traditional occupations, men in organisations and management positions, as well as men's reactions to women, men's constructions of homosociality and obstacles to gender equality when women enter traditional male occupations. She continues:

> Research linked to the gender equality project has been directed to attack 'the problematic male role' or 'masculinity ideology' and detect obstacles to gender equality (for example, Ekenstam et al., 1998; Robertsson, 2002; Nehls, 2003). Some attempts have been made to emphasise men trying to live in alternative more gender equal gender formations (for example, Ekenstam et al., 2001) and analyse new forms of male gender formations (for example, Johansson and Kuosmanen, 2003). Ordinary men's lives and men in power positions, as, for example, politicians, are still neglected. . . .
>
> Two main perspectives, or positions, can be found in the recent research on men and masculinities in Sweden. The main focus is either on *'men as a problem'* or on *'men's problems'*, where a social psychological emphasis is put on the restrictions that masculinity concepts have on men. In the first kind of research, 'men as a problem', men are focused upon from a hierarchical gender order perspective with an emphasis on the reproduction of men's advantages. The emphasis in these studies has mainly, like in the statistics and policies, been more on *power relations between men and women as groups*. The second perspective, 'men's problems', has focused more on how men comprehend masculinity and live their lives and on men as 'victims' of a patriarchal gender order. (italics in original)

The question of men's violences has not been a main focus of research on men in Sweden (Balkmar and Pringle, 2005a; Pringle, 2005). The completion of the first national survey of women's experiences of gendered violence (Lundgren et al., 2001), showing higher levels of violence than expected by many, may prompt more attention to this in the future.

In *Finland*, a Nordic country with a Nordic welfare model, located between Sweden and Russia, there has been a considerable number of research studies that provide information on men and men's practices. Some are focused on men; some are gendered but not necessarily in relation to men; some are not focused specifically on men, and either do not discuss in any detail that they are studying men or do not provide a gendered analysis of men. This applies to many studies on history, men's 'misery', lifestyle, alcohol use and working life. Even studies that are more explicitly on gender, for example, on gender in working life, usually do not include an explicit gendered analysis of men. The gendered re-examination of this material would be most useful. There has not been an extensive development of focused, critical studies on men and men's practices, even though there has been some academic debate on these questions at least since the early 1990s.

There has been some growth of Finnish studies on work, sport and health. This may be changing with an increasing critical research focus on men's violences. A pervasive theme highlighted in Finnish research is the misfortune of some men, in terms of mortality, illness, isolation, alcohol use, working life, culture, rather than the power, privileges and control of resources of certain men or being a man more generally. There is a need for more focused research on men's practices, power and privilege, in relation to both those men with particular power resources, and hegemonic ways of being men. The connections between some men's misfortunes and men's powers and privileges is a crucial area for future research (Hearn and Lattu, 2000; Hearn et al., 2003a, 2006).

There is very little academic literature in *Denmark* that can be considered to be critical research on men.[4] There is a limited amount of academic commentary that calls attention to the need for a focus on men and masculinity (Reinicke, 2002, 2004). The prevailing discourse of gender equality has generally concerned women's equality in the workplace. Recently it has been extended to include men in the context of shifting gender practices with focus on fatherhood and on parental/childcare leave and some research examines men's experiences and perceptions of fatherhood (Madsen et al., 1999, 2002; Olsen 2000). Men are a focus in terms of social exclusion and homelessness, and this includes both Danish and immigrant men, with the context being the failure of the welfare state to meet the needs of certain classes of men (Andersen and Larsen, 1998).

Discussions of men's violence are generally weighted by psychological explanations. An exception to this is work that examines men's violence in Greenland (Sørensen, 2001), yet there is little critical research on men's violence in Denmark itself. Where gender and ethnicity are discussed in the academic literature such studies tend to focus on youth subcultures (Jensen, 2002) and homeless men (Järvinen, 2004). There is virtually no research on the political linkages between men's practices either in relation to being a perpetrator or victim of racism. There is clearly a need for both basic research on men's practices as well as critical studies on men in all areas. While some works address men, there is virtually no explicitly gendered analysis of men's practices. Furthermore, with the exception of one or two scholarly voices, it is the problems of men that get attention and discussions of men's power and men's privilege are conspicuously absent (Iovanni and Pringle, 2005a).

In *Ireland* men as gendered subjects have remained largely outside the gaze of critical inquiry, and academic research into men in Ireland has been limited. One consequence is that it leaves anyone who sets out to review relevant research with a modest enough task, yet there is still sufficient material available to make this something of a challenge. In most research there is a strong taken-for-grantedness about the nature of Irish society, for example, in rural land ownership. Historically, the Catholic hierarchy has expected strict adherence to celibacy and hegemonic masculinity was also cast accordingly, with the family and heterosexual marriage having the purpose of procreation, rather than pleasure. Traditional masculinity in Ireland has also been constructed in terms of the 'hard working man' and 'good provider'. Ferguson (2006) reports that traditionally

> Men were the exclusive breadwinners, while women were constructed as the carers, the 'specialists in love and the emotions' . . . Irish men . . . have traditionally gone to extraordinary lengths to find work and make a living for themselves and their families. . . . at the same time women and men who transgressed the deeply moral norms were severely punished. Women, and unmarried mothers in particular, suffered terribly as they were incarcerated in Magdalene Homes and their children routinely removed to the infamous Reformatory or Industrial Schools, where many were seriously abused (Raftery and O'Sullivan, 1999). Boys were taught industriousness and given the skills to be labourers, . . . girls were prepared as future domestic servants and housewives.

There is increasing recognition of the impact of the climate of rapid social change upon men. Another strong and growing current concern is with men's abuse of children, as is men's violence to women (Ferguson, 2000, 2006).

General works have been produced in *Italy* on male identity and role, relations between male and female genders, and masculinity. There is relatively strong development of work on fatherhood, male sexuality, violence and emotions. One particular focus is on the complexity of family dynamics with more or less traditional forms of fatherhood. Some writing has suggested that it is difficult for men to acknowledge that their own sexual identity is problematic. There is a frequent implicitness in men speaking about themselves, their own identity and life. It is not clear what it means to men to acknowledge that their emotional world is sexual and that any experience they go through is a sexed experience, thus discovering their partiality (as opposed to universality) and their own difference (Ventimiglia and Pitch, 2000).

Estonia is a transitional nation since regaining its nationhood from the former Soviet Union in 1991. In the late 1990s representative surveys, with thousands of respondents, were conducted, on work, home, health, social exclusion and violence. Research coverage is relatively good on work and health, but not on social exclusion. The explicit gendering of men and focus on masculinities is not directly presented in most studies. Gender issues are not seen as a top priority. While such key problems as crime, poverty and unemployment are clearly strongly gender-laden, their gendering is generally ignored in research.

Social problems are manifested in men's short life-expectancy; after Russia, Estonia has the largest difference in life expectancy between men and women in Europe. Interestingly, Estonian men subjectively tend to estimate that their health is better than women's and that they have less chronic diseases and health problems, even though this is not so. Studies are needed on the reasons for this discrepancy. The main problems experienced by men identified in research are: work overload, intensification of working life, pressures to earn more money; neglect of health problems; low educational levels; changes in marriage; and fathers' rights (Kolga, 2000, 2006).

Since the restoration of political independence in *Latvia* in 1991, academic research has never included problems of men and masculinities as a separate area to be financed from the national research council. Gender research has been marginally developing due to the absence of qualified professionals in the academic sphere. In their absence, gender as a category of analysis has been appropriated rather superficially and applied in various research projects within academically well-established disciplines, for example, the sociology of the family and demography. There is no qualitative academic comparative gender research on masculinity discourses in the major ethnic communities (Novikova, 2000a, 2006).

Though in *Poland* there has been a moderate development of research on men in recent years, there is a relatively strong concern in research with questions of unemployment, health and suicide. One general conclusion to be drawn from the review of research literature, especially that on social exclusion, is that masculinity as an independent research topic has enjoyed little popularity among Polish scholars. Despite the research that has been done, there are still many questions, especially around men's health, that are unexplored (Oleksy, 2000; Oleksy and Rydzewska, 2006).

In the *Czech Republic*, there is some limited but growing interest. Šmídová (2006) reports that academic attention to men and masculinities has mostly comprised qualitative research studies on topics such as fatherhood or men's role in dual career families. She continues:

> Apart from studies on conventional heterosexual nuclear families and men's place in it, there has been some academic attention devoted to single men (Cermakova et al., 2000), little concern with sexuality-related research with the exception of transgenderism, and so far almost no studies on men in the public sphere. An exception on the last count was one part of the doctoral thesis of Hana Cervinkova on masculinities in the Czech army (Cervinkova, 2003). A few studies, mostly sociology theses, deal with analyses of social trends in Czech society since 1989 and inclinations of Czech men towards traditional or conventional models of masculinities (for example, normative masculinity represented by the breadwinner model). The possibility of a career based on individual effort and economic power of money are new phenomena to be studied here.

> Different types of masculinities within families are also being discussed. The type of 'men who mother' ('matkové') is the theme of a few recently launched research studies . . . (Šmídová, 2002, 2003). Generally, research attention is directed to types of men and masculinities who do not present competition, power or domination . . .

As is often the case elsewhere, although – or perhaps because – masculinity is obviously very visible, men's issues in *Bulgaria* are invested with an uncanny invisibility, reminding one of a 'natural' power or an elemental force (Bhabha, 1995; also see Kamborouv, 2003). In reviewing the academic field, Kamborouv (2006), concludes:

> Men and their masculinities are not thought to constitute a problem, either for a specialised research and discussion, or for the media, cultural and public sphere. . . . men and masculinity are a taboo topic, or rather a topic considered to be unfathomable for being unquestionable in itself: men and their masculine models are taken as the given, rather unrelated to women's and children's issues, or to the problems that particular groups or types of men face lately. Men and manhood are taken to be essential, and thus not susceptible to shift or elaboration.

The rise of Gender Studies in the *Russian Federation* at the end of 1980s and the early 1990s has resulted in the creation of a curious situation in the social science community. At first glance, the situation seems to reflect the main tendencies in the development of research: the common difference between Gender Studies and Women's Studies exists in Russian social science just as it does in Western social science. However, such impressions turn out to be rather superficial. In reality, the main research stream in the Russian version of Gender Studies is the 'female' one. For the most part research in Russian Gender Studies is directly devoted or has a 'non-direct' relation to studies of women's situation in public and private spheres. Nevertheless, studies on men are not completely absent, with their appearance within the framework of Gender Studies in the mid-1990s (Chernova, 2000).

The Russian Federation discussion on a 'Masculinity Crisis' began in the 1970s (Urlanis, 1978). At that time the basic characteristics of this crisis were: low life expectancy compared with women, self-destructive practices, such as hard drinking and alcoholism, smoking, 'excessive eating', accidents.[5] These problems remain in the 1990s. This has led to the appearance of a particular and rather peculiar 'victimisation theory', in which men are passive victims of their biological nature and structural/cultural circumstances, and can hardly be called 'actively functioning' social agents. Recent qualitative investigations have examined men's relations to violence and the exclusion of some groups, such as homosexuals, from 'normative masculinity'. Despite its rather short history, studies on men in Russia have their own theoretical concepts, conceptual devices and research field. Recent research has recognised both plural forms of masculinity, and the form of hegemonic masculinity within Russian gender culture (see, for example, Kukhterin, 2000; Meshcherkina, 2000; Oushakine, 2002). Social exclusion and men's violences both remain under-researched.

Thematic areas

Home and work

Historically, in many countries and until relatively recently, established forms of masculinity and men's practices could be distinguished on two major dimensions – urban and rural; bourgeois and working class. In these different ways, men have both created huge problems, most obviously in violence, and have also been constructive and creative actors, as, for example, in building industries, albeit within patriarchies. The exact ways these four forms were and are enacted clearly varies between societies and cultures. In addition, many other crosscutting dimensions have been and are important, such as ethnic variations. In recent years, urban bourgeois, rural bourgeois, urban working class, and rural working class forms of masculinity and men's practices have all been subject to major social change. Such changing gender relations in turn both constitute governments and provide tasks for governments to deal with. Thus, governments can be seen as both part of the problem and part of the solution.

Recurring themes in contemporary studies of men's relations to employed and paid work across Europe include: men's occupational, working and wage advantages over women; men's gender segregation, both horizontal and vertical; many men's close associations with paid work. In some cases, men's situation in non-traditional occupations has been studied. There has been a tendency to focus on men in lower and middle-ranking jobs (for example, Collinson, 1992), and a general lack of attention to men's dominance as managers, policy-makers, owners and power holders (see Wahl, 1995; Collinson and Hearn, 1994, 2005; Wahl and Holgersson, 2003; Reis, 2004).

However, despite the fact that work relations provide some, but by no means all, of the most obvious sources of men's individual and collective power, there has been something of an avoidance of these issues even within the general critical field. This tendency is in some ways surprising. Perhaps it is because men's relations with paid and employed work are so obvious or because the analysis of men's situation 'at work' reveals such consistent patterns, across European societies at least, they have not been thought of as so interesting to study. Studies of men and masculinity have often tended to underestimate or even to neglect the significance of work and organisations more generally as sites for the reproduction of men's power and masculinities. This is even though key workplace issues such as organisational power, control, decision-making, remuneration, cultures and structure crucially reflect and reinforce masculine material discursive practices in complex ways.

It is as if the very obvious associations of men with work, organisations and management, at least at the ideological level, have meant that a 'fresh start' has had to be attempted. This might be seen as a reversal of the well-drawn tendency to explain men's behaviour with reference to job, occupational and organisational positions, in contrast with explanations of women's behaviour in relation to the family (Feldberg and Glenn, 1979). Thus this 'fresh start' might involve seeing men in terms of family, friends, health, the body, emotions, sexuality, violence and so on; important though these and other long neglected aspects are, work, organisations and management continue to be major forces in the construction of men, masculinities and men's power.

In many countries there are twin problems of the unemployment of some or many men in certain social categories, and yet work-overload and long working hours for other men. These can especially be a problem for young men and young fathers; they can affect both working class and middle class men, as, for example, during economic recession. In working life, work organisations are becoming more time-hungry and less secure and predictable (Holter and Olsvik, 2000). In a number of studies, time utilisation emerges as a fundamental issue of creating difference in everyday negotiations between men and women (Metz-Göckel and Müller, 1986; Busch et al., 1988; Höpflinger et al., 1991; Notz, 1991; Jurczyk and Rerrich, 1993; Niemi et al., 1991; Tarkowska, 1992). Increasing concerns about men and time-use – in Estonia, Ireland, Norway and Germany (Anttila and Ylöstalo, 1999; McKeown et al., 1998). Also in Italy research is highlighting the importance of quality of time for men in their family relations (Ventimiglia and Pitch, 2000). There is also there a relatively strong development of work on fatherhood, sexuality, violence, emotions, and the complexity of family dynamics with more or less traditional forms of fatherhood.

It is especially noteworthy how much of the recent research on men has focused on men in families and in particular on fathers and fatherhood. For example, Šmídová (2006), reporting on Czech research on masculinities, notes that:

> . . . the concentration of questions concerning men's role in the family life is quite clear. Studies show that men are not the sole breadwinners in the Czech family. Despite this fact, men still take responsible for the finances and women for the housework in the family arrangements. Caring for children is viewed, though, as a task for both parents [CVVM 2003]. The man-father is the key role for men in the family, and men spouses are more satisfied with the family life than their women spouses. As far as domestic chores are concerned, men play the role of helpers rather than equal partners, despite the attested desired ideal for equal sharing (Cermakova et al., 2000, pp. 102–06).

Other common themes are men's benefit from avoidance of domestic responsibilities, and the absence of fathers. In some cases this tradition of men's avoidance of childcare and domestic responsibilities continues for the majority of men. In some cases it is being reinforced through new family ideologies within transformation processes, as in Latvia (Novikova, 2000a). In many countries there is a general continuation of traditional 'solutions' in domestic arrangements, but growing recognition of the micro-politics of fatherhood, domestic responsibilities and homework reconciliation for at least some men. In Norway and elsewhere due to a post-divorce system where most fathers lose contact with their children, higher work pressure and more work mobility, 'father absence' has probably become more widespread in real terms over the last ten years, as has the 'general absence of men' in children's environments, even if more positive trends can also be seen (Holter and Olsvik, 2000).

In many countries there are also counter and conflictual tendencies. On the one hand, there are increasing emphases on home, caring and relationships. This may be linked to 'family values', from either a politically right wing or gender equal status perspective. In Ireland a notable trend is the growth in the number of women, especially married women, working outside the home (Kiely, 1995). By 1996, fathers were the sole breadwinners in only half of all families with dependent children in Ireland. On the other hand, there are tendencies towards more demanding and turbulent working life, through which men may be more absent.

It is not surprising if there may be a degree of cultural uncertainty on men's place in the home and as fathers and a growing recognition of ambivalence, even when there is a strong familism. This theme is taken up in Johansson's (1998) study of divorced fathers in Sweden. This points to male ambivalence between modern fatherhood forms and the traditional breadwinner concept. There is also in some countries, such as Finland, a continuing interest in the reconciliation of work and home; and growing variety of ways of approaching this (Lammi-Taskula, 2000; see also Oakley and Rigby, 1998; Pringle, 1998c, 1998d; Smart, 1999). Given the considerable difference that still exists between men's and women's earnings, it is not surprising that it is the woman who stays at home after the birth of a child. She is usually the person with the lower income, and a couple does not need to be wholehearted advocates of traditional domestic ideology to opt for the traditional solution.

Evidence from Nordic countries shows that parental leave, when left to negotiations between men and women, becomes mostly taken up by women, although most people say they want a more balanced situation (Lammi-Taskula, 1998; Holter and Olsvik, 2000). For example, in Sweden more men take parental leave than in most other European countries. However, women still take the overwhelming majority of such leave. Nevertheless, if massive social policy inputs, such as the Swedish government has committed to increasing men's actual parental leave, can result in such modest results, then that suggests we need to reconsider very carefully whether top-down social policy initiatives are of themselves often sufficient for the changing of men's behaviours. This perspective is reinforced by recent research by Bekkengen (2002) that suggests that the usual explanation for low take-up – that labour market rigidities prevent many men from taking as much parental leave as they would like – have to be questioned as sufficient in themselves. In particular, her study indicates that the most crucial factor is often that men generally possessed much greater power to choose the extent of their involvement than did their female partners (Pringle, 2003).

Even with this relative emphasis on men in families, there is a need for greater consideration of fatherhood in terms of cultural, sexual and other forms of diversity, and more inclusion of the 'voices' of women and children in studies of fatherhood. It would be interesting to see how and when, if ever, women and men form coalitions through a politics of reconciliation, and how gender constellations at 'work' and in the 'private' sphere influence each other. It would be important to research further couples who experience difficult labour market conditions, so, for instance, making the female partner the main earner in the long term or forcing them to accept working times that do not allow traditional distribution of housework.

Relatively little research has been carried out on men as carers. Gaps exist in knowledge on the gender division of domestic labour and parenting in most countries. Irish fathers' accounts of their participation in childcare and domestic life remain to be documented. Little is known, for instance, about why a third of Irish fathers work 50 hours a week or more: whether this reflects the adoption of traditional definitions of masculinity, or because men feel required to earn to meet the family's financial obligations and spend time away from home and children reluctantly. Further exploration of the complex dynamics surrounding negotiations between women and men in relationships regarding housework, parenting and emotional work is also needed. Most research focuses on white heterosexual partners. Research on the intersections of men, the home and labour markets in their diverse configurations, including minority ethnic families and partnerships would be welcome. In seeking to make sense of the albeit limited increases in parental activity by some men in the home, there is the question of to what extent do these changes represent real social 'progress' or sometimes re-creations of patriarchal dominance in new forms.

Social exclusion

This has proved to be the most difficult area to pre-define, but in some ways one of the most interesting. National reports have approached this area differently (see Chapter 7). Social exclusion enters into research literature in many different ways, as unemployment, ethnicity, homosexuality and so on. Different emphases have been respectively inspired by labour market and social policy studies, race and ethnicity studies, and gay studies and queer studies. Each therefore has been subject to quite different traditions and distinct influences. Issues of migration and citizenship are beginning to attract increasing attention, especially with processes of Europeanisation and the changing shape of national borders after the implementation of the Schengen Treaty and recent EU enlargement.

The transitions of economies away from heavy manufacturing and towards lighter manufacturing and service sectors has led to studies on men's, particularly working class men's, coping and adjustment, for example, in the printing industry (Cockburn, 1983) and coalfield localities (for example, Dicks et al., 1998; Waddington et al., 1998). In some cases, there has been a high rate of change in work and workplaces, with large numbers of layoffs. Lifelong security of employment is not guaranteed, not even for the relatively successful and well qualified; so-called 'traditional' working class-based masculinities, most obviously around heavy manufacturing and mining, can no longer be easily sustained unchallenged. This has been very significant in many of the Baltic, Central and East European countries, but also in the UK, Germany and elsewhere. In Poland men aged 55–59 have been most affected by unemployment (Borowicz and Lapinska-Tyszka, 1993). In Czech Republic unemployment figures are generally rather low, but are relatively high for the youngest age group of men (for the age group 15–19 men have outnumbered women in unemployment since 1994) and men with the lowest or no education (*Zeny a muzi v datech 2003*, 2003; Cermakova et al., 2000).

The social exclusion of certain men links with unemployment of certain categories of men (such as less educated, rural, ethnic minority, young, older), men's isolation within and separation from families, and associated social and health problems. These are clear issues throughout all the countries. There is a lack of studies showing the variety of structures and processes that may lead to the marginalisation of men as groups and/or individuals, and what differences and similarities there are to women. For instance, does ethnicity in some respects override gender? In Italy, Estonia and most other countries social exclusion is generally under-researched. In Estonia the most visible example of social exclusion is people looking for something, usually bottles, in trash containers. Nobody knows how many 'container people' there are, but it is clear there are many homeless, mainly non-Estonian, Russian speaking men, aged 30–50 years.

In many former Soviet bloc territories the restoration or transformation of statehood has shifted many welfare measures from state to local levels, leading to new, previously unknown, forms of dependency for people. The new conditions for property acquisition and upward social mobility have, however, benefited selected men-dominated echelons already structured by the vertical gender segregation of the Soviet political and ideological hierarchies and labour market. Industrial closures, less housing construction and withdrawals from the army have drastically changed conditions for many men, and brought unemployment and health problems. Even so, gender issues are not generally a top research priority; explicit gendering of men is not directly present in most studies. Issues of social exclusion are especially important in the Baltic, Central and East European countries with post-socialist transformations of work and welfare and dire consequences for many men.

Even in Nordic countries, which are relatively egalitarian by some measures and have relatively good social security systems, new forms of problems have emerged. In Finland socially excluded men have been extensively studied through men's 'misery' and biographical approaches (Kortteinen, 1982; Alasuutari and Siltari, 1983), rather than through gendered studies of men. On the whole, Norwegian men have experienced relatively little unemployment, alcoholism and migration in recent years (Holter and Olsvik, 2000). However, in the last decade, new forms of marginalisation have developed, with shifts from traditional industry to more postindustrialised society. Globalising processes may create new forms of work and marginalisation. Corporate reorganisation is commonplace; post-Fordist flexibility demands flexibility of men. Some men find it difficult to accommodate to these changes in the labour market and changed family structure. Instead of going into the care sector or getting more education, some young men become marginalised from work and family life. Working class men are often the most vulnerable. The job chances of non-Western immigrants are in many situations much worse, perhaps 5–10 times worse, than for Norwegians and Western immigrants. Discrimination seems to hit non-Western men especially. A similar pattern is found elsewhere.

There is a lack of attention to men engaged in creating and *reproducing* social exclusion, for example, around racism. More generally, the conceptual separation of 'the social problems which some men create' from 'the social problems which some men experience' is often simplistic and there is a need to study the intersections more carefully. There is also a lack of research in work organisations on the intersections of gender and other social divisions along the contours of cultural diversity, ethnicity, sexuality, age, disability and class.

Violences

The major recurring theme here is the widespread nature of the problem of men's violences to women, children and other men, and in particular the growing public awareness of men's violence against women (Ferguson, 2000; Hearn and Lattu, 2000; Holter and Olsvik, 2000; Müller, 2000; Pringle, 2000). Men are overrepresented among those who use violence, especially heavy violence, including homicide, sexual violence, racial violence, robberies, grievous bodily harm and drug offences. Similar patterns are found for accidents in general, vehicle accidents and drunken driving. Directly physically violent crime tends to involve violence by men to those whom they know whereas with property crimes victims tend more to be strangers.

Violence against women by known men is becoming recognised as a major social problem in most of the countries. The abusive behaviours perpetrated on victims include direct physical violence, sexual violence, isolation and control of movements, and abuse through the control of money. There has been much feminist research on women's experiences of violence from men, and the policy and practical consequences of that violence, including that by state and welfare agencies, as well as some national representative surveys of women's experiences of violence, as in Finland (Heiskanen and Piispa, 1998), Germany (Müller and Schrottle, 2004) and Sweden (Lundgren et al., 2001). There has for some years been a considerable research literature on prison and clinical populations of violent men. There is now the recent development of research in the UK and elsewhere on the accounts and understandings of such violence to women by men living in the community, men's engagement with criminal justice and welfare agencies, and the evaluation of men's programmes intervening with such men (Brown and Caddick, 1993; Pringle, 1995; Lempert and Ölemann, 1998; Brandes and Bullinger, 1996; Hearn, 1998). Gendered studies of men's violence to women is a growing focus of research, as is professional intervention.

Child abuse, including physical abuse, sexual abuse and child neglect, is now being recognised as a prominent social problem in many countries. Both the gendered nature of these problems and how service responses are themselves gendered are beginning to receive more critical attention, in terms of both perpetrators and victims/survivors. There is some research, especially in the UK, on men's sexual abuse of children but research on this is still underdeveloped in most countries, including in the Nordic countries (Iovanni and Pringle, 2005a; Pringle, 2005). In some countries, sexual abuse cases remain largely hidden, as is men's sexual violence to men. There is also a need for more empirical and theoretical consideration of the ways that some men use such relations with children as a major means of 'doing domesticity' in their lives.

In Ireland there has been a series of scandals particularly involving child sexual abuse by priests, some of whom were known to the Church hierarchy but not reported or brought to justice by them and then moved onto another parish. There is still a playing down of the significance of violences by hegemonic men and a reluctance to problematise active married heterosexual masculinity and question gender and age relations within the Irish family (Ferguson, 1995). There has been a strong concern with intersections of sexuality and violence in Italy and some other countries (Ventimiglia, 1987; Castelli, 1990); this is likely to be an area of growing concern.

There continues to be an amazing lack of gender awareness in studies that understand themselves as dealing with supposedly 'general' issues around violence, for instance, racist violence. The question of traditional masculinity and its propensity for racist violence has not yet been even articulated in high budget studies. Masculinity seems to be recognised as playing a role when violence against women is the explicit topic. In many countries relatively little academic literature exists on elder abuse and on violence against men. Studies on the reasons for non-violent behaviour in men are lacking completely. There is a lack of studies on connections between violence between men and men's violence against women. Forms of men's violences that are rarely addressed in a gendered way is 'civil disorder' (Power and Tunstall, 1997; see Chapter 8 this volume) and ethnic and sectarian conflicts.

Other key research questions round violences that need more attention concern:

(a) how men's violent gendered practices intersect with other oppressive power relations around sexuality, cultural difference, ethnicity, age, disability and class, and the implications of such analyses for challenging those practices and assisting those abused;
(b) how different forms of men's violences interconnect, for example, men's violence to partners and to children;
(c) how men's programmes against men's violences can be developed, particularly research into the promotion of successful initiatives at school, community and societal levels;
(d) men's sexual violences to adult men;
(e) men's violences to lesbians and gay men; and
(f) men's violences to ethnic minorities, migrants, people of colour and older people.

Health

The major recurring theme here is men's relatively low life expectancy, poor health, accidents, suicide, morbidity. Some studies see traditional masculinity as hazardous to health. In some countries, such as Estonia, this is argued to be the main social problem *of* men (Kolga, 2000). Men constitute the majority of drug abusers and are far greater consumers of alcohol than women, though the gap may be decreasing among young people. Yet surprisingly there has been relatively little academic work on men's health from a gendered perspective in many countries.

Men tend to suffer and die more and at a younger age from cardiovascular diseases, cancer, respiratory diseases, accidents and violence than women. Socio-economic factors, qualifications, social status, life style, diet, smoking and drinking, hereditary factors, as well as occupational hazards, can all be important but seem to be especially important for morbidity and mortality. Gender differences in health also arise from how certain work done by men is hazardous. Evidence suggests that generally men neglect their health and that for some men at least their 'masculinity' is characterised by risk-taking, an ignorance of men's bodies, and reluctance to seek medical intervention for suspected health problems. Risk-taking is especially significant for younger men, in smoking, alcohol and drug taking, unsafe sexual practices, road accidents.

In this context it is interesting that Estonian research finds that men are over-optimistic regarding their own health (Kolga, 2000). Men's suicide, especially young men's, is high in the Baltic countries, Finland, Poland, Russia. In these countries there is also a high difference in life expectancy between men and women. In Ireland and Norway, men perform suicide about three times as often as women; in Poland the ratio is over 5:1 (*Human Development Report 2000*, 2000). In several countries the suicide level has been related to economic downturns. In many countries men tend to use more overtly and dramatically physically violent means to kill themselves, as compared with women. Studies on men, sport, and the body are likely to be a growing area of research; they have attracted particular attention in the Nordic region (Ervø and Johansson, 2003a, 2003b).

Neglected health issues include the intersections of men's well-being with age, disabilities and other social divisions. A lack of comparative studies on men's and women's health statuses and practices is obvious. There has been relatively little academic work on men's health from a gendered perspective in many countries. Despite the mass of information on men's health outcomes, there is relatively little on men's healthcare practices.

There are, however, signs that this may be one of the major growth areas of scholarship and policy development around men in the future, with much interest being shown by governments, industry and political interest groups, albeit for a variety of different reasons and interests. Following the 'Men's Health Report of Vienna 1999' (Schmeiser-Rieder et al., 1999) and the WHO 'Men, Ageing and Health' Report (WHO, 2000), the First World Congress on Men's Health was held in Vienna in November 2001. The *International Journal of Men's Health, The Journal of Men's Health and Gender* and the *American Journal of Men's Health* have recently been launched.

Gaps

There is still a need for basic research on men in positions of power, politics, management, associations, and friendship and support networks. Other areas need more explicit, critical gender analyses, such as age, generation, work and family; men's relations with women; gay men; disabled men; rural men; poorly educated men; men, ethnicity, racism; violence to women and children; racist violence, homophobic violence; suicide; men's healthcare practices; men and alcohol; health and violence.

Among the significant areas urgently requiring further research, three that are particularly important are: the intersections of gender with other social divisions clustered around dimensions such as culture/ethnicity, sexuality, age, disability, class; how to promote programmes to challenge men's violences; the promotion of further transnational and comparative research in relation to all the themes. There is a lack of research in work organisations on the intersections of gender and such other social divisions. Similar gaps exist around men's violences.

Concluding remarks

European transnational comparative research on men has begun but there is scope for much more such work, exploring the continuities and discontinuities between cultural locations and national systems. Transnational comparison can also help to elucidate central theoretical, empirical and policy debates on men and masculinities.

Men's relations to power

The most pervasive aspect of this review of the state of academic research on men is the repeated finding of the centrality of men's relations to power. Data on men's practices reveal the pervasive and massive negative impact of patriarchal relations of power across all societal sectors. The importance of the ongoing challenge to these persistent gendered relations of power and privilege throughout the countries cannot be over-emphasised. There is a very major lack of attention to men in powerful positions and men's broad relations to power, both in themselves and as contexts to the four themes.

Unities and differences

There are both similarities between the nations and clear differences, in terms of the extent of egalitarianism, in relation to gender and more generally; economic growth or downturn; post-socialist transformation; strength of the women's movement and gender politics. There are also differences between men in the same country, for example, West German men tend to be more traditional than East German men. Future research could usefully examine regional variations amongst men within nations, for example, how the different cultural contexts of Northern or Southern Italy or the regional parts of the UK have framed the social relations associated with men. Unities and differences between men need to be highlighted between countries and amongst men within each country.

Recent structural changes

This kind of transnational, comparative research review prompts more focused attention on current social changes in Europe, and how these both reproduce and challenge existing patriarchal structures and practices. Those questions are likely to be major concerns for future European theory, research and policy. Analyses of men need to take into account the fact that many of the countries have experienced recent major socio-economic change. This applies especially to the transitional nations, though one should not underestimate the significance of changes elsewhere, such as the late 1990s economic boom (Ireland), and recovery from the early 1990s recession (Finland). In the transitional nations economic changes were often viewed as positive (more freedom, independence, individual initiative) compared with the Soviet experience. They have also often brought social problems. While there is no exact concordance between economic and social change, there is often a clear relation, for instance, weakening of the primary sector leading to social and geographical mobility. In the transitional nations people never expected that economic freedom would be associated with a decrease in population and birthrate, high criminality, drugs, diseases such as tuberculosis, and often negative impacts on welfare. The various national and transnational restructurings throughout all the countries raise complex empirical and theoretical issues around the analysis and reconceptualisation of patriarchy and patriarchal social relations. These include their reconstitution, both as reinforcements of existing social relations and as new forms of social relations. New forms of gendering and gendered contradictions may thus be developing, with, through and for men's practices.

Interconnections, power and social exclusion

There are many important interrelations between the various aspects of men's positions and experiences, and their impacts on women, children and other men. There are strong interconnections between the four main focus areas. This applies to both men's power and domination in each theme area, and between some men's unemployment, social exclusion and ill health. Men dominate key institutions, such as government, politics, management, trade unions, churches, sport; yet some men suffer considerable marginalisation as evidenced in higher rates of suicide, psychiatric illness and alcoholism than women.

The mapping of interrelations is one of the most difficult areas. It is one that deserves much fuller attention in future research and policy development. This applies especially as one moves beyond dyadic connections to triadic and more complex connections. A considerable body of research has been conducted across many countries illustrating a correlation between poor health, including the poor health of men, and various forms of social disadvantage associated with factors such as class or ethnicity. In fact, more generally the theme of social exclusion and inclusion can be seen as an important element entering into the dynamics of all the other themes regarding men's practices outlined here. This again emphasises the requirement for particular policy attention to be given to social inclusion and the need for more research on men's practices and social exclusion and inclusion. Patterns of men's violence interconnect with the other three issues to some extent but also cut across these social divisions. Social exclusion intersects with all three other themes. More generally, the intersection of gender with other power relations, such as 'race', ethnicity, age and disability, in the lives of men needs much more attention.

Of the many interconnections between the four themes, one further example can be cited. With regard to the interrelations between the topic of fatherhood and men's violences, in most parts of Western Europe, a striking tendency is to treat these two topics as separate issues. Indeed, countries can be found that both enthusiastically promote fatherhood and, quite separately, address men's violences, but without 'joining up' the two issues. It would seem that the two topics should be joined up. In other words, there is no contradiction between positively promoting the role of men as carers and emphasising at the same time the prime requirement of protecting children from men's violences. What is striking in terms of European research and policy-making across Europe is how rarely such an integrated dual approach is adopted: the question as to why it seems to be so hard to do is one that researchers and policy-makers should ponder deeply.

Theoretical, methodological and empirical questions

There are a large number of theoretical issues raised by this kind of network-based inquiry. These include: the difficulty of constructing comparative grounds; the relation of studies on men to studies on women and gender; the extent to which research on men's practices can be separated from other social science fields; and the relation of social science research and that deriving from the humanities and other disciplines. Such concerns can be understood as both epistemological and methodological, and practical matters in the conduct of research.

There is a strong sense in which the taken-for-granted agendered nature of society continues in both academic and more everyday constructions of society, and this means that men continue to be (un)seen as agendered, and not a suitable focus for research. There has been a considerable amount of research providing information on men and men's practices. Some is focused on men; some is gendered but not necessarily in relation to men; some is not focused specifically on men, and either does not discuss in any detail that it is studying men or does not provide a gendered analysis of men. Indeed there is often 'opacity' in men speaking about themselves, their own identity and life. It is often unclear what it means to men to acknowledge that any experience they go through is a sexed/gendered experience, thus discovering their partiality (as opposed to universality) and their own difference. Interrogating this is part of the broader gendered social analysis, both empirical and theoretical.

Across the European field, there is a need for further consideration of theoretical issues which have important material implications: Has it become more or less important to be a 'man'? What does 'being a man' mean both in terms of practices and discourses? What is the relationship between practices and discourses in the context of this field of study? What are the precise inter-relationships between macro level systems of power relations which contextualise men's practices and the micro level of individual men's everyday engagements and understandings of their worlds?

3
Statistical Information

Jeff Hearn, with Ursula Müller, Elżbieta H. Oleksy, Keith Pringle, Harry Ferguson, Voldemar Kolga, Emmi Lattu, Irina Novikova and Teemu Tallberg

This chapter presents some findings on the review of statistical information on men's practices in the Network's countries: Czech Republic, Denmark, Estonia, Finland, Germany, Ireland, Italy, Latvia, Norway, Poland, Russian Federation, Sweden and the UK. Separate national reports were prepared for ten of the nations on these four themes of home and work, social exclusion, violences and health, and these were supplemented by national reviews in Czech Republic, Denmark and Sweden. The time framework in the national reports generally focuses on the 1990s. Information is provided on the 1980s in some cases in order to compare the situation over time. This is especially important in the transitional nations.[1]

In this chapter we set out, first, the broad context of the examination of statistical information on men and men's practices. This is followed by discussions of how statistical information on men is handled in the different national contexts, and then of the four main themes of home and work, social exclusion, violences and health.

The general state of statistical information

There is a very wide range of cross-national statistical sources available, from the UN and its agencies, especially UNDP (for example, *Human Development Report 2005*); WHO; Eurostat; OECD; national governments (for example, Research and Development Statistics (http://www.homeoffice.gov.uk/rds/index.htm)), as well as some commercial publications (for example, Mackay, 2000). However, in many areas gender-disaggregated statistics are still not available. Some basic information on demography, economy, polity and violence is presented on the fourteen nations in Tables 2.1 and 2.2 (pp. 30–33).[2]

In the previous chapter, we discussed how, in academic research, there has been a strong emphasis on the different political academic traditions that operated in studying men in the different national contexts, as well as distinct historical conjunctions for the lives of men. We also noted how in some countries, especially in Germany, Norway, Sweden and the UK, but also to an extent elsewhere, it can be said that some form of relatively established tradition of research on men can now be identified, albeit with different orientations. Interestingly, national surveys of men have been conducted in all of these four countries (for example, Jalmert, 1984; Metz-Göckel and Müller, 1986; Holter and Aarseth, 1993; Mintel, 1994; Holter, 1997).

We have also identified variations in the framing of research, in particular the extent to which research on men has been conducted directly and in an explicitly gendered way, the relation of these studies to feminist scholarship, Women's Studies and Gender Research more generally, and the extent to which research on men is focused on and presents 'voices' of men or those affected by men. Other differences stem from different theoretical, methodological and disciplinary emphases and assumptions.

Such political and academic differences are generally less apparent in national reports on statistical information. All countries have a system of national statistics though there are variations in their reliability. Furthermore, national statistics are largely the outcome of the work of large-scale bureaucratic government agencies, often with established ways of doing things, and a relatively long time lag in developing and changing systems. National statistical practices tend to change rather slowly. Increasingly, changes have been in response to external, transnational pressures, and indeed there are multiple pressures to accumulate national statistics from the UN and its agencies, such as UNDP, the EU (for members and prospective members), Eurostat, and so on. In addition, there are in some countries national statistical studies by academic researchers, newspapers and other media, and market research companies.

Rather, the state of statistical studies on men in the national contexts varies in terms of the volume and detail of statistical information. The general extent of national statistical resources is an important factor affecting the extent of available statistics on men. This is in addition to differences arising from the substantive differences in men's societal position and social practices, as the social and cultural contexts in which national statistics are collected are very varied indeed. In most countries, though there may not be a very large body of statistical information specifically focused on men's practices, a considerable amount of analysis of men is still possible.

As regards sources used, previous knowledge of members has been supplemented by reviews of the available statistical information from national statistical offices. For example, in Estonia this is the Statistical Office of Estonia; in Finland it is Statistics Finland; in Poland the Chief Statistical Office; in the UK the Office for National Statistics, and so on. In some cases much of this material is available electronically, through websites, diskettes and CD-ROMs; in others, extensive library work and examination of printed paper reports has been necessary; and in some cases there have been further contacts with key governmental statisticians and other researchers. In many cases key statistical information is produced by governmental ministries or other national bodies. In some cases, some national statistics are produced in both national languages and English.

Sources arising from international co-operation are also sometimes important, for example, in Estonia, the report issued by Fafo Institute for Applied Social Science (Norway) in co-operation with Ministry of Social Affairs of Estonia, Statistical Office of Estonia and University of Tartu. This collaborative survey, NORBALT, was carried out in 1994 and 1999 by these institutions on living conditions in the Baltic states and the two Russian regions of St Petersburg and Kaliningrad.

The amount and detail of statistical information stems from the priority that is given to different policy areas and problem definitions within governmental systems. This is especially important in the fields of labour market and employment, health and illness, and violence, statistics for all of which are generally relatively well developed. Governmental statistics on violence are usually collected by police, courts, other criminal justice institutions and victimisation surveys, so giving different pictures of levels of men's violence. Such statistics on violence are often compiled in terms of crime and criminal actions, alleged or proven, rather than in terms of the perpetration or experience of violence. There is frequently a lack of statistical information on social exclusion, such as ethnic or sexual minorities. The emphasis on different areas of social exclusion varies between the countries. The large amount of existing material is often scattered within a wide variety of statistical locations.

National statistics are frequently framed within an ideological presentation of neutrality, objectivism and facticity. The frequent lack of critical commentary might suggest that the figures are often meant to 'speak for themselves'. This is not to suggest that the figures are specifically 'wrong', but rather that they may be presented or interpreted as the most objective account of social arrangements, even though they may not explicitly highlight key issues of, for example, power, conflict and gender.

One aspect of this assumed 'neutrality' is that there is considerable national variation in the extent to which statistics are gender-disaggregated. In some countries, for example, Finland, there had been a long-term effort to make national statistics more explicitly gendered (Veikkola, 2002). However, a relative lack of gendering of data continues in many statistical sources. Detailed statistical sources directed towards a gendered analysis of men's practices are relatively rare. There is little statistical information and analysis that is explicitly focused in an explicitly gendered way on men, variations amongst men, and the relationship of those patterns to qualitative research on men's practices and lives.

National contexts

In the *Russian Federation* and other former socialist countries, sex, or gender, was, during the Soviet times, an important variable regularly used in statistical surveys particularly regarding the labour market, employment, family, health, demography and migration. Soviet policy-makers were sensitive to the results of statistical surveys by sex in paying political lip service to 'sex equality'. At the same time, violence as a gendered social problem was considered to occur rather randomly and as such was not explicitly considered a serious social issue. While the transitional countries of the former Soviet bloc have been reorganising their statistical data collection, it would be wrong to overgeneralise about them. Moreover, although after the breakup of the Soviet Union all republics were formally at the same point of departure, it is now obvious that they have developed in very different ways and are located in different socio-cultural spaces. Some examples are given below.

The form and development of statistical sources thus intersect in complex ways with the substantive form and nature of socio-economic change. This is perhaps clearest in some of the transitional nations, where changing governmental systems, including statistical data collection, are dealing with rapidly changing social and economic conditions. For example, *Estonia*, one of the Baltic republics that gained independence after the breakup of the Soviet Union, has gone through a major period of transition. While governmental data generally seem to be quite reliable in Estonia, social statistics are poor, compared with that on the environment, finance, industry, fuel and energy, housing, trade and construction. Statistical coverage is relatively strong on men's relations to work and health, but not social exclusion and violence. On the other hand, there are general representative surveys, with thousands of respondents, conducted in the late 1990s, on work, home, health, social exclusion and violence. In 2000 the Estonian population census produced very unexpected results. In all statistical yearbooks Estonia's population was forecast as 1,439,000 (as of 1 January 2000, calculated on the base of 1989 census data); however the figure, according to preliminary census data, was 1,376,743. The real decrease of population has been larger than expected or known before the census. There have been strong critiques of recent Estonian census survey by demographers (Kolga, 2001c). Statistical assessments should be considered within this context.

Statistical studies, surveys and researches in *Latvia* have been in a period of transition since the restoration of independence in 1991. The 1990s can be characterised as one of social, economic and psychological depression that has overlapped with the consequences of economic stagnation of the Soviet period. Demographic and family policy is central to the processes of post-socialist nation- and state-building, contextualised within the changing ethnic composition of the population and application to the EU. Thus, the major priorities in national statistics are the demographic situation, fertility, family policy, actual and desired family models, children's health, unemployment and changes in length of working life.

On the other hand, international standards are being introduced, in particular, with the *The Statistical Yearbook of Latvia* and the *UNDP Human Development*

Reports. However, current statistical surveys and specialist competence are still not sufficient in terms of analytical capacity to formulate informed policy recommendations in the major public policy spheres. 'Local colouring' of statistical surveys acts against the production of independent analyses in proposing policy decisions to policy-makers. The Soviet silencing of statistics on violence has been reproduced in post-Soviet state-building discourse. Gender, usually rather than sex, is used as a categorisation, but 'men' is not as a subcategory of gender analysis. Statistical data are gathered mainly around social, demographic, 'normal family' issues; the underlying argument of the biological reproduction of the nation excludes studies on the intersections of ethnicity, sexuality and gender. Gender-specific statistics remain absent from studies of the educational, political and cultural spheres. Gender and separate men-only statistical methodologies, such as on men and sexuality, urban or rural unemployment, age, and ethnicity, are very rare (Novikova, 2001c).

In *Poland* public statistics have devoted much attention to work-related issues. For example, public statistics in Poland provide reliable and independent data derived from surveys conducted by the Chief Statistical Office and its subsidiaries. As for home-related matters, pilot surveys are the only source of information on the division of labour and duration of housework in the 1990s. There are no data on the relationship between housework and employed activity, and no data on the relationship between the job or the type of work and home activities are given in the publications on time-use. Researchers have measured differences in time spent on individual activities in the context of age, education and source of income, but not sex. Of the various socially excluded groups, such as the unemployed, homeless, ethnic minorities, gay minorities, alcoholics, drug users, offenders and prostitutes, the unemployed receive most statistical attention. Data on the use of financial and non-financial social benefits do not include distributions by sex. There are no data on ethnic and gay minorities. The problem of racism and xenophobia, as well as homophobia, has appeared in surveys related to public opinion polls. They do not include in the questions sex differences of the groups to which the questions refer (such as national minorities, foreigners residing in Poland, homosexuals). Polish public statistics offer numerous data on health-related issues and welfare, though there are still significant gaps on health statistics (Oleksy, 2001c).

In the *Czech Republic* in the last ten years there have been a few sociological studies, mainly statistical surveys, conducted on women. Official statistical evidence recognises data based on sex but some key information that would provide more detail on the gendered structure of society is not available. An example of such missing information is the combination of sex/gender and education or other relevant stratification criteria in statistical measurement (Šmídová, 2006).

In some countries there are very large amounts of statistical information available. For example, in *Finland* a great deal of statistical information is produced by Statistics Finland, and much of that available on their website database, in annual yearbooks and on CD-ROMs. Statistical information is also produced by the National Research and Development Centre for Health and Welfare (STAKES) and the Social Insurance Institution of Finland (KELA), as well as different ministries. There have been recent increases in the extent to which such statistical sources are gender-disaggregated, but further disaggregation is still needed. Gender-focused statistical sources include those on gender equality in working life and the 'gender barometer' measuring attitudes to gender equality (Melkas, 1998, 2001, 2004). There is little statistical information specifically focused on men, variations amongst men, and the relationship of statistical patterns to qualitative research on men's practices. Labour Force Surveys and Employment Statistics are based more on quantifiable measures than subjective experiences of work and family. Statistical information on social exclusion is relatively scattered. Statistics Finland publishes a series on living conditions, but not homelessness. KELA produces reliable data on the use of social benefits, and alcohol use is relatively well surveyed. There is not much regularly produced statistical information on foreigners, immigrants and ethnic minorities. Statistics Finland research on the social conditions of immigrants in 2002 will contribute information in this area. While information on men's health outcomes is generally good, further information on men's healthcare practices is desirable (Hearn et al., 2001c).

Norway is a 'relatively egalitarian' country in gender terms, and yet despite the presence of relatively good statistical sources, many important indices and measures are still missing or can only be assembled through much detailed work. For example, more information is needed on the main factors affecting the gender gap in mortality, the main patterns of gender segregation, and the composition of research and the level of gender research investment. Other data not easily found include: men's mapping of household time-use; work hours for relevant groups of men and women; wages and breadwinners in relevant sectors, different levels, job types; couple (married, cohabiting, etc); household income composition (his and her share) by relevant job variables (sector, level, job type, pay), as well as more information on men's violences against women and children (Holter, 2001c).

In *Sweden* there is useful information easily available from the Swedish Institute's information site (www.sverige.se) and the national statistical pocketbook (SCB, 2002). Gender equality has been politically implemented since the 1970s. Gender equality laws were introduced 1980 and 1992, when gender equality statistics also became a part of the official statistics. Every year a pocketbook 'På tal om kvinnor och män' (On Men and Women) with statistics concerning gender equality is distributed. Organisations with more than ten employees have to produce gender analyses of salaries and a gender equality plan; gender analyses are mainstreamed in all political areas and decisions. Thus there are close connections of statistics, policies and research to the gender equality project (Nordberg, 2006). However, on some issues where gender is clearly important – such as the over-representation of men in fatal road traffic accidents – statistics are not easily available (Balkmar and Pringle, 2005b).

What is known about men in Sweden both in statistics and research is mainly connected to the gender equality project, even though strong gender segregation persists in the labour market. Men are mostly highlighted as a problem and looked upon as an obstacle for gender equality, a focus that has been maintained in gender equality policies. Statistics and research are often constructed to show gender differences between men's and women's time use for work, family, childcare and household responsibilities. Gender differences concerning power, economy, crimes, education and health are also highlighted. Statistics concerning gender equality take their point of departure from a heterosexual couple, a standpoint that is not problematised very much. The 'good gender equal life' is taken for granted to be in a family consisting of a heterosexual couple, man and wife – both of whom are wage earners. Men and women living in other kinds of relations are not focused on in the same way as are heterosexual couples, and same-sex couples are not compared with heterosexual couples concerning gender equality and unpaid household work (Nordberg, 2006).

Denmark is relatively well provided for in terms of statistical sources, and these are co-ordinated by Statistics Denmark.[3] These cover family, household and demographic patterns, the gendering of the labour market participation, wage gap, occupational and management distributions, and many other areas. In addition, there are some studies on gendered health statistics. With respect to diseases affecting both women and men that can lead to hospital admissions, 2002 data (Kruse and Helweg-Larsen, 2004) revealed some gender differences. For example, although the difference is more pronounced in the younger age ranges, in all age groups there were more men than women admitted to hospitals for cardiovascular disease, the gender ratio being 1:81. There appears to be adequate statistical material in Denmark on gender differences in health, morbidity and mortality, but more statistical study of men's health and health care practices would be desirable.

There is some growth of interest in statistics on violence. A survey of 10,434 respondents conducted by the National Institute of Public Health based on interviews and questionnaires included questions about exposure to interpersonal violence (Kjøller and Rasmussen, 2002). Another study of nearly 6,000 Danish youth surveyed at the age of 15 via computer assisted self-interview has examined experiences of sexual assault (Helweg-Larsen and Larsen, 2002), with girls reporting them two and a half times as often as boys. Official statistical information on men's violences is available primarily through crime statistics with victim information based on reports to the police available only since 2001. One large national prevalence survey was conducted in 1995–96 (Rigspolitichefen, 1998) specifically in the context of violence. Overall, there has been little statistical study of men's use of and experiences of violence (Iovanni and Pringle, 2005c), until recently (Balvig and Kyvsgaard, 2006).

In *Germany* there are many statistical sources available on the labour market, family formation and health. The Federal Statistical Office produces a yearbook that covers, amongst other things, developments in the labour market, family and households, health, mortality, parental leave, and poverty, relying on officially produced data. The Federal Office produces more specific data, for instance on qualifications and training. The problem with these data is that they still show the characteristics of their mode of production; their presentation often does not answer any research question. Other data are collected by huge official surveys and other agencies. The Federal Institute of Health and the Federal Criminal Institute analyses officially produced data, and also conduct studies of their own. These data often react to questions seen as politically urgent. A huge range of data is produced by investigations on social problems financed by political authorities, especially ministries (Müller, 2001b). Recent national surveys have addressed women's (Müller and Schröttle, 2004) and men's (Jungnitz et al., 2004) experiences of violence.

The quality of statistical information on men in *Ireland* is mixed. The state has pursued aspects of a gender equality strategy since the mid-1970s. However, with some notable exceptions, the impact of such policies is not routinely evaluated in official statistics on the gendered nature of family responsibilities, work, violence and health. Research studies, some sponsored by government departments, have begun to address these gaps, but progress is slow. Ireland has experienced huge economic growth since the mid-1990s, so that fewer men are now unemployed than for 20 years. Despite this growth, levels of poverty and social disadvantage remain significant. Concepts of social exclusion have broadened to take account of not only poverty, but educational disadvantage, racism, homophobia and drug misuse. Official statistics on the gendered nature of violences and health are becoming more sensitive to disaggregating men and women's experiences, but remain partial. While more is known about the gender of victims of violent crime, nothing is produced by government departments or police criminal statistics on the gender of perpetrators. There a similar lack of official data on the gender of perpetrators of child abuse, a gap being filled to some extent by research (Ferguson, 2001c).

The picture is also mixed in *Italy* where there has been a strong emphasis in recent statistical information on demographics, marriage, poverty, health, suicide, crime and violence (Ventimiglia and Pitch, 2001).

A different situation operates in the *UK* (Pringle et al., 2001). Especially since the advent of the Labour Administration in 1997 statistical data have expanded on topics such as poverty, unemployment, the labour market, crime (including violences to women), health, ethnicity, and often with a relatively strong gender focus. There is an immense amount of official statistical data on gender in relation to the labour market: it dwarfs the amount of data on other topics, even those relatively well-covered such as crime. In contrast, there is much less produced on areas of disadvantage such as disability, sexuality or crimes against children. This pattern reflects the governmental policy agenda focusing on social exclusion defined in rather narrow labour market terms; and crime, with some areas highlighted more than others. Thus the form of statistical information is interrelated with the form of socio-economic, political and policy change.

Overall, there is an urgent need for broader official statistical data gathering in relation to gender and social disadvantage, particularly on disability, sexuality, age, men's violences to children. Government statistics pay considerable attention to men's violences to women within heterosexual relationships (or as officially termed 'domestic violence') and racist crime (or 'racially motivated' crime as in official statistics), but relatively little attention to men's violences to children, gay men and lesbian women. Government statistics focus far more on men's health in relation to poverty, the labour market or ethnicity than disability or sexuality. This confirms the importance of understanding the complex intersections of disadvantage associated with gender, ethnicity, class, age, sexuality, disability. Issues of home and work, social exclusion, violences and health overlap and intersect in complex ways.

Thematic areas

Home and work

There is a very large amount of statistical data on men's relations to home and at work. This area frequently constituted the major part of the national reports on statistical sources. There is also much more complexity in the variables and relations presented than for the other themes. On the other hand, much of the data continues the tradition of dealing with home and work separately, so reinforcing the 'public/private' division. Men are constructed primarily as workers or unemployed or retired, on the one hand, and as family or household members, on the other.

In terms of men 'at home', the general national systems of population and census statistics are clearly a useful starting point. These statistics need to be read in association with census and other statistical information on economic activity, employment and status, and labour markets. General demographic patterns include the higher mortality of men relative to women, and thus the larger numbers of women in the older population. There are also a wide variety of statistics on patterns of family formation, childbearing, separation and divorce. These have generally been constructed as descriptive demographic variables rather than measures of men's family or household practices or dynamics more generally.

The pattern of family forms and men's relations to them is probably becoming more varied in many parts of Europe. While the so-called 'nuclear family' is not the majority type of household in most countries, it does remain an important minority form. For example, in Estonia despite the growth of divorces, the traditional family – officially married or cohabiting, with children – remains the largest family type. In Germany and elsewhere there is a trend toward smaller households. In Italy the process of decline of marriage continues, even as cohabitations increase. This is also observable in Norway, where there has been a marked increase in cohabitation and, in that sense, decline in marriage. In the UK cohabitation has increased amongst young people. Similar changes in marriage patterns in Poland have meant increasing numbers of single, unmarried men.

Another important trend that has been typical of practically all EU countries since the 1980s is the noticeable rise in the age at which people get married. Housework is still mostly women's work, and this is clearly statistically documented. There is much less statistical information on men's caring and associated activities at home, and on the interrelations of men's home and work, including the reconciliation of home and work life, men as carers and the sexual division of labour within households. For example, in Ireland government departments gather no data whatsoever on this and have been slow to commission research into this area.

In many countries the option of a child-induced career disruption continues as the normal case for the mother and a special case for the father. There is a growing research and statistical literature on men's and women's differential take-up of various forms of state and occupational parental leave. This is an especially significant research area in Germany, Norway and Sweden. In Norway, cash support reform for families with small children has created a new trend where the mother reduces wage work while the father works as much or more than before. The proportion of fathers taking long parental leave has decreased (Holter, 2001c).

In the Czech Republic the figure of men staying at home caring for children and household has risen slowly from a statistical zero in 1990 when the new legislative Act enabled men to stay at home on parental leave and officially become a caregiver (Marikova, 1999, 39) to an estimate of 0.5–2% today (Šmídová, 2006). Men have become entitled to financial assistance in the form of parental benefit only since 1995. One feature of this situation is that fathers tend to more usually take care of older children. This view is supported also by figures of single parent households, where only 2% of children live with their fathers as sole parents at their age of 0–17, and dependent children at ages of 18–24 live with their fathers in 3% of all cases according to the Census in 2001 (*Zeny a muzi v datech 2003*, 2003).

Recurring themes in employment include men's occupational, working and wage gap over women, gender segregation at work, differences in patterns of working hours, many men's close associations with paid work. In recent years the primary sector has diminished and the tertiary sector has grown. Male domination of the public sphere becomes obvious both in male/female ratios of economic activity rate and Gross Domestic Product. Unemployment seems to apply relatively equally to men and women, though these figures may not be very reliable due to different definitions used. Many countries have suffered from severe unemployment during the recessions of recent decades, leading to social exclusion of certain groups. Men dominate formal decision-making and are in a large majority in most parliaments (Hearn et al., 2002c).

Polish data show that more men worked full-time, in the private sector in particular, of all employees; part-time female employees dominate in both sectors. In Finland and Sweden women work both in the private and in the public sector, while men work mostly in the private sector. These two countries embody both relative gender equality and traditionally high labour market participation of both women and men, along with strong labour market segregation. Fifty-six per cent of the Czech labour force in 1999 was men in the 'civil sector' of the labour market (*Zeny a muzi v cislech*, 2000, 118); this sector excludes 'duty or service contracts', such as the military, police and firefighters. Data from these are not made public even though these jobs have some gender specifics and even equal opportunities policies (Šmídová, 2006).

Another important variable is the relation of women's salaries to men's. The ratio of men's wages to women's have not changed greatly during recent years: there is still a gap of about 20%–27%. In Sweden which has been at the forefront of gender policy development, men still often have higher salaries than women in the same occupation, and men in general have 122% of women's salary (Nordberg, 2006). In the Czech Republic men earned 135% of the average women's wage or salary in 1997 (or to put this another way, women earned 73.4% of what men earned) (*Zeny a muzi v cislech*, 2000). In the 2001 Census the gender pay gap was still 26% (Šmídová, 2006).

There are also national differences in class structure and the extent of variation in salaries between men: in Estonia one man may earn 16–17 times more than another man. There has been a general lack of attention to men as managers, policy-makers, owners and other power holders. There are now some studies of this in Finland. The change of women entering into senior management has been slow and the proportion of female senior staff and upper management has largely remained stable during the first half of the 1990s; 21% in 1990 and 22% in 1995. The salary of managers depends strongly on gender, but less so in the case of lower level occupations. In Czech Republic relatively small differences in earnings in different segments of the labour market visible today can be traced back to the totalitarian times of 'equal distribution of wealth' – almost equal pay and living standard to anybody employed (and almost everybody was employed) (Šmídová, 2006).

Many other major patterns of change are identified. In Norway, there has been a slight decline of non-standard employment forms over the last years (Holter, 2001c). In some countries, for example, Ireland, there has been a notable increase in women's employment in recent years, with associated effects upon men. Primary breadwinning is no longer the monopoly of men. Structural economic changes have been especially significant in the transitional countries, where they have brought major change for women and men at home and work. In some cases, there is also the problem of a high rate of change in work and working place, with high amounts of layoffs.

Such changes have been very significant in many of the Baltic, Central and East European countries, but also in the UK and elsewhere. Moreover, it is incorrect to consider all post-socialist countries in the same vein. For example, Bulgaria, Czech Republic, Estonia, Latvia, Poland and the Russian Federation are at different points of economic development, which may account for different forms of the social problem of men, and different patterns of occupational mobility for women and men. In some cases, notably Estonia and the Russian Federation, there has been a decline in population, and the growth of the 'economically inactive' population and relatively high rate of unemployment. In Estonia men, especially rural men, are the subjects of structural economic changes during the last ten years which appeared in the diminishing of the primary sector and the expansion of the tertiary economic sector.

The gender pattern of unemployment is variable between countries; in official figures at least, these may mask other realities by excluding many categories of people. In some official figures, men are more likely to be unemployed; in others, women. In the Czech Republic in 1997 the rate of unemployment was similar for women and men at about 7% of the labour force, according to the OECD-CCET Labour Market Database (cited in UNICEF, 1999, 28). Rates for long-term unemployment lasting a year or more were in 1998 very similar for women and men at 31.5% and 30.9% respectively of the total unemployment (*Human Development Report 2000*, 2000, 241). According to the *Human Development Report 2003* (2003, 299), the rate of men's unemployment was in 2001 substantially below that of women's, at 68.5% of the women's rate (with the general rate at 8.2% of the labour force) (Šmídová, 2006).

There is a growing amount of detailed statistical data on time. In Poland from the point of view of the mean time of the duration of the activity, men devoted to their jobs twice as much time as women on the average. They also used mass media more frequently. They spent nearly twice as much time on sports and leisure activities. Women devoted almost three times as much time to housework, slightly more time than men to studying, as well as to religious practices. In the context of the mean time of the performance of the activity, professionally active men devoted to work more time than women by 33 minutes every day on the average.

The number of hours worked outside the home is a crucial determinant of the level of contact between parents and children. In Ireland men work an overall average of around 46 hours per week, with fathers tending to work slightly longer hours than non-fathers. A third of fathers (33%) work 50 hours per week or more compared to only a quarter of non-fathers (27%). Mothers, where they are employed, work an average of 31–32 hours per week outside the home, exactly 15 hours less than the number of hours worked outside the home by father. Non-mothers work longer hours in employment than mothers. It appears that fathers' work patterns are influenced by the employment status and earnings of their partners. Fathers whose partners are working outside the home spend less hours at work than fathers whose partners are not working. A further crucial variable is the time of the day or week when the work is done. A small proportion of fathers in Ireland do shift work, nearly half do evening work, a quarter do night work, two-thirds Saturday work and two-fifths Sunday work. Fathers are much more likely to work unsocial hours than mothers.

In Ireland the proportion of mothers in full-time employment is, however, much lower than for fathers, with much higher proportions of women doing part-time work. Still, fathers were the exclusive breadwinners in only half of all families with dependent children. In all countries fathers are more employed than non-fathers. In Norway fathers with young children are 'the most stable labour power in the market' (Holter, 2001c). This applies especially to younger fathers in employment. In Finland educated men tend to have more children; men have been asked in a national survey for their views on state support to families. More men than women considered the support satisfactory; about 33% of men born in 1953–1957 and 1963–1967 thought it was completely or somewhat insufficient, whereas more than half of the women of the same age groups considered it insufficient. The majority of men thought that a lower level of taxation would be the best way to support families, whereas women wanted more services.

The relative wage-earning working life of men has shrunk for a number of reasons. The training phase is becoming longer, careers start later, working life is shorter, and life expectancy (in some countries) is increasing. However, a quantitative time gain does not necessarily mean a qualitative gain, because the shortened working life has become more intensive, less tranquil and more uncertain. One of the most significant trends is the demand for productivity and an increasing pace of work. Work has also become mentally, if not physically, more wearing and uncertainty, competition and fixed-term employment contracts are more common, with associated health effects (Vahtera et al., 1997; Kivimäki et al., 2000).

Social exclusion

As with the academic research, this has been the most difficult area to predefine, but in some ways one of the most interesting. National reports on statistical sources have approached this area very differently, in view of the different ways in which social exclusion is recognised (see Chapter 7, this volume). Social exclusion appears in the statistical literature in many, sometimes related, different ways, such as unemployment, ethnicity, education, homelessness, imprisonment and so on.

The most recurring form of social exclusion that has been identified from statistical sources is poverty and unemployment of certain groups of men. Other key dimensions include exclusions of ethnic minorities, foreign nationals, migrants, especially non-Western immigrants, and asylum applicants, whose exclusion can relate to the criminal justice system, education, unemployment, health, or some permutation thereof. In some countries there is growing recognition of education as a site or source of social exclusion for some men, especially young men, by class, region and ethnicity. Accordingly, consolidated and multiple forms of poverty (by low level of education, class, unemployment, skills, age, ethnicity) are increasingly recognised. There is growing concern with statistical information on forms of social exclusion that are health-related, including alcohol and drug addiction, disability and imprisonment. For example, men make up the very large part of the prison population, as much as 98%. In some countries, the proportion of women is increasing. The typical profile of a male prisoner in many countries is of profound social disadvantage. In the UK minority ethnic men and women accounted for relatively high proportions of the prison population. Regional differences are also recognised, notably in Germany, between the former East and West Germanies.

The social exclusion of certain men frequently links with unemployment of certain categories of men (such as less educated, rural, ethnic minority, young, older), men's isolation within and separation from families, and associated social and health problems. These are clear issues throughout all countries. Statistical sources have shown the factors associated with long-term unemployment for men of working age, including giving up active job search and withdrawal from the labour force into the 'inactive' category: poor educational qualifications; living in public housing especially in larger cities; being in the older age groups; sharing a household with other unemployed or officially defined 'economically inactive' persons; being single or having a large family. Unemployment is also often higher for immigrant and minority ethnic men. Long-term unemployment is a problem for a relatively small but significant group of men in 'consolidated poverty' in many countries, including those that are more affluent, such as Germany, and those that have gone through a recent economic boom, such as Ireland. With increasing refugees and economic migrants arriving since the mid-1990s, the shift to a multicultural society is showing latent Irish racism, including violent attacks on many men and women of colour, for which no official figures are available.

Issues of social exclusion are especially important in the Baltic, Central and East European countries with post-socialist transformations of work and welfare, with dire consequences for many men. There is clear statistical evidence of health problems of men in the Russian Federation, while Estonia and Latvia have experienced rapid increases in HIV/AIDS infection. In Poland, the term social exclusion refers mainly to the unemployed, homeless, ethnic minorities, sexual (gay and other) minorities, and those thought to be pathologically unable to change, such as alcoholics, drug users, offenders and prostitutes. Unemployed people receive most statistical attention from amongst these groups; there are no data, however, on ethnic and homosexual minorities. The problem of racism and xenophobia, as well as homophobia, appears in surveys related to public opinion polls. They do not, however, include questions on gender differences within the groups to which the questions refer, for example, by ethnicity, nationality or sexuality.

Few statistical studies give attention to men engaged in creating social exclusion, doing discrimination, and reproducing social inclusion.

Violences

As in the review of academic research in the previous chapter, the recurring theme here is the widespread nature of the problem of men's violences to women, children and other men. Men are strongly overrepresented among those who use violence, especially heavy violence including homicide, sexual violence, racial violence, robberies, grievous bodily harm and drug offences. Similar patterns are also found for accidents in general, vehicle accidents and drunken driving. In all the countries, men commit suicide more than women.

Violence is also age-related. The life course variation in violence with a more violence-prone youth phase has been connected to increasing exposure to commercial violence and to other social phenomena, but these connections have not been well mapped. Most robberies and violent crimes are committed by men between 21 and 40 years old. Directly physically violent crime tends to involve violence by men known to those concerned, while with property crimes victims tend more to be by strangers.

Much of official statistics on violence need to be treated with caution. In many countries there is a large amount of statistical data on crime, as a more general organising principle than violences. For example, the problem of violence in Polish public statistics is limited to cases registered by the police and adjudicated in courts. There are no data for the whole country that specify types of violence used and data on non-registered cases. The source of data for the Chief Statistical Office is the information of the Chief Police Headquarters, which also present on their webpages the most important data on perpetrators of offences connected with domestic violence, rape, sexual abuse of children, infanticide and desertion; they do not, however, specify the sex of perpetrators or characterise the victim.

There are clear gender differences in the kinds of crimes reported. For example, in Italy men report being victims of violent crimes, women more crimes against property. However, in Finland figures in *Crime and Criminal Justice 1995–1996* (Rikollisuus ja seuraamusjärjestelmä tilastojen valossa,

1997), an overview of crime and the criminal justice system, were not separated by gender. This needs to be remedied in future work. Recent publications on homicide (Kivivuori, 1999) give gender-disaggregated data on victims and offenders. The national surveys of women's experiences of violence from men in Finland (Heiskanen and Piispa, 1998) and Sweden (Lundgren et al., 2001) might be paralleled by statistical studies of men's use of and experiences of violence. This has happened in Germany, where the national representative survey of women's health, well-being and personal safety (from violence) (Müller and Schröttle, 2004) has been accompanied by a smaller scale survey of men's experience of receiving violence (Jungnitz et al., 2004).

A form of violence that is repeatedly highlighted is men's violences to women. The range of abusive behaviours perpetrated on victims include direct physical violence, isolation and control of movements, and abuse through the control of money. Estimates range from 10 to over 40% of women experiencing such violations. There has been a large amount of feminist research on women's experiences of violence from men, and the policy and practical consequences of that violence, including by state and welfare agencies, as well as some national representative surveys of women's experiences of violence, as in Finland and Sweden. Such focused surveys of women's experience of sexual violence (in the broad sense of the term) tend to produce higher reports than from general crime victim surveys. In turn, the latter tend to produce higher figures than police and criminal justice statistics. Thus some non-governmental sample surveys of the general population have produced higher figures than police and criminal justice statistics for levels of men's violences to women. For instance a local study in North London suggested that a third of women will experience a form of 'domestic violence' in their lifetime and that just over 20% are raped by a husband or partner (Mooney, 1999). Another local survey in Glasgow estimated that 40% of women have experienced rape or sexual assault (Glasgow Women's Support Project/Glasgow Evening Times, 1990).

Child abuse, including physical abuse, sexual abuse and child neglect, is being recognised as a prominent social problem in statistical sources in many countries. Both the gendered nature of these problems and an appreciation of how service responses are themselves gendered are beginning to receive more critical attention, both in terms of perpetrators and victims/survivors. A markedly 'male' offence is the sexual abuse of children. Around 90% of child sexual abusers are men (see Pringle, 1995). One Polish survey found that boys were physically or emotionally abused by their fathers and sexually abused by their relatives, teachers, friends of the family, neighbours and friends more often than girls (Kmiecik-Baran, 1999, 110–11). However, girls contacting a Polish 'domestic violence' hotline 'Niebieska linia' (Blue line), reported being victims of violence twice as frequently as boys who contacted it (Oleksy, 2001c). Out of nearly 6,000 Danish young people surveyed at the age of 15 via computer assisted self-interview, 657 youth (11.3% of the total; 15.9% of the girls, 6.7% of the boys) reported having experienced a sexual assault punishable in law. Of these 657 young people, 44% (n = 287) reported that the assault was perpetrated by a person over at least five years. This number represents 4.9% of the total respondents (7.9% of the girls, 2.0% of the boys) (Helweg-Larsen and Larsen, 2002).

In Ireland official statistics do not gather data on the gender of perpetrators of child abuse, a gap that is being filled to some extent by research. Retrospective Prevalence Surveys within general adult populations always reveal far higher levels of child sexual abuse than official crime statistics. The most quoted retrospective British prevalence study amongst young people used successively narrower definitions of sexually abusive experiences in childhood to gauge the differences in reported prevalence levels. Using the broadest definition produced figures of 1:2 for females and 1:4 for males (Kelly et al., 1991).

Health

The life expectancy of men has increased markedly since the beginning of the 20th century. There is a persistent theme of men's ageing in many, though not all, countries. This is especially notable in Italy, which also has a low birth rate. As with the review of academic research in the previous chapter, the major recurring theme in terms of health is men's relatively low (compared to women) life expectancy, poor health, accidents, suicide, morbidity. Men suffer and die more and at a younger age from cardiovascular diseases, cancer, respiratory diseases, accidents and violence than women. Socio-economic factors, qualifications, social status, life style, diet, smoking, drinking, drug abuse, hereditary factors, as well as occupational hazard, seem to be especially important for morbidity and mortality. Gender differences in health arise from how certain work done by men are in hazardous occupations. Generally men neglect their health and for some men at least their 'masculinity' is characterised by risk taking, especially for younger men (in terms of smoking, alcohol and drug taking, unsafe sexual practices, road accidents, lack of awareness of risk), an ignorance of their bodies, and reluctance to seek medical intervention for suspected health problems. Thus 'traditional masculinity' can be seen as hazardous to health. There is some growing statistical information on perceptions of health and also health care use. In this context it is interesting that Estonian research finds that men are over-optimistic regarding their own health.

Morbidity and mortality are central topics of public discussions in some countries. For example, in Latvia, there is recognition that men fall ill and die with cardiovascular diseases more frequently than women, and life expectancy for males has decreased by four years, and two years for females. There has been attention to gendered health, with occupational health problems of work with asbestos, in chemico-pharmaceutical enterprises, and chronic lead poisoning, often mainly affecting men. Statistics indicate to a rapid decrease of fertility and growth of mortality, with a stress on the negative effects upon ethnic Latvians. The notion of depopulation is articulated in nationalist discourse. The most recent studies have shown that reproductive health in Latvia is characterised by the following problems: Latvia's birth rate is one of the lowest in the world; male life expectancy trends are downwards, and much lower than for women; male participation in the choice of contraception, family planning and child-raising is insufficient (Novikova, 2001c).

There is some information on the social care sector, and the overlap of health and welfare. For example, of residents in Polish stationary welfare centres including children, in 1992, men constituted 44%, women 56%. Men (55%; 45% women) were more numerous only amongst mentally handicapped residents. Female pensioners – 62% (nearly 38% men), chronically ill women – 66% (34% men), disabled – 58% (42% men) were among adult residents in the centres. Data on underage centre residents revealed a contrary trend: boys were more numerous in all groups – chronically ill, disabled and mentally handicapped. The number of the homeless who stayed in shelters increased greatly in 1998, of whom 91% were men (Oleksy, 2001c).

Men's suicide, especially young men's, is high in the Baltic countries, Poland, Russian Federation and Finland. In these countries there is also a relatively high difference in life expectancy between men and women. In Ireland, Italy and Norway, men perform suicide about three times as often as women; in Poland the ratio is over 5:1. In Italy over the last ten years there has been a clear prevalence of men in comparison to women, while as regards suicide attempts, the trend is reversed: more than 50% are by females.

Globally, the rate of suicide tends to increase with age; however, the rising figures for young men's suicide have attracted particular attention in recent years. While Ireland has one of the highest known differences internationally between young male and female suicides (7:1), it does not have the highest overall 15–24 year old male suicide rate. With an overall male rate of 20.3 per 100,000 Ireland comes 28th in the World Health Organisation table (of 97 countries). Lithuania has the highest figure, with a rate of 80.7, followed by the Russian Federation (69.3) and Belarus (60.3) (http://www.who.int/mental_health/prevention/suicide/en/Figures_web0604_table.pdf). There is a very low level of take up of services by young male suicides prior to their deaths: this group does not see the services, as presently structured and delivered, as being relevant to them. Suicide rates have generally fallen across the UK over the last 15 years, except among young men aged 15–44; suicide rates for Scotland are considerably higher than other UK countries. Local areas where suicide rates were significantly high tended to be those characterised as having high 'deprivation' levels.

Many of the health issues addressed here have clear policy implications. While these are focused on more specifically in the next chapter, one example may be useful at this point. In discussing national statistics on reproductive and sexual health in Latvia, Novikova (2001c) highlights these policy issues: insufficient exchange of information between statistics organisations and research organisations; lack of co-ordination between government, local government and non-governmental organisations; the need to promote gender equality and men's participation in addressing reproductive health; the absence of adequate gender equality and reproductive and sexual health education at schools. In such ways, statistical sources and policy questions are closely linked.

Concluding remarks

The explicit gendering of statistics on men's practices

National and comparative statistics are frequently framed within an ideology of neutrality, objectivism and facticity. Their frequent lack of critical commentary might also suggest that the figures 'speak for themselves'. Key statistics are still not always gender-disaggregated. Men ands men's practices can easily remain strangely invisible in both gender-aggregated statistics and their interpretation.

In the previous chapter, we noted that an interesting and paradoxical issue is that the more that research, especially focused gendered research on men, is done the more that there is a realisation of the gaps that exist, both in specific fields and at a general methodological level. While a lack of gendered statistical data on men hinders research development, this conclusion cannot be said to have been reinforced in any clear way with regard to the development of statistical questions.

On first reading it might seem that relatively few specific gaps have been identified in the statistical sources. In some senses there is indeed a wealth of information, especially on employment, demography, family arrangements, health, illness and mortality. However, a closer reading shows that while the national statistical systems provide a broad range of relevant information, they usually have significant shortcomings. Explicit gendering of statistics is still not usual. Moreover, there is an absence of focused statistical studies of men, especially differences amongst men. Many statistical studies are rather cautious in their critical commentary. Many provide data for further analysis, interrogation, comparison with other data, critical comment and theory development. This is partly a reflection of traditions around the rules of statistical inference, and partly as many studies are produced within a governmental context where such further analysis and critique is not seen as appropriate.

Moreover, a problem with the huge amount of data available is that the foci of data production and collection, as well as the respective basic populations studied, differ to such an extent that, until now, it has been a difficult task to find any ground for comparing and relating the data to each other in order to find comprehensive and interpretive information about men. For example, in Germany there is a lack of middle range studies which might close the gap between theoretical concepts of masculinities and gender relations, empirical data produced in small case studies providing deeper insight into the microstructure of problems, and the official statistics level that, until now, has produced a 'big picture', albeit with mainly unclear aspects.

The source and methodology of statistics

There is a need to attend with great care to the source and methodology of statistics on men's practices. For example, focused surveys of women's experience of sexual violence, in the broad sense of the term, tend to produce higher reports than general crime victim surveys. In turn, the latter tend to produce higher figures than police and criminal justice statistics. Thus the use of statistics on men's practices is a matter for both technical improvement and policy and political judgement.

Unities and differences

As with the review of academic research (Chapter 2), there are both clear similarities between nations and clear differences, in terms of, for example, the extent of egalitarianism, economic growth or downturn, and experience of post-socialist transformation. However, statistical data on men's practices also reveal the pervasive and massive negative impact of patriarchal relations of power across all sectors of society. The importance of the ongoing challenge to these gendered power relations cannot be over-emphasised. There is neglect of attention to men in powerful positions and to analyses of men's broad relations to power, both in themselves and as contexts to other themes. Unities and differences between men need to be highlighted, between countries and amongst men within each country, as with differences between men in the former West Germany and the former East Germany, and within groups of men.

Recent structural changes

Analyses of the social problem of men should take into account that many of the countries have experienced recent major socio-economic changes, with implications for the social construction of men. In the case of the transitional nations the political and economic changes, often viewed as positive compared with the Soviet experience, have also often brought social and human problems. As noted in the previous chapter, while there is no exact fit between economic and social change, there is often a clear relation, for instance, a weakening of the primary sector leading to social and geographical mobility. In the transitional nations, people never expected economic freedom would be associated with a decrease in population and birth rate, high criminality, drugs, and diseases such as tuberculosis. During the transition period there has often been a negative relation between economy and welfare.

Interconnections, power and social exclusion

There are strong interconnections between the four focus areas. This applies to both men's power and domination in each theme area, and between some men's unemployment, social exclusion and ill health. Statistics reveal the overall contradictory nature of men's positions and experiences. Few statistical studies give attention to men engaged in creating social exclusion, 'doing' discrimination, and reproducing social inclusion. Men dominate key institutions, such as government, politics, management, trade unions, churches, sport; yet some men suffer considerable marginalisation as evidenced in higher rates of suicide, psychiatric illness and alcoholism than women. Men make up the majority of prisoners, are more often the long-term unemployed, and experience lower life expectancy than women. Social exclusion applies to and intersects with all three other themes: home and work, violences, health. When one maps the academic research onto statistics, patterns of men's violence can be seen to interconnect with all the themes to some extent, as well as cutting across social divisions. Statistics are mainly focused on dyadic analysis, for example, poverty and men/women, or poverty and ethnicity. Developing triadic statistical surveys and analyses of, say, poverty, gender and ethnicity is much rarer, and an altogether more complex task.

4
Law and Policy

Keith Pringle and Jeff Hearn, with Ursula Müller, Elżbieta H. Oleksy, Harry Ferguson, Voldemar Kolga, Emmi Lattu, Irina Novikova, Teemu Tallberg and Hertta Niemi

Introduction

While there is stubborn persistence in some aspects of men and masculinities – most obviously in men's domination of the use of violence – there have also been major historical changes in some forms of men's practices. Moreover, men and masculinities are set within changing policy contexts. Changing gender relations both constitute governments and other policy-making institutions, and provide tasks for governmental, partnership and third sector agencies to deal with. In this sense governments and other policy institutions can be seen as both part of the problem and part of the solution.

To understand the national and transnational policy context also involves considering the relevance of 'the social problem of men' within organisational and governmental policy formation, national, regional and indeed EU institutions. It is necessary to analyse and change the place of men within the gender structures of governmental, transgovernmental and policy-making organisations. This includes the questions of the relative lack of attention to men in power, including men in the EU, the implications of mainstreaming for men, and men's relations to gender equality. The social problem of men relates closely to existing EU social agendas, including EU policies on equality, gender equality, social exclusion and racism. There is a need to develop policy options on men, including critical, well informed practices and policies on men.

Addressing policy around men and masculinities is an important and urgent matter. There are indeed risks and dangers in non-action, for example, in the intersection of various 'new' and 'old' masculinities, nationalisms, racisms and xenophobias. There are also key issues around the changing policy context in Europe – including the relation of the EU to recent eastward expansion and the conditions of application and accession; questions of migration, especially of young men, and their implications for women and men, in countries of both emigration and immigration; trafficking in women, children and men, especially the actions of men as consumers within EU member countries. The social problem of men is of central and urgent interest to EU and applicant countries.

Many other transnational organisations and groupings, for example, the Council of Europe, the UN, UNESCO, UNICEF, ILO, the Nordic Council of Ministers, the EU Women's Lobby, and various NGOs have come to recognise the importance of the place of men in the movement towards gender equality. The UN held a Beijing + 5 Special Event on Men and Gender Equality in New York, June 2000 (http://www.undp.org/gender/programmes/men/men_ge.html#Beijing + 5 Special). The first EU Conference on 'Men and Gender Equality' was held at Örebro, Sweden in March 2001. Further governmental and transgovernmental interest seems likely to develop. In March 2003 the UN Division for the Advancement of Women (2003) organised a worldwide online discussion forum and expert group meeting in Brasilia on 'the role of men and boys in achieving gender equality' as part of its preparation for the 48th session of the Commission on the Status of Women in 2004.[1] In particular, we should highlight how men's violence to women and children is receiving more attention from the EU, the Council of Europe and other transnational organisations, such as UNICEF and UNESCO (Breines et al., 2000; Ferguson et al., 2004; Edwards and Hearn, 2005).

It is necessary to analyse and change the place of men within the gender structure of governmental and other policy-making organisations. There is also a need to develop policy options on men, including best practices and policies on men. Addressing policy around men and masculinities is an important and urgent matter.

In this chapter, first we set out the general state of law and policy on men and men's practices. This is followed by a discussion on the four main themes: home and work, social exclusion, violences, health. We then present some policy recommendations that follow from the analyses of this chapter, together with those in Chapters 2 and 3. Finally, we highlight a few broad issues that need to be addressed within policy agendas if the detailed policy recommendations are to have a chance of success.

The general state of law and policy addressing men's practices

The state of studies on men in national contexts varies in terms of the volume and detail of law and policy, the ways in which this has been framed, as well as substantive differences in men's societal position and social practices. In this section, we address the following questions: information sources; some broad substantive patterns; and some interconnections of sources and patterns.

First, we make some remarks on sources. Existing academic knowledge of members has been supplemented by extensive reviews of the available information on law and policy from national governmental, quasi-governmental and related sources. In some cases much of this material is available electronically, through websites, diskettes and/or CD-ROMs; in others extensive library work and examination of printed paper reports have been necessary; and in some cases there have been further contacts with key governmental contacts and other researchers in the theme areas.

Importantly, in examining law and policy, there is a need to distinguish between several different levels and layers of forms of law and policy, and hence their analysis. These are principally: the broad legal and constitutional arrangements; the specific embodiment of formal policy in law; the development of explicit governmental policy; the often changing forms of local and agency-based policies, sometimes operating more implicitly; and the practice of policy implementation in day-to-day policy practices. The balance between these various forms of 'law and policy' varies between the national reports. The importance of the comparative evaluation of legal and policy support for some form of the provider model (or other models) needs to be stressed.

The amount and detail of policy information stems from the priority that is given to different policy areas, problem definitions and extent of problematisation within governmental systems. This is especially important in the fields of labour market and employment, health and illness, and violence, all of which are generally relatively well developed. There is frequently a lack of clearly and easily available policy information on social exclusion, such as ethnic minorities. The emphasis on different areas varies between the countries. The large amount of existing material is often scattered within a wide variety of governmental locations.

In terms of substantive patterns, we may note the connections and differences that there are with both academic research and statistical information on men's practices. In Chapter 2, we discussed how in some countries, especially in Germany, Norway, Sweden, the UK, but also to an extent elsewhere, there is now some form of relatively established tradition of research on men that can be identified, albeit of different orientations. We addressed variations in the framing of research, that is, the extent to which research on men has been conducted directly and in an explicitly gendered way, and the relation of these studies to feminist scholarship, Women's Studies and Gender Research more generally, and the extent to which research on men is focused on and presents 'voices' of men or those affected by men. There are also very different and sometimes antagonistic approaches to research within the same country, for example, between non-gendered, non-feminist or even anti-feminist approaches and gendered and feminist approaches. Other differences stemmed from different theoretical, methodological and disciplinary emphases, assumptions and decisions. Addressing these differences has been part of the task of the Network (Hearn et al., 2002d). These differences in traditions were less observable in the national reports on statistical information (Hearn et al., 2002c; Chapter 3 this volume).

To some extent, and in some perspectives, it might be presumed that academic research and statistical information provide two, often interrelated, ways of describing, analysing and explaining men's practices, whether dominant, subordinated or different. At the same time, they construct those dominant, subordinated and different patterns of men's practices in their own ways. Meanwhile law and policy might be initially understood as governmental and quasi-governmental regulations of those dominant, subordinated and different patterns of men's practices. Yet, law and policy are also themselves modes of describing, analysing, explaining and indeed constructing men's practices. Thus political and academic differences are both apparent and to some extent obscured in the specific form of the legal and policy modes examined here.

There are both similarities and differences in the substantive patterns of national laws and policies. The social and cultural contexts in which these national reports are written are very varied indeed, and need to be understood to make sense of the different orientations of national reports. The general state of law and policy in the countries under scrutiny is the product of several factors. These include their diverse broad historical and cultural traditions; their legal and governmental institutions; their more recent and specific relations to the European Union (EU); and their welfare and social policy frameworks and practices.

As regards the impact of EU Law and policy-making structures on individual members, we need to remember that the EU itself is part of the historical legacy that has been based on the attempt to develop broad social democracy and stop fascism from happening in Europe again. Furthermore, it is relevant to look at the EU, the European Commission and the associated organisations as gendered institutions. This includes the question of the lack of attention to men in power, including men in the institutions of the EU itself. The EU and the EU application process are themselves becoming important parts of the public politics of comparative European welfare development, including the comparative development of gender policies, and policies in relation to men. This is especially significant as regards the EU's eastward expansion, including the specific conditions for application and accession.

There is a growing recognition of the impact, albeit differential, of the EU itself on the heterogeneous gender politics and gender regimes of the member states (Liebert, 1999). This is partly through the operation of various equal opportunities policies at the supranational and national levels, most obviously in the fields of family, welfare, labour market and education policies, but also more generally in migration and environmental policies (Walby, 1999). In most cases these debates on and indeed in the EU have focused on (increasing) women's participation in the public spheres of employment and education, along with the development of women's rights in social protection and welfare.

Throughout their development there have been strong legal and policy emphases on equality and gender equality within the EEC and the EU. Key measures here include:

- Article 119 (EC) of the 1957 Treaty of Rome on the principle of 'equal pay for equal work',
- the 1975 Equal Pay Directive (75/117/EEC),

- the 1976 Equal Treatment Directive on Employment, Vocational Training and Promotion, and the Working Conditions (76/207/EEC), and
- the subsequent related directives, especially the Social Security Directive (79/7/EEC),
- Article 13 (EC) of the 1997 Treaty of Amsterdam on general anti-discrimination in employment,
- the Community Framework Strategy on Gender Equality (COM (2000) 335 final of 7.6.2000) and the related Programme (Decision 2001/51/EC),
- the Employment Framework Directive 2000 (Council Directive 2000/78/EC).

According to Articles 17 and 18 of the Employment Framework Directive 2000, all EU member states are required to implement national legislation prohibiting discrimination in employment on the grounds of sex, racial or ethnic origin, religion or belief, age, disability or sexual orientation by 2 December 2003. Similarly, Paragraphs (1)(c) and (1)(d) of Article 3 address 'pay' (including travel allowances and occupational pension schemes) and 'benefits', respectively. Article 12 prohibits discrimination on the grounds of nationality. In addition, there are numerous other Declarations and Recommendations around equal opportunities, which have had the effect of shaping policy norms and creating a policy climate towards this direction (Bulmer, 1998).

Overall policy development in the EU is to some extent framed by the development of the European Social Agenda (2000–2005) (Communication . . . , 2000) This seeks to advance a range of 'future orientations for social policy', of which the most relevant to the topic of men's practices are the following:

- 'Fighting poverty and all forms of exclusion and discrimination in order to promote social integration';
- 'Promoting gender equality'; and
- 'Strengthening the social policy aspects of enlargement and the European Union's external relations'.

There is, however, much to be done in order to give explicit attention to the full implications of achieving gender equality within the European Social Agenda, in terms of what this means for men and changing men's practices. The policies of the existing EU social agenda (including EU policies on equality, gender equality, social exclusion, racism) imply the development of policy options on men. There have already been some steps in this process, for example, the EU 'Men and Gender Equality Conference', Örebro, held in March 2001 under the auspices of the then Swedish presidency, and the EU conference on 'Gender and Social Exclusion', Copenhagen, September 2002 under the auspices of the Danish Presidency. It is likely that this process of considering the implications for men and changing men's practices will increase in the coming years, albeit from a variety of political interests and motivations.

In focusing on men within this European context, a persistent challenge is how to examine law and policy that specifically addresses men, whilst at the same time being aware of the broad range of laws and policies that are not explicitly gendered that are likely to bear on men. In one sense almost all laws and policies can be said to be relevant to men as citizens (or indeed as non-citizens, for example, as aliens). In another sense, in most countries, though there may not be a very large body of law and policy information specifically focused on men, there is still a considerable amount of analysis of law and policy in relation to men that is possible. These questions are affected by both deeply embedded historical constructions of citizenship, and more recent reforms around gender and 'gender equality'.

On the first count, it is important to note that in many countries citizenship has historically been constructed as 'male', onto which certain concessions and rights of citizenship, for example suffrage, have been granted to women. However, there is variation in the extent to which this pattern applies, and in some cases citizenship has taken different gendered forms, with citizenship for women and men being more closely associated with relatively recent nationalisms for all citizens. This is not to say that such latter 'nationalistic' citizenship is non-gendered, far from it; it may indeed remain patriarchal in form, not least through the continuation of pre-nationalistic discourses and practices, sometimes around particular notions of 'equality', as in the Soviet regimes. Indeed it might be argued that some forms of (male) citizenship, based on notions of individualism and even exclusion of community and similarity, are often in tension with some forms of (male) nationalism, based on notions of cultural lineage, culture and language, and exclusion of individuality and difference.

On the second count, the contemporary societal context of law and policy on men is often formally framed by the ratification, or not, of such international agreements as:

- the ILO Convention 100 on Equal Remuneration for Men and Women for Equal Work 1957,
- the ILO Convention 111 in Respect of Discrimination in Employment/Occupation 1957 (http://www.unesco.org/culture/worldreport/html_eng/stat2/table13.pdf),
- the UN Declaration on Human Rights, the European Convention on Human Rights,
- the UN International Covenant on Civil and Political Rights,
- the International Covenant on Economic, Social and Cultural Rights, and
- the Convention on the Elimination of All forms of Discrimination Against Women (CEDAW) (and reporting thereon) (http://www.unhchr.ch/html/intlinst.htm).

These are often supplemented by a '(Gender) Equality Act', a Bureau of Gender Equality between Women and Men, Convention on the Rights of the Child, and various forms of gender mainstreaming. Some of these international agreements are open to reservations and different interpretations.

The constitutions of all the nations reviewed here in different ways embody equality for citizens under the law; non-discrimination on grounds of sex/gender. Most have a written constitution. Moreover, even in the case of the UK, which does not have a written constitution, the signing of the European Convention on Human Rights and EU membership more generally may be tending to override this anomaly. Gender-neutral language is generally used in law and policy, though often also for different reasons and within different legal and political traditions. In the case of the last tranche of recent entrants to the EU, considerable efforts have been put into the harmonisation of law and policy with the pre-existing EU members and directives, including in terms of non-discrimination and gender equality. EU enlargement appears to contribute to strengthening initially the formal law and policy on gender equality. These various formal apparatuses may contradict with both historical tradition and contemporary legal and policy practice and implementation. The effectiveness of these policy measures, at least in the short term, is also in doubt, in view of the lack of gender equality (Hearn et al., 2002b, 2002c).

Gender equality legislation may indeed remain without clear consequences for policy and outcomes, for women and men. There is often a gap between the governmental rhetoric and everyday conduct in society, with men and women mostly unaware of discussions about gender equality in the labour market and elsewhere. For example, the Russian constitution stipulates that 'Man and woman' shall have equal rights, liberties and opportunities. The problem is in the realisation of these principles in every branch of legislation, social relations and everyday practice. In addition, governmental responsibility for gender equality is frequently delegated to one ministry, or one part thereof, and in some countries there are significant legal and policy variations between different national or regional governments, and between ministries.

These broad national variations need to be put alongside contrasts between different welfare state policy regimes. In the case of the study of differential European welfare regimes, the most common general model applied in this specific fashion is that devised by Esping-Andersen (1990, 1996). There has been an extensive critique of such models, partly in terms of their insufficient attention to gender relations. There is a need for greater attention to conscious gendering in and of assumptions that are brought to bear in such analyses. Contrasts between Neo-liberal, Social Democratic, and Conservative welfare regimes in Western Europe have thus been critiqued in terms of their neglect of gender welfare state regimes and gender relations. As noted in Chapter 1, such models need to be refined by the specification of differences with and amongst gender welfare policy regimes in former Soviet bloc nations; and specification of differences amongst men and men's practices.

There is also national variation in the extent to which laws and policies are gender-disaggregated. As noted, a relative lack of gendering of law and policy continues in most cases. Detailed laws and policies directed towards gendered interventions with men and men's practices are relatively rare. There is relatively little law and policy explicitly focused on men, variations amongst men, and the relationship of those patterns to men's practices and lives. Exceptions to this pattern include, in some cases, law and policy on:

Home and work
- specification of forms of work only for men (for example, mining);
- men as workers/breadwinners/heads of family and household;
- fatherhood and paternity (including legal rights and obligations as fathers, biological and/or social, and paternity leave of various kinds).

Social exclusion
- social assistance, according to sex and marital status;
- fatherhood, husband and other family statuses in immigration and nationality;
- gay men, gay sexuality and transgender issues.

Violences
- compulsory (or near compulsory) conscription into the military;
- crimes of sexual violence, such as rape; and
- programmes on men who have been violent to women and children.

Health
- men's health education programmes;
- reproductive technology and reproductive rights.

The form and development of law and policy also intersect with the substantive form and nature of socio-economic change. As we saw in Chapter 2, there was a strong emphasis on the different political and academic traditions that operate in studying men in the different national contexts, as well as distinct historical conjunctions for the lives of men. More specifically, in terms of policy development that has addressed men, a simple, perhaps over-simple, differentiation may be made between the countries in this review as follows:

- the Nordic nations (Denmark, Finland, Norway, Sweden) – that have had both gender equality apparatus, and at least some focused policy development on men, through national committees, since the 1980s (thus prior to Finland's joining the EU), operating in the context of the membership and work of the Nordic Council of Ministers; this included the 'Men and gender equality' programme (1995–2000) (http://www.norden.org/jaemst/sk/maend.asp?lang=4).
- the established EU-member nations (Ireland, Italy, Germany, the UK) – that have developed their 'equal opportunities' and 'gender equality' policies in the context of the previous EU-15, and with some specific emphasis upon men; and

- the former Soviet nations and former 'Eastern Bloc' countries (Bulgaria, Czech Republic, Estonia, Latvia, Poland, the Russian Federation) – which in a variety of ways have a recent political history of formal legal equality but without developed human rights, and are now in the process of developing their gender equality laws and policies post-transformation, also with very limited specific emphasis upon men. Four of these nations are now, since 2004, part of the EU-25.

In addition, the nations have experienced different socio-economic changes, for example, the German unification process, and post-socialist transition in Estonia, Latvia, Poland and the Russian Federation. These changes set the context, the ground and the challenges for law and policy. Other major social changes include those in Ireland with rapid movement from a predominantly rural society through a booming economy, as well as its own nearby political conflicts, challenges and changes in Northern Ireland. Somewhat similarly since the 1950s Finland has gone through a shift with migrations from the countryside to the suburbs in search of work.

As a way of looking at these varying situations in a little more detail, we shall contrast the situations in the two Nordic countries, two of the post-communist countries, and the UK. In Norway, as in many other countries, the period after the second World War was characterised by extended policy declarations concerning gender equal status, yet it was mainly in the 1960s and 1970s, with increased demands for women's labour power, that more detailed and binding policies were created. A national Gender Equality Council was created in 1972 as a partially independent organ with the task of monitoring equal status progress. In 1979, a new Gender Equality Act entered into force, with an Ombudsman arrangement and an Appeals Board. In 1986, the government created a Male Role Committee to look into and create debate about men within an equal status perspective. The Committee which existed until 1991 surveyed men's attitudes and conditions through broad co-operation among feminist and other researchers (Holter, 2001a). In the early 1990s, there was a slowdown of the gender equality process. Economic setbacks were accompanied by a shift to the right, with the welfare state increasingly targeted by neoliberal political views. In recent years, national politics have become noticeably less gender-balanced, with all the major parties led by men, although the figures do not yet show a clear setback.

National legal and governmental policy in Finland is framed and characterised by a complex formal mixture of statements favouring gender equality in principle and statements using gender-neutrality as the major form of governmental communication; statements typically promote and favour gender equality, and this is generally done through gender-neutral laws and policies. This means that there are relatively few explicit governmental statements on or about men. Most laws are constructed in a gender-neutral way. The Finnish Act on Equality between Men and Women came into force in 1987. As with other Nordic predecessors of the Finnish Act, it is mostly a passive law to be used when it is alleged that someone is discriminated against. Gendered exceptions to this generally gender-neutral pattern in which men are explicitly or implicitly named include: compulsory conscription into the army; a strongly pro-fatherhood policy and ideology; a national programme against violence; and recent political debate on same-sex marriage. In addition there has been a variety of extra-governmental political activity around men of varying gender political persuasions. Since 1986 there has been a 'Men's Section' (the Subcommittee on Men's Issues), a subcommittee of the Council for Equality between Women and Men. This has recently produced a publication (Kempe, 2000) that sets out ways in which gender equality can be developed to men's advantage. There is a lack of consideration of how men might assist the promotion of gender equality in ways that assist women; there is a lack of consideration of how different aspects of men's practices might connect with each other, for example, fatherhood and violence.

The situation in the post-communist countries is very different. A gendered examination of Russian legislation allows one to talk about gender asymmetry. According to the Russian Federation Constitution (Part 3, Article 19, Cited in Zavadskaya, 2001), 'Man and woman have equal rights and freedoms and opportunities for its realisation.' At first sight, this constitutional principle is reflected in contemporary legislation. However, not only does everyday practice and the reality of institutional life contravene it, but legislators do not always understand the principle of gender equality. The formal legislation reflects the idea of gender equality, but does not reflect nor guarantee its realisation for both sexes. Women have equal rights to be elected (equally with men), but they do not have equal opportunity for achieving equality with men's rights. Absolutely another situation is found in the sphere of labour legislation. The legislation reflects the idea of gender equality. In this legislation we see a system of actions for the defence of women's rights, especially the 'unwed mother'. In this sphere it is most important to address objective necessity and produce appropriate measures. Discrimination of men exists in family legislation. A man finds it very difficult to have the right to bring up a child. Gender research into Russian legislation testifies to ambiguities in understanding gender equality in different spheres of society. Gender legislation is still at the formative stage, as shown by the examination of some specific branches of Russian legislation.

Recent developments in the Latvian legal process have reflected the commitment of Latvia to join the European Union. Thus, a number of the international and EU documents and conventions have been ratified by the Latvian government. In 2001 new strategies and initiatives were introduced, as expressed in such documents from the Ministry of Welfare as *The Gender Equality Initiative. Draft document* [Koncepcija dzimumu līdz tiesības īstenošanai, 2000] and *Equal Opportunities to Everybody in Latvia. Draft document* (2000). In 2000 a new Family Act was introduced in which the idea of paternity leave was introduced and the necessity to struggle with family violence was stated. Both documents mainly deal with issues of men and women in home, health and work. The family is defined as a reproductive heterosexual partnership for securing the economic and social 'body' of the society. Neither document contains the language of differences, sexual, ethnic or racial. Issues of ethnicity and cultural differences are to be resolved through policy developments in ethnic and social integration to overcome the ethno-political divisions of Latvian society. Indeed the rigidly 'disciplinary' character of the documents issued both by The Ministry of Welfare and by The Department of Naturalisation are to the disadvantage to future policy developments because the language of gender equality and gender mainstreaming is excluded from the ethnic integration policies, and the language of ethnic integration is excluded from the gender equality initiatives. There are no explicit statements addressing men and ethnicity/race, or men and sexuality, thus pointing out as yet 'untouchable' questions of social exclusion in family, work, health, violences. Since the restoration of political independence, the political climate of Latvia has never been stabilised, and rapid changes of governments have been detrimental to the principle of continuity in implementing the initiatives in policy development and pursuing the principles of transparency, accountability and policy responsibilities.

Since the advent of the Labour Administration in the UK in 1997, topics, such as poverty, unemployment, the labour market, crime (including violences to women), health, ethnicity, have become major focuses of policy attention – and often with a relatively strong gender dimension. By contrast, there is much less policy focus on areas of disadvantage such as disability, sexuality or crimes against children. This pattern largely reflects a government policy agenda on: social exclusion defined in rather narrow labour market terms; and on crime, highlighting some areas more than others. For example, men's violences to women and other men receive considerably more policy attention than men's violences to children. It is striking that men figure so little explicitly in UK governmental discourses compared to their prominence in much of the critical, and not so critical, UK academic literature (see Chapter 2). When men are addressed explicitly in government produced material, this is far more likely to be in early stage consultation documents or inquiry reports than firm recommendations, advanced consultative documents or Acts of Parliament. Thus in these very different ways the form of law and policy is interrelated with the form of social, economic and political change (Pringle, 2001).

Finally, in this section it is important to mention men's organising outside the state with its uneven impacts on policy-making on men. One might think that there might be considerable focus on such a visible social category as men, albeit from different vantage points. But generally this is not explicitly so – though there is more interest in Western than Eastern Europe, with some very active groups in the field of fathers' rights and men's health. There are many organisations consisting mostly of men but usually without any explicitly articulated, conscious awareness or agenda linked to the male gender. The difference that such politics, movements, organising and groups of men are not explicitly gender-conscious; they supposedly 'just happen' as 'normal' ways of doing things in government, business and civil society. In addition, even groups or organisations (more or less dominated by men) that do not *appear* have or operate with an explicit gender consciousness may well articulate very clear statements on gender and the place of men in society. This is perhaps clearest with far-right political groups, which often present very dominating models of and for dominant group men, in contrast to women and dominated group men.

Although there is a mass of organisations dominated by men, the great majority are not explicitly gender-conscious. For example, Oleksy (2001a) suggests that, with perhaps surprisingly little explicit interest in 'men's' issues, 'it is difficult to talk about men's politics' in much of Central and Eastern Europe. In reviewing the field in Poland in 2001 only one organisation explicitly and exclusively addressing men in a *gender-conscious* way, the Association for the Defence of Fathers' Rights (*Stowarzyszenie Obrony Praw Ojca*) (Oleksy, 2001a), was identified, that is, apart from gay groups such as Lambda Warsaw and the Campaign Against Homophobia (KPH) (ILGA, 2000). Across many parts of Central and Eastern Europe, and especially the large urban centres gay organising is becoming increasingly active (Long, 1999; Stychin, 2003; Binnie, 2005), with the support of the International Lesbian and Gay Association (ILGA); some other men are interested in organising fathers' groups and some men's groups are analogous to the mythopoetics.

The term 'men's movements' is more usually applied to the practice of *gender-conscious* organising by men. Such organising can take a wide variety of forms and have a range of political orientations and interests. Messner (1999) suggests, rather than a continuum of positions, a three-way dynamic between men's organising that is based in opposing patriarchy, engaging with differences between men (such as by 'race', ethnicity or sexuality), and (re)asserting men's rights. Men's politics then becomes a three-way process of contestation. Thus men's movements can include profeminist groups, gay groups, men's rights groups, as well as others in an ambiguous relation to feminism and gender politics. Men's organising and 'policy on men' is the subject of further research in Estonia, Finland, Ireland, and Latvia, Sweden and the UK (Hearn and Niemi, 2005). Meanwhile, many, perhaps most, mainstream (malestream) business and governmental organisations remain places of men's organising, often in effect 'men's organisations' themselves full of unnoticed, unnamed 'men's groups'. Men routinely organise in such groups and organisations, without naming them as such.

Thematic areas

Home and work

Although there may not be a very large body of law and policy information specifically focused on men, the various historical and national traditions in the constructions of citizenship have large implications for the place of men in law and policy. These constructions of citizenship have often been presented as 'gender-neutral', even though they have clear historical gendering as male. Such constructions have clear relevance for the formulation of law and policy on men in relation to home and work.

Throughout the countries within this study there is a general use of gender-neutral language in law and policy, and this has been reinforced in recent years through the ratification (or not) of such international agreements as the ILO Convention 100 on Equal Remuneration for Men and Women for Equal Work 1957, the ILO Convention 111 in Respect of Discrimination in Employment/Occupation 1957, the UN Declaration on Human Rights, the European Convention on Human Rights, the UN International Covenant on Civil and Political Rights, the International Covenant on Economic, Social and Cultural Rights, and the Convention on the Elimination of All forms of Discrimination Against Women (CEDAW). In all the countries there is some form of equality or anti-discrimination legislation, and in many there are a '(Gender) Equality Act', and some form of Equal Opportunities Office or Bureau of Gender Equality between Women and Men. Various forms of gender mainstreaming are also being increasingly promoted, in word at least, in government. In terms of the EU, the main areas of activity, for member and applicant nations, include:

- equal pay;
- equal treatment for women and men at work and in access to employment;
- balanced distribution of work-related and family duties;
- training and informing of social partners about equality policy and norms in the EU;
- participation in EU equality framework programmes.

The general tradition here is gender equality in formal treatment and process rather than gender equality of outcome. There is also in EU countries the Directive on the restriction of working time, though again its practical implementation is varied. These and other formal 'gender-neutral' national and transnational apparatuses and objectives may contradict with both national historical tradition and contemporary legal and policy practice. Importantly, these include the different traditions of welfare capitalism or welfare patriarchies, that are themselves commentaries on home and work, such as:

- Strong, Modified, Weak Breadwinner States (Lewis, 1992; Ostner, 1994; Duncan, 1995, 2001);
- Latin Rim, Bismarckian, Anglo-Saxon, Scandinavian (Langan and Ostner, 1991);
- Transitional from Private Patriarchy, Housewife Contract, Dual Role Contract, Equality Contract (Hirdman, 1988, 1990).

- Private Patriarchy with High Subordination of Women, Public Patriarchy with High Subordination of Women, Private Patriarchy with Lower Subordination of Women, Public Patriarchy with Lower Subordination of Women (Walby, 1986, 1990, Waters, 1990, Hearn, 1992; Duncan 2001).

The various national governmental and constitutional frameworks intersect with the everyday patterns and realities of home and work. Housework is still mostly women's work; men's family statuses are still, despite rises in separation and divorce, defined mainly through marriage and fatherhood; recurring themes in employment include men's occupational, working and wage gap over women, gender segregation at work, differences in patterns of working hours, many men's close associations with paid work.

In all countries there are elements of the provider-breadwinner model, though the strength of this is very variable. Taxation is sometimes and increasingly an untypical arena of policy. Marriage and paternity law have been and largely remain basic ways of defining different men's statuses in law, with fatherhood generally assumed for men whose wives have children. These have been and, to varying extents, are ways of defining men's relation to work as providers-breadwinners. In all the nations apart from the Russian Federation there is some kind of parental/paternity leave, but the conditions under which this operates are very variable. There are, however, major changes, complications and contradictions, with the growing politics around fathers' rights, some degree of shared care/parenthood, and leave for fathers and as parents.

Policy development around men's parental and paternity leave has been active in the Nordic countries. The outcomes have, however, been variable from one country to another. Supporting fatherhood is a central part of governmental policy in Finland (Hearn, 2001). In Norway a proposal from the Male Role Committee for the father's quota, or 'the daddy's month' (now two months) has been enacted (Holter 2001a). The results were remarkable. Soon after its introduction in 1993, two-thirds of eligible fathers used the reform, which gave the father one month of paid leave (of a total of 10 months). This reform, like most of the debate on men as caregivers, had women as the main subject – to the extent that the father's pay was stipulated on the basis of the mother's labour market activity. As regards Sweden, it is also true that more men there take parental leave than in most other European countries. However, women still take the overwhelming majority of such leave. Indeed one reason why a 'daddy's month' of parental leave was introduced was because men's take-up was so slow (Bergman and Hobson, 2001). In 2002, a second 'daddy's month' was introduced because, although take-up had improved a little, it was still a relatively small increase. A similar picture exists in Denmark (Iovanni and Pringle, 2005a, 2005b, 2005c). On the other hand, the experience in some other Nordic countries, for example, Norway, has been somewhat better. Nevertheless, if massive social policy inputs, such as the Swedish government has committed to increasing men's actual parental leave, can result in such modest results, then that suggests we need to reconsider very carefully whether top-down social policy initiatives are of themselves often sufficient for the changing of men's behaviours (also see Bekkengen, 2002; Chapter 6, this volume).

All countries have some kind of equal wage legislation on such grounds as an employee's sex, nationality, colour, race, native language, social origin, social status, previous activities, and religion, yet gendered inequalities persist in terms of unequal pay for work of equal value (see Chapters 2 and 3, this volume). There are also clear gendered policies and laws for the armed forces, and for some other areas of work, such as religious workers and ministers.

In many countries the increasing neo-liberal and market-oriented trends in the 1990s, such as 'turbo capitalism', globalisation, restructuring, more intense jobs, has brought a more individualist approach to gender. These have strong implications for policy, for example, the structuring of time, family and care responsibilities and work–home relations (see Chapter 6). At the same time, there are limited moves towards greater equality planning and reform in workplaces, for example, in Finland, Sweden and Norway. While there are growing governmental and related discourses about men at home and work, including the reconciliation of the demands of home and work, there is usually a lack of explicit focus on men, especially in clear and strong policy terms. This is being addressed in the 2005 EU policy priority by the DG Employment, Social Affairs and Equal Opportunities. There remains a lack of linkage between men as parents and governmental documentation on men as violent partners or violent parents.

Social exclusion

As was the case also in Chapters 2 and 3, this has proved to be the most difficult area to pre-define, but in some ways one of the most interesting. The ways in which social exclusion figures appear rather differently in the countries reviewed here. However, even with this variation there is still frequently a lack of gendering of law and policy in relation to men. This is despite the fact men often appear make up the majority or vast majority of those in some of the socially excluded sub-categories.

To illustrate these considerable variations, we may note, for example, how in Norway, there is a focus on the relation of citizens to the social security system, and on rural and urban youth. In Estonia government is increasingly recognising social exclusions, such as men's lesser education than women, non-Estonian men's lower life expectancy, homophobia, drugs, HIV/AIDS. Such problems have been denied a long time; however government is close to recognising these problems, especially drugs and AIDS. The government has developed several programmes to deal with men social problems, including the prevention of alcoholism and drug use (1997–2007), and of HIV/AIDS. However, there is no clear plan on how to deal with these men's social problem. In Germany there has been extensive debate on same-sex partnerships.

Although this has not yet yielded the same status as for heterosexual marriages, there has been some extension of rights, for example, old age care, housing rights, medical, and educational rights regarding the partner's children.

In Ireland men are generally not gendered in public policy. Yet, through EU funding, men's groups for men have been set up in disadvantaged localities, usually based within a personal development model. At the same time outside the state father's rights groups are exerting greater pressure (Ferguson, 2001a). There is in Ireland limited gendering of men in relation to social exclusion, the most significant being in relation to the vulnerability of men who are socially disadvantaged and long-term unemployed. Since 1994, the Department of Social, Community and Family Affairs has been funding men's groups in socially disadvantaged areas. While there is no single model of 'menswork' going on in such groups in Ireland, the most common orientation appears to be personal development, as a support for men who feel excluded and are struggling to find a role for themselves.

Gendered power relations and sexism intersecting with other dimensions of oppressive power relations, such as racism, disablism, heterosexism, ageism and classism, are a major dynamic in generating patterns of social exclusion. Yet most governmental strategies to counter social exclusion do not explicitly address the issue of men; and where they do, an acknowledgement of oppression towards women and children is largely absent. Somewhat paradoxically, countries with a stronger hegemonic masculinity, represented by great concentrations of capital and power, may in fact offer some more options for diversity among some groups of men, compared to smaller tightly-knit 'male-normative' societies. Occasionally we hear of men as the socially excluded, rarely of men who perpetrate the various social exclusions. The oppression, and violence, perpetrated by many men on many women and on many children in the countries under review here, need to be urgently reconfigured by policy-makers as serious forms of social exclusion. Similarly, there is a lack of policy attention in all countries to men engaged in creating and reproducing social exclusions, for example, around racism, and the intersections of different social divisions and social exclusions.

Violences

The context of law and policy is set here by the recurring theme of the widespread nature of the problem of men's violences to women, children and other men. Men are strongly over-represented among those who use violence, especially heavy violence including homicide, sexual violence, racial violence, robberies, grievous bodily harm and drug offences. Similar patterns are also found for accidents in general, vehicle accidents and drunken driving (see Chapter 8).

Formal gender-neutrality operates in law in most respects. Exceptions to this include in some cases the specification of sexual crimes, of which rape is a clear, though complex, example, with fine differences between countries. While the codification of crime and punishment is ancient, the issue of violence against women is a relatively new topic for policy development for many countries. In many countries this is still constructed as 'family violence' rather than 'violence against women'.

In some countries, notably Germany, Sweden and the UK, 'domestic violence' has both received far more attention and been far more defined as a gendered crime in recent government guidance and legislation than any other form of men's violences. Men as violent partners have been the focus of some considerable attention in governmental discourses: certainly more than men as violent fathers – and this discrepancy needs some urgent investigation, partly because much international research (see Hester et al. 1998; Hester, 2000 for a summary of this research) suggests that violent partners may often be violent fathers too. There is gradual change in terminology from 'domestic violence' or 'family violence' to 'violence against women'. In Finland a national policy programme was established in the late 1990s on violence against violence, along with other initiatives against prostitution and trafficking, on a temporary basis, but not extended beyond its five year span (http://www.stakes.fi).

In most of the Western European countries there is some system of refuges for battered women but these are generally very much lacking in funding. In contrast, in Estonia there is no network of shelters for women or indeed consultation services for violent men. Overall in most countries there is little intervention work with men who are violent to women. In Norway there has been the development of alternatives to violence projects for men on a voluntary basis; some progress has been made in reducing violence and developing research, most of it from below, in the form of voluntary activities, activists and networks, rather than governmental policy decisions (Råkil, 2002). In the UK there is some use of men's programmes in some localities on a statutory basis. In many countries the concern with men's aggressive behaviour is still regarded in traditional stereotypes and is explained in terms of impoverishment, value crisis, alcohol and drug addiction.

The results of Norwegian research indicating the possibly significant impact of bullying on men's violence is under-explored (Holter, 1989; Råkil, 2002). In the UK and elsewhere there is often a lack of consistency regarding violence against women with governmental policy advocating greater involvement of men in families/greater fathers' rights whilst at the same time pressing for recognition of the possibility of father's violence to mothers/children after separations. While this is not necessarily any contradiction in these approaches, what is worrying is a frequent lack of dialogue between them (Pringle, 1998b, 2001). In Germany there has also been policy attention to other diverse forms of men's violence, including in the army, sexual harassment, and violence in education.

Even with the rather uneven set of responses to violence against women, it is important to consider that other forms of men's gendered violences have not received the same attention. For example, in the UK little recognition is afforded to the predominantly gendered nature of child sexual abuse in governmental documents/legislation despite the fact that this gendered profile of perpetrators is virtually commonplace as acknowledged in research, practice and (to some extent) public domains. In that country there have been numerous official enquiries into cases of child sexual abuse. Hardly any of them acknowledge one of the few relatively clear facts from research about this crime, namely that it is overwhelmingly committed by men or boys. It is to be hoped that the increasing numbers of studies by mainly feminist researchers, highlighting the very real linkages between 'domestic violence' and child abuse, may focus attention on child sexual abuse as a gendered crime. Overall, there is generally a lack of attention paid to the gendered quality of violences inherent in, for instance, pornography, prostitution, child sexual abuse, trafficking in people. As already noted, there is a need for more coherent government policies regarding men as child carers recognising *at the same time* both men's real potential as carers and the equally real problems of gendered violences by men against women and children (Pringle, 1998b).

Last, but not at all least, men's violences to ethnic minorities, migrants, people of colour, gay men and older people are being increasingly highlighted more, but are still very unexplored. They remain important areas for further policy development.

Health

The context of law and policy in relation to men's health has several contradictory elements. The life expectancy of men and thus men's ageing has increased markedly since the beginning of the 20th century. Yet the major recurring health theme is men's relatively low (to women) life expectancy, poor health, accidents, suicide, morbidity. Men suffer and die more and at a younger age from cardiovascular diseases, cancer, respiratory diseases, accidents and violence than women. Socio-economic factors, qualifications, social status, life style, diet, smoking, drinking, drug abuse, hereditary factors, as well as occupational hazards, can all be important for morbidity and mortality. Gender differences in health arise from hazardous occupations done by men. Generally, men neglect their health and for some men at least their 'masculinity' is characterised by risk taking, especially for younger men (in terms of smoking, alcohol and drug taking, unsafe sexual practices, road accidents, lack of awareness of risk), an ignorance of their bodies, and reluctance to seek medical intervention for suspected health problems. Thus 'traditional masculinity' can be seen as hazardous to health.

Despite this, law and policy on health is often non-gendered, or rather, as with violences, is a mix of non-gendered and gendered elements. In Poland both men and women are entitled to social welfare and health care use on many grounds. There are only government programmes on the protection of women's health and no programmes on men's health have been identified. Similarly, in Latvia policy is directed towards the health of mother and child, and stress is put on the importance of women's well-being in terms of their reproductive health. In several countries there are now national health education programmes. There are the beginnings of health education in Ireland, though the construction of health is mainly in physical terms. In Norway a number of health campaigns and measures are related to men's health, such as attempts to reduce the proportion of smokers, but masculinity is not a main focus. Some research on men's health is ongoing or planned, but it cannot be described as a coherent research field. Indeed it is only recently that women's health has achieved this status. National programmes for the prevention of alcoholism and drug use, tuberculosis, and HIV/AIDS and other sexually transmitted diseases, are all relevant for men.

There is growing concern with young men's health in a number of countries, for example, in Finland with young men's accidental mortality. Much needs to be done on men's and young men's suicide, and on the very high level of deaths from accidents (especially road traffic accidents) in young men. UK reports have noted how class factors intersected with gender regarding suicide rates for the highest risk age group (under 44 years), thus making an explicit link with some men's social exclusion. However, in many countries there are no policies. For example, there are no relevant provisions in Polish law exclusively on men's health. Men are referred to in individual provisions related to self-inflicted injuries or incapacitation of health carried out in order to evade compulsory military service (both of which are treated as offences). No data were found on Polish organisations that deal exclusively with problems of health, social welfare and suicides concerning men or on nationwide initiatives and programmes in this area (they are mainly aimed at women and children).

The health of men is just beginning to be recognised as a health promotion issue in Ireland, in the context of growing awareness of generally poor outcomes in health for men compared with women and generally lower resource allocation to men's health. The Irish government published a new health strategy in 2001 (Ferguson, 2001a) with a specific section on men's health. Health is still tending to be conceptualised in physical terms, with a neglect of psychological well-being. While increases in male suicide, especially by young men, are increasingly the focus of public concern, there has been little attempt to develop gender-specific policies and programmes which can help men to cope with their vulnerability and despair (see Chapter 9, this volume).

What is almost wholly absent from national governmental policy discourses, as opposed to some research, in relation to men's health, is any recognition that high levels of accidental and suicidal death might link with more critical approaches to men's practices, such as risk-taking, self-violence, problems in emotional communication, being 'hard'. Overall there is virtually no consideration of how problems of men's health link more broadly with a critical analysis of men's oppressive social practices.

Conclusions

It is not possible to provide a neat, brief list of conclusions from such rich and complex material as reviewed in this chapter. Therefore, in this final section, we only highlight some general issues that it is essential to address in policy analysis and development.

Gender-neutral language

Gender-neutral language is generally used in law and policy, though for different reasons within different legal-political traditions. The national constitutions embody equality for citizens under the law; non-discrimination on grounds of sex/gender. Despite these features, major structural gender inequalities persist.

Gendered welfare state policy regimes

The different traditions of gendered welfare state policy regimes have definite implications for men's practices; this is clearest in men's relations to home and work, including different constructions of men as breadwinners. The implications for men's social exclusion, violences and health need further explication.

We also wish to make a specific point about welfare state policy regimes and men's violences to women and/or children. If we look at various welfare systems in Western Europe in terms of the extent to which they demonstrate an awareness of the problem and a willingness to respond to it, then the transnational patterns that emerge in Europe are almost a reversal of the standard Esping-Andersen-type classifications. The criteria which can be used to look at each country would include: the levels of research carried out on the topic in different countries; the extent to which the prevalence of men's violences has been researched and/or acknowledged publicly; the extent to which legal frameworks are focused on men's violences; the extent to which there are welfare initiatives aimed at dealing with the outcomes of men's violences; the extent to which welfare professionals are trained to address men's violences.

If such criteria are used, then arguably the UK emerges as perhaps the most advanced welfare system in this case whilst some of the Nordic countries do rather badly or would only rate in the middle rank. In other words, on this important dimension of men's violences to women and to children, one of the relatively 'Neo-liberal' welfare systems in Europe performs much better than many of the 'Scandinavian' welfare systems. This is significant for a number of reasons at various levels of policy: first, it suggests that much needs to be done in the Nordic states to make their welfare responses in this field as relatively comprehensive as they certainly are in other fields of welfare; second it suggests that using Nordic welfare systems as models in social policy (as often occurs in some welfare areas) may be more hazardous than has generally been assumed: one has to choose which aspects of welfare to use as models; finally, it suggests that social policy-makers should be wary of relatively global welfare typologies.

Gender equality provisions

The implications of gender equality provisions for men are under-explored. Different men can have complex, even contradictory, relations to gender equality and other forms of equality. Men's developing relations to gender equality can include: men assisting in the promotion of women's greater equality; attention to the gendered disadvantage of certain men, as might include gay men, men with caring responsibilities, men in non-traditional work; men's rights, fathers' rights, and anti-women/anti-feminist politics. There is little attention to how men might assist the promotion of gender equality in ways that assist women.

Gender mainstreaming

Efforts towards gender mainstreaming in law and policy are often, quite understandably, women-oriented; the implications for such policies for men need to be more fully explored, whilst at the same time avoiding anti-women/anti-feminist 'men only' tendencies that can sometimes thus be promoted.

The intersection of men, gender relations and other forms of social division and inequality

These other forms, such as ethnicity, remain an important and undeveloped field in law and policy. Both the substantive form and the recognition of these intersections in law, policy and politics vary considerably between the nations. There are clear overlaps in the governmental material between the four areas of this analysis: for instance, social exclusion and health; social exclusion and home and work. Partly because gender, and particularly men, generally figure far less prominently in governmental material than in the academic or even the statistical data, the overlaps are much less obvious here. These intersections are likely to be a major arena of political debate and policy development in the future. Let us consider two examples.

First, there are the interrelations between the topic of fatherhood and men's violences. In most parts of Western Europe, it seems there is a striking tendency to treat these two topics as separate policy issues. Indeed, one can find countries which both enthusiastically promote fatherhood and, quite separately, address men's violences: but do not join up the two, as they should. Indeed, in terms of research and policy-making across Europe, such an integrated dual approach is rarely adopted: the question as to why it seems to be so hard to do this is one which researchers and policy-makers should ponder deeply. This has to change.

Another example of interconnections between the policy themes is between social exclusion and men's health. Much research illustrates a correlation between poor health, including that of men, and various forms of social disadvantage associated with factors such as class or ethnicity. More generally, the theme of social exclusion/social inclusion can be seen as an important element entering in to the dynamics of all the other three themes regarding men's practices. This again emphasises the need for particular policy attention to be given to social inclusion and far more research on men's practices in both social exclusion and inclusion.

Policy recommendations

The Network was asked by the European Commission to provide policy recommendations based on the data gathered. Many recommendations were nationally specific, and so we drew up Policy Option Papers for each government of the countries represented in the original network. In addition, we formulated more general, transnational policy recommendations (http://www.cromenet.org). These are located under the four major themes – together with some comments on interrelations between these themes, in the four chapters, on: home and work (Chapter 6), social exclusion (Chapter 7), violences (Chapter 8), and health (Chapter 9).

5
Media and Newspaper Representations

Jeff Hearn, Elżbieta H. Oleksy, Joanna Kazik and Keith Pringle, with Ursula Müller, Emmi Lattu, Teemu Tallberg, Harry Ferguson, Voldemar Kolga and Irina Novikova

In recent years there has been a large expansion of European scholarship on the representation of men and masculinities in a wide variety of media, including film, television, video, magazines, painting, fine art, music, dance, Internet, photography and advertising (for example, Middleton, 1992; Pedersen et al., 1996; Edwards, 1997; Nixon, 1997; Sterr, 1997; Penttilä, 1999; Jokinen, 2000). However, relatively little attention has been given to the mundane medium of daily newspapers. When studying men, the daily press appears to have been frequently taken-for-granted, unlike, say, Hollywood film. Newspapers are literally everyday phenomena; their very ordinariness may mean that they are not taken as seriously in studies on men, gender relations and media as other 'more dramatic' or 'glamorous' media such as film, video and television. Furthermore, newspapers are generally designed for more local, national or regional audiences and markets than some other media, such as Internet websites, mailing lists and newsgroups.

In this chapter we first set out some comparative and methodological issues in studying newspapers and other media, including our own methodological approach. This is followed by an examination of newspaper and media representations on men and men's practices in the countries concerned, with special attention to the relation of nation and transnationalisation. A more detailed discussion on the four main themes of home and work, social exclusion, violences and health, follows, before some concluding comments.

Comparative and methodological issues

Much research on gender and media, along with cultural studies more generally, has highlighted the deep embeddedness of gender in cultural artefacts, including newspapers. The study of such contextual aspects of representation are a major gap in current research on men in the media and thus need to be explored further in future work. Indeed, it could be important to examine in which kinds of journalistic, and indeed other media contexts, men are given meaning *as a gender* or *as gender* (in a comparable way to how women are sometimes equated with sex/gender). It is quite apparent that those kind of contexts where men are given meaning as gender are rather untypical and could perhaps for their part change the typical man–woman segregation prevalent in mainstream journalism.

This foregrounding of men *as a gender* or *as gender* is currently done, or performed, in rather limited and specific ways within mainstream news media. This includes occasional 'men's supplements' or 'fathers' supplements' (as, for example, on Father's Day), which are presented, sometimes in a humorous or ironic way, as parallel or equivalents to 'women's supplements' or 'women's pages'. Not only daily newspapers would be worthy of analysis, but also information-orientated magazines – weeklies, biweeklies, or monthly papers. The press of this type sometimes presents problems directly or indirectly bearing upon men or related to 'men's' issues. There are of course other media that directly foreground men, in the texts and as readers and consumers. These include pornography of many different types, men's health (such as various national language European versions of the originally US-published *Men's Health*), style and other 'men's' magazines (largely but not exclusively for younger men and sometimes including what might be described as 'soft porn'), gay media, and a relatively small anti-sexist/profeminist media. There is a limited development of literature and other media on other non-profeminist 'men's movements', such as Christian or 'fathers' rights'. There is a huge variety of 'specialist' hobby and special interest magazines and other media, that appear to focus very much indeed on men consumers and readers, and are explicitly or implicitly on men; these range across sports, games, fishing, computers, Internet, cars, motorcycles, even pipe smoking.

Interestingly, in one sense, the press provides clear and explicit representations of men, in sport, politics, business and so on. In most sports journalism there is a transparent taken-for-grantedness of men, so that within the confines of the text it is not necessary to focus specifically on men or women as genders. In such textual orders 'man' is the norm and 'woman' the exception. Within (mainstream) journalism, dominant assumptions about men, gender and (hetero)sexuality pervade the texts and can be taken as a starting point in their interpretation and deconstruction. In journalism, as elsewhere in society, taken-for-granted heterosexual gender segregation and assumptions are so transparent that there is no apparent need in the texts to specifically and explicitly emphasise gender. In this way 'gender' is said and shown by not saying so and not explicitly showing it in the various forms of 'gender-neutrality' (Hearn, 1998a; Hanmer and Hearn, 1999).

This apparent 'gender-neutrality' is a very widespread mode of representation in newspapers. When referring to notions of 'gender-neutrality' we do not mean that gender is not present or does not matter. On the contrary, 'gender-neutrality' is a taken-for-granted and widespread mode of representation in which the object is represented *as if* gender is not present or does not matter;

this supposed 'gender-neutrality' is a form of gendering. Similarly, extensive use of 'factual' styles of reporting and various forms of 'facticity' and 'objectivity' (Tuchman, 1973) in news journalistic genres, that may appear to be presented as simply 'neutral', does not mean that such news is 'gender-neutral'.

The kind of 'silence' or 'absence' regarding men through apparent 'gender-neutralisation' helps explain why investigating men can seem 'difficult', and even perhaps why men and boys often find it difficult to change or break with the established, dominant and neutralised pattern. This pattern seems to express or embody a broad resistance. In some situations women are given a similar form of 'main person' neutralisation, as, for example, in the dominant representation of women in nursing journals, even though there have historically been long traditions of male nurses. The same kind of meta-message can be found in journals and material from various parts of professional and work life and organisation: that there is a 'right' gender and then there are 'exceptions'.

In order to develop a grounded comparative data on newspaper representations, three (national) newspapers were selected for analysis in each country, as follows:

- the largest circulation 'serious'/'quality'/'broadsheet';
- the largest circulation 'popular'/'yellow'/'tabloid';
- one other to be chosen at the discretion of the national member.

The selected newspapers were as follows:

Estonia: *Eesti Päevaleht, Postimees, SL-Öhtuleht*
Finland: *Aamulehti, Helsingin Sanomat, Ilta-Sanomat*
Germany: *Bild Zeitung, Frankfurter Allgemeine Zeitung, Süddeutsche Zeitung*
Ireland: *The Irish Examiner, The Irish Independent, The Irish Times*
Italy: *Libero, La Repubblica, La Stampa*
Latvia: *Chas, Diena, Vakara Zinas*
Norway: *Aftenposten, Dagbladet, Klassekampen*
Poland: *Express Ilustrowany, Gazeta Wyborcza, Trybuna Lódzka*
Russian Federation: *Izvestia, Komsomol'skaya pravda, Sovetskaya*[1]
UK: *Daily Telegraph, Guardian, The Sun*

These were acquired for May 2001. While all of May's papers were available for use, detailed qualitative and quantitative analysis was conducted in seven countries: Estonia (Kolga, 2001b), Finland (Hearn et al., 2001b), Germany (Müller and Jacobsen, 2001), Ireland (Ferguson, 2001b), Italy (Ventimiglia, 2001), Poland (Oleksy, 2001b), and the UK (Raynor et al., 2001). This focused on weeks 19 and 20, that is, Monday 7 May to Sunday 20 May, as these were the first two *full* weeks. In addition, broad qualitative reviews were conducted in Latvia (Novikova, 2001b) and Norway (Holter, 2001b).

The main method of analysis was qualitative analysis of the relevant articles on men and men's practices. We used the following guidelines in the process of selecting articles:

- Include articles which explicitly discuss masculinity or masculinities.
- Include articles which implicitly discuss masculinity or masculinities, that is, those articles whose focus is *centrally* on the activities of a man or men, even if they do not explicitly make links between the subject and masculinity.
- Exclude material where a man or men are mentioned but the focus is not centrally on them. For example, an article where (men) footballers are mentioned but where the focus of the article is on, for instance, the start of the season rather than those men as players. This example would thus not be included.

Quantitative calculations were made for each paper for each day of the number of articles addressing men in relation to the four main themes. Calculations were also made for each paper for each day in total square centimetres (including title of the article and any pictures attached to the article) of articles addressing men in relation to the four themes noted above, along with the additional 'other' category noted above. These quantitative calculations were completed with pre-designed proformas.

However, the operationalisation of this methodology was far from unproblematic. This was for several reasons. Firstly, there is the very pervasiveness of 'men' and 'masculinity' throughout much newspaper coverage. Thus attempts to focus on only those articles that discuss masculinity or masculinities implicitly or explicitly is fraught with difficulties of definition. Secondly, the main categories for both the quantitative and qualitative analyses of the press material – home and work, social exclusion, violences, health – have been taken from the themes that have been the structured focuses throughout the Network's work, as discussed in the previous chapters. In this sense a somewhat artificial structure has been imposed on the analysis of the newspapers concerned. There are, for example, many overlaps and interrelations between the coverage of the four themes, for example, between the *representation* of social exclusion and violence, or homelessness and home and work.[2]

Thirdly, the period of study of the newspapers is also important. The period of four weeks devoted to the analysis is too short to define the representations of men. For instance, in the Polish case the amendment of the Labour Code, in which the Parliament granted fathers the right to a part of maternity leave was important from the point of view of 'men's' issues at that time. A very different pattern of reporting would have been apparent, for example, during the weeks following the September 11 attacks. One may wonder whether the data are representative and whether conclusions drawn on the basis on the analysis of this sample are indicative of longer-term or more general patterns.

Newspaper representations of men's practices

The general context and situation of newspapers is very different across the countries, partly because of the huge variation in the population size and geography of the countries, and partly the sheer range in the size and complexity of their newspaper and other media markets. There are also considerable variations in the extent of research on the gendered representation of men in the media and newspapers in the countries. The sheer variety of newspapers in, say, the Russian Federation contrasts with the relative simplicity of the structure of the newspaper market in smaller countries such as Ireland. While many countries have relatively few market leaders in both the more 'quality press' and the more 'tabloid press', there is great diversity in the form of newspapers at the national and especially regional levels. There are also variations in the social positioning of newspapers in different societal contexts. For example, Norway has a state support system for small newspapers and scores highly on the number of papers per inhabitant (Holter, 2001b), and Finland one of the highest per capita rates of newspaper production and reading.

In general, the markets are diversified, starting from mainstream newspapers mainly distributed in cities and newspapers of smaller, regional or local scale whose circulation is relatively low, addressing a very specific target audience. Newspapers are both very large business, and in particular advertising, activities, and also other ventures surviving partly through their donors' financial support; in some cases they may be distributed for free or at subsidised, reduced price. There is also a recent growth of free newspapers, sometimes distributed in the larger cities with the co-operation of transport authorities, and supported by advertising or sponsored by larger normal priced newspapers. Another key growth area is Internet newspapers and the Internet versions and archives of paper printed newspapers. These archives are in some cases a huge potential resource for research, basic information and analysis of representations of men and men's practices.

The coverage of different themes in relation to men in the national newspapers surveyed varies between the countries (Table 5.1). Overall, printed media generally devote little *explicit* attention to men, masculinities and men's practices. The overall space devoted explicitly to men is low – generally no more than a few per cent and sometimes less than 1% of the total coverage. To an amazing extent, the three most widespread newspapers generally avoid reflections on masculinity in a thoroughgoing way. Masculinity appears as presupposed referring to economic activities – women figure only as an exception. Although in a different context, the absence of clearly defined themes dealing with men's issues or matters connected exclusively with men or unequivocally referring to them is the most striking observation from the analysis of the three selected Polish newspapers. Men play the main role primarily in events in the context of politics, economy and sport.

Table 5.1 Percentages of articles and space devoted to men and men's practices in three analysed newspapers in selected countries

		Home and work	**Social exclusion**	**Violences**	**Health**	**Other**	**Total**
Estonia	Number of articles	7	8	15	7	NC[1]	37
	Percentage of articles	19%	22%	40%	19%		
	Space	30%	18%	33%	19%		
Finland	Number of articles	41	12	134	33	15	235
	Percentage of articles	17%	5%	57%	14%	6%	
	Space	36%	2%	33%	20%	9%	
Germany	Number of articles	62	104	76	22	118	382
	Percentage of articles	16%	27%	20%	6%	31%	
	Space	19%	23%	13%	4%	41%	
Ireland	Number of articles	25	65	41	5	NC[1]	136
	Percentage of articles	18%	48%	30%	4%		
Italy	Number of articles	28	9	103	18	8	166
	Percentage of articles	17%	5%	62%	11%	5%	
Poland	Number of articles	5	3	43	1	3	55
	Percentage of articles	9%	5%	78%	2%	5%	
	Space	9%	10%	73%	1%	6%	
UK	Number of articles	102	18	161	60	87	428
	Percentage of articles	24%	4%	38%	14%	20%	
	Space	30%	3%	40%	10%	17%	

[1] NC = Not Calculated

The extent of explicit coverage on men is greater in the Western European countries than in the Eastern European countries. The greatest number of articles in most countries is on violences, with the second greatest number usually on home and work. However, in both Germany and Ireland the largest category of articles was on social exclusion, followed by violences in both cases. The articles on violences are often relatively short, so that home and work is often the largest category by space covered. The range of the amount of the number of articles by theme is: home and work (9%–24%), social exclusion (4%–48%), violences (20%–78%), health (2%–19%). The greatest coverage is for men's relations to violences, and home and work. Apparently 'gender-neutral' ways are commonly used for reporting on all four themes. The explicitly gendered representation of men in the press is not strongly visible. When gender is explicitly presented, then traditional views are often reproduced. The image of men that emerges from the above analysis, is often necessarily incomplete and partial, even oddly negative.

Contrary to some expectations, the most 'serious' newspapers are not always those that allocate the greatest surface area to these issues. Such 'quality' papers do not necessarily have less advertising, catering as they often do for more affluent sections of the population. In Finland the proportionate emphasis on men in spatial coverage is by far the greatest in the afternoon 'tabloid' paper, *Ilta-Sanomat*, except for the social exclusion theme. In the UK *The Sun* devotes considerably less space to news compared to the other two papers, and yet, in absolute terms, it gave by far the most attention to men and masculinities, especially regarding violences and health. Whilst the emphasis on violences is not so surprising, the attention paid to health is more striking, and worthy of further study. Conversely, the *Guardian*'s overall low relative coverage warrants further consideration, given it is regarded as one of the most 'socially concerned' newspapers.

In none of the UK papers analysed was there significant discussion of men and masculinities in relation to the development of government policy. This contrasts with the considerable attention paid to men in *some* areas of UK governmental and quasi-governmental policy discussion (Pringle, 2001). This finding is surprising for two reasons: first, the period reviewed was part of the 'run up' to the General Election when one might expect policy issues to be prominent; and, second, two (*Daily/Sunday Telegraph*, the *Guardian*) of the three papers reviewed are recognised as among the most 'heavyweight' and serious in the UK regarding policy issues as a whole.

The extent of separation of 'quality' from 'tabloid' press (and thus the continuum of market segmentation) is also very variable by nation. For example, in Ireland there is a clear preference for the better quality, serious newspapers. The relatively non-tabloid nature of the Irish press is partly due to strict libel laws restricting aggressive investigative journalism; the 'naming and shaming' of gay men, politicians, child sex abusers and so on, as occurs in the UK, for instance. The traditional power of the Catholic church which, since the formation of the Irish state in 1922, has heavily regulated discourses and images surrounding socio-moral issues is also important. The press has a clear role in broadly reproducing normative assumptions about men and gender relations. Though there are no Irish-produced tabloids, interestingly, there are Irish editions of UK tabloids. A striking example of how the two editions, Irish and UK, of the largest selling UK newspaper, *The Sun*, can operate differently was reported by the *Guardian* newspaper in January 2002, with the launch of the new Euro currency in Ireland, but not in the UK:

> Jakki, blonde and only lightly sequined, gazed from the top half of the front page of both the British and Irish editions [of *The Sun*] with an identical promise of more on page 3.
>
> But the screaming banner headlines underneath were disconcertingly different. 'Dawn of a new €rror,' proclaimed the Sun (30p), while the Irish Sun (€.63) used equally bold type to hail 'Dawn of a new €ra.' (Black, 2002).

There are several well-established genres that are relevant to the representation of men. These are most obvious in the field of violence, specifically through crime reporting. There are also clear genres in sport, politics and business. The field of home and work is more diverse, though some articles are research-based or produced in response to governmental or academic research. The fields of social exclusion and health are also less clearly organised in their reporting, though it may be that there are emerging genres in both, in terms of the public debates on men's health problems, and the awareness of the social exclusion of some groups of men.

An important issue is the primary focus of coverage that addresses men in terms of social problems and the problematisation of men: individual, group/cultural; societal; other; unclear. This is most obvious in relation to reporting on violences. In the 'tabloid' press, articles often have an individual focus. Even when implicitly addressing a problem that is unique to, or at least more common for, men this still tended to be through an individual's story. This was somewhat less so in the 'quality' press, though societally-focused articles were still unusual. The gender political positioning of articles is also highly significant. In some cases journalism is explicitly anti-feminist. This is having a distinct effect on gender politics in Ireland. While that development may, in one sense, have helped the problematisation of men and masculinities in public discourse, it seems to have made it more difficult for stories about violence against women, and women's issues in general, to be a legitimate focus of comment in their own right. In some journalism, defeating feminism seems more important than promoting men's welfare.

While broad political positions can be identified in press and other media, specific interpretations of possible meanings and structures of articles need to be related to context and genre. The contexts in which the male gender is given importance or meaning are themselves gendered. For example, when male company managers are presented as supposedly non-gendered, this can itself be seen as a means of obscuring gendered practices whereby female managers are seen as 'exceptions'. Thus the question can be asked: to what extent are there established genres regarding the four main themes?

One interesting strategy or genre is that of 'scandalisation', as in some German and British newspapers, for example. This seems to aim to get readers to shake their heads in disbelief about the things that are happening in the world, especially 'elsewhere'. This can be geographically and culturally far away, far away from the reader's social situation, or closer to home in terms of the evil things that could happen to them themselves or in their close neighbourhood. In particular, items around violence are presented in this way. On the other hand, in some countries, notably Ireland, forms of scandalisation are not so frequent as elsewhere. The political and public service culture in Ireland is such that resignations for being outed as gay, or as having failed in one's public duty are very rare. Politicians are simply not held to account in the same manner as, for example, in the UK, or at least they do not take the ultimate step of resigning; nor are they sacked. On the other hand, there has been extensive public debate in Ireland in recent years on the 'paedophile priest' (Ferguson, 1995), preceding that in the US (Inglis, 2002).

In some cases a particular news issue concerning men has special prominence for a considerable period of time – almost a life of its own in the press. For example in Ireland, the most prominent reporting in all categories of men's issues during the study period concerned the dismissal of the Managing Director of the national airline, Aer Lingus, for alleged sexual harassment. The rights and wrongs of the action were hotly debated, with some commentators questioning the motives of the women who made the complaint and whether men can ever properly prove themselves innocent of such charges. While at least some journalists were concerned about natural justice, some of the commentary fitted with a sense that has grown in the Irish media that feminism has gone too far and men are being unfairly discriminated against and always losing out (Ferguson, 2001b).

Nation and transnationalisation

Questions of strategy and genre are culturally and historically specific. While national data has been used as the basis of comparison, the growing importance of transnational media developments is vital. With more transnational contacts, information, technologies and exchange, possible models of men's behaviour in families and jobs, and men's sexual identifications are translated into local and national societal impacts and meanings. In practice this often means Western, especially US, corporate imaging and representations of men. This applies throughout Europe. Apparent media diversity and competition can lead to a strange uniformity, in the shape of endless series material, mostly from the US, on most television stations, advertising and apparently superficial commercial or commercial-style radio – the so-called 'dumbing-down' of the media.

One crucial aspect of historical change in the media, that affects European representations no less than elsewhere, is the movement towards the visual, and thus visual strategies and genres, in the mass media. While there are many forms of visual mass media, in the case of newspapers, advertising is a particularly potent source of cultural imagery. Advertising images can even be seen as an educational instrument of forms of 'gender literacy'. The ideology of what it means to be a 'real man' is translated into advertisement images of expensive businessmen's clothing or young stylish men or, in some countries, working clothes. Such images are inferential of certain models of masculinity – public/individual/young/acting/building/achieving/enjoying – and are provided by the advertisement sponsors, whether or not they have consciously concerned themselves with the textual productions of men and men's practices and representations of men.

The overall media scene has generally become much more commercialised in recent years, including advertising targeting children and other groups. In some countries debate on recent, and sometimes somewhat paradoxical, attempts to diversify television and radio channels is generating much attention. The nature of this increasingly transnational debate around satellite, cable, digital, multichannel, multi-media developments needs to be placed in their specific national media and newspaper contexts. Younger generations of men appear to often prefer Internet sources and other informational sources that are largely beyond the exploration of the topic here. Many use Internet, television or radio, rather than be regular readers of national newspapers. It might be that the power of newspapers to influence their target audiences and shape their opinions is undergoing significant long-term change and reduction. For example, in several Estonian Internet portals there have been very lively and active and non-censored discussions on gender equality, and the position of men and women in society. This would suggest that Estonians, especially the younger and active sections of society, are not indifferent to gender equality issues. Unfortunately it is quite common for articles written by feminists to receive very aggressive responses, even personal attacks. However, such Internet activity can compensate for the relative passivity of print newspapers and other media.

Other important information and communication technology media developments include email lists, bulletin boards, websites, chatrooms, virtual worlds, and interactive and multimedia, for example, combining mobile phones and internet. The monitoring and control of media is thus increasingly becoming a very difficult transnational question, with contradictory implications. These include, on the one hand, the increasing availability of pornography, much produced from Eastern Europe (Hughes, 2002), along with the harmful sexually violent effects for those involved (Månsson and Söderlind, 2004; Jyrkinen, 2005), and yet the potentially democratising possibilities of much of the new media (Loader, 1997; Liberty, 1999).

The impact of these various transnational trends and processes in individual countries is, however, variable. This is clear in the transitional nations where there have been considerable changes in the structure and operation of news media in recent years. During the Soviet period media was very much the tool of state, party and communist ideology, with high levels or printing and circulation of state newspapers. In some cases, counter-government newspapers were also very important in the lead up to the collapse in the communist regimes. Following this, there has been further development of mass media markets, including the informational universe of international mass media, cable stations and Internet. National television and press are often lagging behind some Western European media, in terms of professionalism, social engagement and competence. Let us look at the situation in the Russian Federation and Latvia in a little more detail.

The Russian newspaper and other media industries have undergone considerable transformation during this period. Commenting on the earlier situation, Tartakovskaya (2000, 118–19) notes that:

> The Soviet media was strongly unified in terms of values and all the newspapers were essentially tools in the same ideological system. Certainly there were subtle differences in the positions of Soviet newspapers, but nevertheless their general characteristics of the role of men, women and the family were very similar ... the assumption that the 'higher goal' of individual men, women and their families was to assist the building of communism.

Izvestia tended to endorse functional families with an egalitarian domestic division of labour; *Komsomol'skaya pravda* tended to emphasise the lives of women, especially single worker-mothers, and their heroic individual contributions to the state rather than to individual men; and *Sovetskaya Rossiya* 'seemed to point to the idea that needs of the state could be reconciled with traditional familial relations in which the man retained his dominance' (p. 119). This last newspaper thus appeared to have the most openly pro-male reporting: 'A man was allowed to be master in his own home, but only on condition that he proved himself at work' (p. 128).

In the post-Soviet period newspaper reporting on men and gender relations has taken quite different forms, with much depending on the political affiliation of the newspaper concerned. In *Komsomol'skaya pravda* both men and women are represented as freed from the state, able to pursue their own affairs, in both senses of the word, with fuller individual liberation. *Izvestia* reports on the transformations more soberly, describing 'a world of gender conflict, a Hobbesian nightmare in which brute strength prevails' (p. 128); and *Sovetskaya Rossiya* is even more pessimistic, with family and personal life severely disrupted by the decline of the state and its services. Tartakovskaya (2000, 135) describes these respectively as: hedonist-patriarchal; liberal-patriarchal; and a 'more nationalist position in which gender relations are still subordinate to a greater good'.

Since the late 1990s the conditions in which the Russian media have operated have changed further and often indeed quite radically, with economic and political crises, downturn in advertising partly through the exit of foreign advertisers, increasing production costs, distribution failures, newspaper closures and layoffs, and drastic reductions of salaries in the industry. This has been especially serious at the regional newspaper level (Fossato and Kachkaeva, 1998).

The Latvian mass media also presents a very diverse picture, even for such a small country. The television channels are state-owned, and, trying to be receptive to social issues of the day, have to financially survive, and so show many serials, soap operas and action movies. The Internet is becoming a widely spread type of mass media, particularly with its cheap or free access and seemingly more diverse informational space. The newspaper market is divided into two sub-markets: Latvian-speaking and Russian-speaking. This results in two readerships with little unity around shared issues. The Russian language press pays more attention to what is going on in Russia and other former USSR republics, and takes a more critical slant on events. These newspapers are very important because some of Latvia's Russian speakers do not speak or read Latvian; other Russian speakers who can speak and read Latvian still buy Russian language newspapers, as Latvian-language newspapers tend to have relatively more restricted agendas. Russian-language newspapers also pay more attention to the problems of 'aliens' in the country.

These two media communities hold different views upon such issues as ethnic and social integration, thus, not only reflecting the politically-shaped opposition in the country, but themselves (re)producing this societal division between Latvians and Russians. This not only exposes the power of political forces behind the media in both languages, but also averts journalists from shared discussions of common social issues, including men's issues. This lack of shared issues, including men's issues, is an explanation of silencing/marginalising of social exclusion among men in society. Thus the form and content of these newspaper representations of men are best understood as a relation of national specificities and transnational constructions (Novikova, 2001b).

Discussion of the four thematic areas

Home and work

This theme covers a very wide range of issues, and as such it is perhaps not very surprising that it is relatively well represented in the newspapers of many countries. In many countries it had the second biggest coverage after the theme of violences. However, in some countries, such as Poland, the representation of this theme remained small. Conversely, this theme sometimes included relatively longer, more detailed articles, especially in the 'quality' press. The overall range of the amount of the number of articles for this theme is 9%–24%. There are a small amount of articles, sometimes based on research, on the changing role of (some) fathers and parenthood models for promoting gender equality more generally. Indeed, with some exceptions, representations of men as fathers, sons, brothers and other male family members appear to be relatively excluded in the press. This is less so and may be becoming even less so, especially in Nordic, UK and other Western European countries. However, overall men or a man in his family context are still relatively rarely represented in a focused way.

On the other hand, men play the main role primarily in events in the context of politics, economy and sport. These categories were not specifically considered for this report, unless the focus on men was central. In Latvia, for example, it was noted that most articles on professional men politicians are written with a critical or ironic tone on the men's national political activity. The very few articles in the genres of 'outstanding man's biography', 'model life story', 'achievement story', and so on are on men in business in contrast to a number of articles on men and their 'work' as hockey-players. Indeed business as a traditional 'men's sphere' has acquired ambiguous connotations in the context of economic crimes, government corruption, murders of businessmen and fear of mafia groups. In some countries, there is a widespread tendency to trivialise or spectacularise (Neale, 1983) references to men, as in the titles of such Estonian articles as 'Men satisfy love of adventure by travelling and forgetting their career' or 'Top businessmen earned millions last year'. Gender has been clearly though implicitly presented in these titles. Somewhat parallel themes around hegemonic and business masculinities are found in Western Europe in terms of what has been described in the Norwegian context as 'greedy boys are at it again' (Holter, 2001b). This kind of sceptical coverage is an interesting and incipiently critical engagement with questions of men and men's power.

More generally, there is often an explicit absence of representations of many of the jobs and professions that men do beyond the traditional set of businessman/doctor/soldier/ performer/sportsman. In some countries, especially the post-communist states but also elsewhere, the military can act as an instrument of shaping certain dominant images of masculinity. This has received attention in the light of bullying of soldiers and 'initiation rituals'. Politics, economy and, in some cases, the military are central interests of the state, the media and their dominant ideologies, and as such this involves imagery of manhood and masculinities based on 'traditional', 'progressive' or sometimes 'foreign' models.

In addition, there are sometimes more focused discussions of men and gender equality in relation to home and work. In several countries, for example, Latvia, Norway and Finland, there was some more specific discussion of men and equality issues. In Latvia, the Gender Equality Draft was during this period drawn up and proposed for discussions in NGOs. In Finland the most discussed gender-explicit topic was the possible introduction of a men's quota in teacher education. In 1989, when the Equality Act came into effect, the quota that guaranteed that 40% of the students would be men, was eliminated. The majority of teachers are women and this led to worries that lone mothers' children especially might need a 'father figure'. There has thus been some pressure to make the quota valid again. Interestingly, the articles were mostly *against* a men's quota, and instead the personal qualities of the teacher were seen as more important than gender. State feminism and gender equality ideology has been to some extent internalised within Nordic mass media.

Social exclusion

The social exclusion of certain groups of men is often a relatively less reported theme than home and work. However, in Germany and Ireland it constituted the largest category, and is also very significant in Estonia. Social exclusion constituted between 4% and 48% of the articles on the four main themes on men. The mainstream press often does not deal with men's gendered experiences around deprivation, poverty, unemployment and disadvantage. This is despite the fact that in the transitional nations and indeed in other countries, many men have had to face social downward mobility. Questions on homeless men are sometimes discussed, and issues of men's health are rarely discussed, even if they might be mentioned. The relationship of issues of gender, class and ethnicity in terms of men do not figure much in the press as well. There are occasional reports on racism and racist attacks. For example, in Estonia a big story was when a racist announcement was found in a bikers' bar – 'no dirty men in bar' – referring to black men. In some countries, such as Italy and the UK, there is a continuing media interest in scandals around sexuality and violence, such as homophobic scandals, rent boys, and child sexual abuse.

Interestingly, in Finland the theme of social exclusion received the least coverage in every newspaper in the time period. Two of the newspapers did not report on men and social exclusion in any way. This is despite the fact that during this time period, there were discussions going on nationally on the so-called poverty package of the government and measures to be taken to combat unemployment. This also contrasts with the earlier academic and media debates on 'men's misery' (Hearn and Lattu, 2000), and may indicate that this perspective is now less in fashion, with the economic upturn of recent years.

In many countries the press is relatively fixed within representational clichés that do not embrace a wide variety of positions of identification that are accessible to men, including those of social exclusion. This could be for a variety of reasons, including sometimes low social engagement and low professionalism of journalists; editorial censorship; in some cases weakness of the press in opinion-formation; and the more general preference for mainstream events and personalities. On the other hand, there are also continuing debates amongst a significant minority of more gender-sensitive journalists on how to foster social and political engagement on gender issues.

Violences

Violences is overall the most well represented theme, constituting 20%–78% of articles on men. Relatively less reporting appears to be found in the German and Latvian presses. In the latter, general discussions on forms of violences and men's involvement in them are marginal in the press. However, some of this variation may be accounted for by methodological difficulties and differences in interpretation. Indeed some articles do not even state directly that it is men who are concerned as perpetrators of violence; common knowledge, however, suggests that men are concerned in many of these instances, as, for example, in the articles that deal with socially marginalised groups. Without very detailed and comprehensive criteria, this makes for great difficulties in quantitative analysis.

Perhaps surprisingly, all three Finnish newspapers generally wrote about violence in a gender-neutral way. The fact that men are far more often the perpetrators, and in some respects the victims, of violence was not discussed in any newspaper in this period, although it has been at other times. Short reports on violent acts or crimes comprised the majority of the articles related to violence. In all three newspapers, violence was the most widely covered of the four themes, in which men are reported in a gender-explicit way. In Germany masculinity and violence against known women is treated in a 'commonsense' way to a very large extent; in particular, violent attacks on women when they want to leave their male partners, or because of jealousy are portrayed as something to be expected, or at least understandable, often picturing the perpetrator himself as a victim.

Frequently in the newspapers surveyed, men as perpetrators of crimes, as a threat to society and, often, to the safety and lives of innocent people, are reported as relatively dominant parts of social life. Men are described as perpetrators of crimes in the majority of articles, and yet that does not necessarily mean that crimes committed by men are seen as an important social issue. On the other hand, most articles on violences are short. Such reports on violent acts or crimes comprised the majority of the articles related to violence. The cases described included: violence perpetrated by men upon men, women or children, and even a dog (battery, harassment, rape and murder), and other breaches of the law by fraud, theft, robbery and organised crime. There were certain particular topical violent cases, such as rape cases, which received a relatively large amount column space.

Men's violence against women and children is often presented as a frightening, yet expected event; in case some things happen, that in fact happen every day. For example, if a woman wants to separate from the male partner she is living with, this may 'cause' danger, even death, to herself or her children, or to the new partner she starts to live with instead, or even to people who just happen to be around. Thus, many newspapers reproduce the view that violence against intimate partners and children makes for a non-surprising element of masculinity, given a situation of marital or similar separation.

The analysis of the articles recorded shows that descriptions of *individual* cases constitute the main way of reporting on violences. However, there are several kinds of exceptions to this pattern. An interesting alternative is the reporting in both the Polish and the Finnish press on honour killings in Muslim countries that addresses the phenomenon from the point of view of *culture*. A UK article addressed the alleged fact that a boy with a mobile phone is said to be more at risk of violence than a pensioner outside; this article took a *more societal* focus as well as explicitly recognising a problem for boys. Other articles have focused on the *group and cultural* aspects of gang formation on the streets. Another UK article discussed how some boys carried out muggings because they needed the money whilst others did so to enhance their reputation or because it was easy since there was no one and nothing to deter them, so bringing a societal focus onto the issue. A *social* focus was also used to look at the circumstances surrounding five men being held in custody as a result of the pregnancy of a 12 year old girl. The article discussed the social problems of the area in the context of regional steel and coal closures. Some articles dealt with *historical* or *international* crimes perpetrated by men. In Poland, the case of crimes against Jews perpetrated by Poles in 1941, as well as compensation for compulsory work in the Third Reich, repeatedly featured in the papers in this period (Oleksy, 2001b).

Although it is seldom stated explicitly, there is often an appeal to the view that 'men are (inherently) bad'. More precisely, men are seen as bad in domestic and children matters. The appeal to men's bad nature may be used as a political angle to avoid debate on wider gender political changes. Such a tone may not be so different from the nineteenth century message that men are barbarous, and need to be kept in the marketplace or away from home, while women are the moral elevators (Holter, 2001b). What we have here is a complex intertwining of gendered and non-gendered aspects and reporting. Most reporting about violence remains in 'gender-neutral' mode. The fact that men are far more often the perpetrators, and in some respects the victims, was usually not specifically discussed. An important intersection of gender, nationality and ethnicity is that newspapers often also mentioned the perpetrator's nationality, if it was known not to be a national.

Health

Men's health is the least reported theme in most countries, ranging from 2%–19% of the articles in the newspapers surveyed. The definition of health can be relatively complicated, for example, whether to include reports on traffic accidents, which are often reported in a gender-neutral way just mentioning the victim's gender. Sport could also be seen as part of health. In most newspapers the great majority of sports news was on men and men's sport events. However, these were not specifically included as they were generally reported in a supposedly 'gender-neutral' way. There appears to be much less reporting on men's health in the transitional nations. No articles or information dealing explicitly with men's health as a social, economic and medical issue were found in Latvia in the period. Only one article, dealing with free prostate examination arranged for men, addressed the problem of men's health in Poland. In Estonia there was slightly greater attention to men's health. In Ireland the theme constituted 0.02% of the entire newspaper coverage.

The greatest number of reports was found in the UK press. These were sometimes individually focused. For example, an article on autism, though giving background information, focused on an individual boy and his circumstances, and did not mention the relatively high prevalence rates among boys. Explicit men's issues did sometimes bring in a group focus but these were few. One article briefly addressed men's need to talk more about illness, go to the doctor more and not ignore symptoms within a man's cancer diary. Another brief article reported research suggesting that men feared impotence more than cancer, AIDS or even death; only heart disease worried them more. Only prostate cancer was addressed as an explicit issue for men. This was given a group focus but even in the 'quality' press the majority of the articles were about individuals or used individual accounts.

At the more detailed level still, it is important to note that there are some newspapers that appear to place relatively greater emphasis on health and men's health. This applies, for example, to the German newspaper, *BILD*, which includes numerous articles talking about dramatic cases of death. In *BILD*, the health of men seems to be always in danger (Müller, and Jacobsen, 2001). 'Men's health' is thematised mostly in terms of risks, in traffic and in work, as a result of irresponsible behaviour, and as a result of violence. This points to the need to be sensitive to the specificities of particular media and media outlets, including variations in newspapers' coverages, rather than to stay with broad generalisations.

Concluding remarks

Research development

While in recent years there has been increasing research on representations of men in the media, there has been relatively less concern with mundane, everyday media representations of men in newspapers. In this sense, this analysis has been founded on a less firm research base than the three phases discussed in the three previous chapters. On the other hand, this also raises many opportunities for further research and opens up many questions for future research on men in newspapers, and men's relations to newspapers, that is relatively easy to undertake with the ready availability of this medium.

Methodology

This qualitative and quantitative research raises complex issues of measurement and analysis. There are major methodological and even epistemological issues in assessing forms of representation of 'men', 'men's practices' and 'masculinities'. This is especially so when a large amount of newspaper reporting is presented in supposedly or apparently 'gender-neutral' terms. Men are routinely taken-for-granted and not problematised in the press. There are also significant forms and genres of reporting, especially around politics, economy and business, and sport, that are often 'all about men', but without addressing men in an explicitly gendered way. Furthermore, the framework of the four main themes has been to a large extent imposed on the newspaper material surveyed. While the overall extent of explicit coverage on men is relatively small, there is noticeably more coverage in the attention to men in families and, to an extent, gender equality debates in Western European countries than in the transitional nations.

Distribution

The most reported themes were generally 'violences', usually followed by 'home and work'. 'Social exclusion' was reported to a variable extent; it was the most reported theme in Germany and Ireland. 'Health' was generally the least reported theme, especially so in the transitional nations, with, for example, no articles in Latvia and only one in Poland. Significantly, men in these nations generally have on average a far worse health record and life expectancy than men in Western Europe. This low reporting in the press there on health contrasts with the higher number of articles in, for example, Finland and the UK.

Variations among newspapers

There are major variations in the pattern of reporting on men amongst particular newspapers. It cannot be assumed that the 'more serious' or 'quality' newspapers devote more explicit attention to men or present more explicitly gendered representations of men than those that are more populist or tabloid. Whilst it is not be surprising that the latter such newspapers might emphasise reporting on violences, attention paid to other themes, such as men's health, is perhaps more surprising and worthy of further investigation.

Violences

The theme of violences needs special mention as it figured so strongly in some countries. While there is limited attention to group, cultural, social, societal, historical and international perspectives on men's violence, a relatively large amount of reporting is often of short articles, much of it reported on an individual basis.

Further studies

Apart from the representation of 'men' in newspaper articles and visual depictions, advertisements and photographs accompanying articles, there are many other aspects of newspapers worthy of further study in relation to men and men's practices. These include: broad socio-economic questions around men and men's practices in the ownership, production, circulation and consumption (Hall, 1997) of newspapers; the interconnections of newspapers and other media; and representations of men in apparently mundane aspects of newspapers, such as announcements of 'births, deaths and marriages', obituaries, listings and reviews of film, television and other media, and personal small advertisements, for 'soulmates', sexual services, and buying and selling of goods.

Acknowledgements

We wish to thank Irma Kaarina Halonen and Tarja Savolainen for advice on media studies.

Part 2
Themes

6
Home and 'Work'

Jeff Hearn, Keith Pringle, Marie Nordberg and Iva Šmídová, with Ursula Müller, Elżbieta H. Oleksy, Emmi Lattu, Teemu Tallberg, Harry Ferguson, Voldemar Kolga and Irina Novikova

Introduction

The social relations of home and work represent some of the most fundamental aspects of gender relations in society, and thus some of the most important elements in the construction of men and masculinities. The separation of home and work is both a very real one and an ideological construction. It is at the root of much liberal social science, as well as figuring, in more or less sophisticated ways, in non-feminist (Habermas, 1984, 1987) and feminist (Fraser, 1989) critical theory. In some ways it refers to the distinction between production and reproduction; but an over-simple division into dual spheres has been shown to be theoretically flawed, historically inaccurate (Bose, 1987; Hearn, 1992) and contrary to the experience of some people and some social categories, for example, women of colour (Collins, 1990).

In many countries and until relatively recently, established forms of masculinity and men's practices could be distinguished on two major dimensions – urban and rural; bourgeois and working class. These four forms and their various historical, societal, national, cultural and local variations have been centrally concerned with different gender arrangements of home and work – in the city and the country, in mental work and manual work. The exact ways these four forms were practiced varied between societies and cultures. In addition, many other crosscutting dimensions have been and are important, such as variations by age, ethnicity and sexuality. In recent years, urban bourgeois, rural bourgeois, urban working class and rural working class forms of masculinity and men's practices have all been subject to major social change.

'Work' is a socially contextualised phenomenon: it refers to both activities that are necessary for survival, that are strictly controlled by others, and that are not personally or collectively sought. For some people, work is linked to salvation or actualisation. The meaning and naming of work is heavily linked to broad societal organisation. It does not only mean paid work in the public sphere. Feminist studies have been highly influential in naming childcare, housework and domestic labour as work. They have highlighted the importance of unpaid domestic labour as an important site of gendered 'work' and of men's domination of women. Meanwhile, the home is still often not seen as a workplace at all. For women, this is one of the many ways in which they and their work remain less visible and undervalued.

In many societies women are mainly or solely responsible for housework; there are also major differences between the kind of domestic tasks performed by men and women. Men tend to 'specialise' in putting children to bed, taking out and playing with children, waste disposal, household repairs and do-it-yourself. Such tasks are generally preferred by men over the much more time-consuming, supposedly mundane and indeed socially subordinated tasks of cleaning, daily shopping, washing, ironing, cooking and the routine care of infants and children (Oakley, 1985).

'Work' also encompasses domestic, unpaid, non-employed labour outside formal organisations in the private sphere. It includes what have come to be called reproductive labour (O'Brien, 1981, 1986; Hearn, 1983, 1987). Furthermore, work is organised across these boundaries of public and private, paid and unpaid, within what has been called the total social organisation of work (Glucksman, 1995). Work is socially and societally organised, according to what has generally come to be called the sexual or rather gender division of labour.

There are a number of different traditions of theorising on forms of capitalism, socialism, welfare society or welfare patriarchies, that are themselves commentaries on home and work. Welfare, whether in state welfare, welfare state, mixed economy, 'third way' or neo-liberal forms, can be seen partly as intervening between home and work. Additionally, welfare work itself is a significant employer of women.

The home–work relation is fundamental in theorisations of patriarchy, including the historical move from private patriarchy to public patriarchy. These include the extent to which nation-states can be characterised as strong, modified or weak breadwinner states. A more structural form of analysis has distinguished different historical forms of patriarchy, including the shift from private patriarchy to public patriarchy (Brown, 1981; Walby, 1990; Hearn, 1992). This latter approach can be combined with the extent of subordination of women, so giving the following societal contexts:

- Private Patriarchy with High Subordination of Women,
- Public Patriarchy with High Subordination of Women,
- Private Patriarchy with Lower Subordination of Women,
- Public Patriarchy with Lower Subordination of Women (Duncan, 2001).

The gender arrangements of home and work interconnect with social exclusion, violences and health. Men's social exclusion from home or work is likely to create problems in the respective other arenas. This is likely to have even more impact on the women, children and other men in that arena, as partners, work colleagues and so on. Men are also active in assisting and reproducing the social exclusion of both women and men, at both work and home. Much violence occurs in the home, in the form of men's violence to known women and men's child abuse, including child sexual abuse. The home is a major site of men's violence. There is increasing recognition of the scale of violence, including bullying and harassment, at work. Violence at home is clearly antagonistic to equality and care at home, and is detrimental to performance at work. Home and work both provide potential social support and networks, to both reproduce and counter men's violence.

Home can also be or be seen as a 'protection' against work or indeed against racism or other antagonisms in the wider society. Home and work are thus sites for increasing or decreasing men's health. Men, especially men in positions of power or with access to power, are able to affect the health of women, children and other men in their realm of power. This can apply to men as managers in, say, restructuring of workplaces, and to men as powerful actors in families and communities. Men's health and indeed life expectancy is also often affected by relative material wellbeing arising from work, and by dangers and risks in specific occupations.

In this chapter we consider work on men and work, home and home–work relations, by considering academic studies, statistical sources, and the development of law and policy, before outlining some policy recommendations.

Academic studies

In academic studies on men at work recurring themes include men's occupational, working and wage advantages over women, gender segregation at work, many men's close associations with paid work, men in nontraditional occupations. There has been a general lack of attention to men as managers, policy-makers, owners and other power holders. Most obviously, there is the continuing dominance of men in management, especially at the very top and more highly paid levels. Davidson and Burke (2000, 2) report that 'in the European Union countries fewer than 5 per cent of women are in senior management roles and this percentage has barely changed since the early 1990s'. There is evidence of some increases in women's representation in middle management and in small business ownership, and thus in management in total (Davidson and Burke, 2000; Vinnicombe, 2000). However, at CEO and highest executive levels the numbers of women, sometimes as low as 1–2%, may be reducing, static or increasing very slowly indeed (Institute of Management, 1995; Veikkola et al., 1997; Institute of Management / Remuneration Economics, 1998).

There are signs of some change in small and medium size enterprises. While in 1996 50% of SMEs in the European Business Survey (1996) countries had only men in management, the 2002 figure was 44%; and the proportion of

SMEs with one or two women in management had also increased (*European Business Survey . . .* , 2002). However, according to Eurostat (2002), only in Italy, the Netherlands and Austria was the proportion of men employed as 'Directors and chief executives' less than three times that for women. In Sweden it was fifteen times higher, and indeed Swedish research has pointed to homosocial bonding among men in higher positions as a specific problem (Wahl and Holgersson, 2003).

Also, there are clear national policy pressures, especially in Norway and Sweden, to address and change this situation, and particularly in relation to the membership of boards of directors. Men managers are more likely than women managers to be better paid, to be in more secure employment, to be on higher grades, to be less stressed, to be older at each responsibility level, and to have not experienced prejudice and sexual discrimination (Davidson and Cooper, 1984; Institute of Management, 1995; Institute of Management / Remuneration Economics, 1998).

Strong gender divisions within management specialisations persist, often underwritten by gender divisions in education and training, for example, men's domination of most engineering and technology sectors. In many organisations, management has been and continues to be represented as gender-neutral, whether as part of supposedly non-gendered bureaucracy or taken-for-granted managerial imperative. Management and other organisational practices often involve homosocial practices, with men's preference for men and men's company, and the use of masculine models, stereotypes and symbols in management, often from sport, the military and evolution, such as the 'law of the jungle'. Male homosociality that combines emotional detachment, competitiveness and viewing women as sexual objects, and perpetuates hegemonic masculinity, also suppresses subordinate masculinities and reproduces a pecking order among men. Management and especially what is often understood as effective business management have often been assumed to be consistent with characteristics traditionally valued in men (Alimo-Metcalfe, 1993). There have been significant historical transformations of management, from male near-monopoly, to dominant traditional managerial masculinities, and to more modern forms of gendering (Kerfoot and Knights, 1993; Roper, 1994; Collinson and Hearn, 1996).

The question of remuneration and other benefits, fair or unfair, is a central gender issue. The gender pay gap persists. In the OECD, women are still paid 16% less per hour than men, on 'raw' unadjusted figures. This is the figure unadjusted for the effects of, first, the remuneration rates by observed characteristics of jobs, and second, the whole national wage structure. If these two factors are taken into account the gender wage gap as measured is altered, for example, to a lower figure by 2–4% for the UK, and by a higher figure of up to 6% in the Netherlands (*OECD Employment Outlook*, 2002, 94–106). There are indications of slow narrowing of the gender gap in Europe, though some recent figures also suggest a slight widening in some countries.

Work organisations are becoming more time-hungry and less secure and predictable. While it is necessary not to overstate the uniformity of this trend that is relevant to certain groups only and not all countries, time utilisation emerges as a fundamental issue of creating difference in everyday negotiations between men and women (Metz-Göckel and Müller, 1986; Busch et al., 1988; Höpflinger et al., 1991; Notz, 1991; Jurczyk and Rerrich, 1993; Niemi et al., 1991; Tarkowska, 1992). Increasing concerns about men and time-use have been reported in Estonia, Ireland, Norway, Germany and elsewhere (McKeown et al., 1998; Anttila and Ylöstalo, 1999). In Italy research is highlighting the importance of the quality of time for men in their family relations (Ventimiglia and Pitch, 2000). In many countries there are twin problems of the unemployment of some or many men in certain social categories, and work overload and long working hours for other men, especially for young men and young fathers.

The state of knowledge on men, home and work is uneven, especially in Central and East Europe. Not only is there typically an under-resourced research infrastructure, but there are also the difficulties of researching and measuring the informal or 'grey' economy and second-job market that are especially important in many such countries. In the Russian Federation and other countries plot work can be a significant economic activity providing food and sometimes a surplus. In the Czech Republic there are almost no studies on men in the public sphere (see Chapter 2). Academic research on men and masculinities mostly comprises qualitative studies on topics such as fatherhood or men's role in dual career families (Marikova, 2000; Cermakova et al., 2000). There has been some research on single men (Cermakova et al., 2000). Studies show that men are not the sole breadwinners in the family and important decisions are often made by both partners together. The father is the key role of men in the family, and men report being more satisfied with family life than their spouses. As regards domestic chores, men play the role of 'helpers' rather than partners despite the pretended desired ideal of equal sharing (Cermakova et al., 2000, 102–06).

Other recurring themes are men's benefit from avoidance of domestic responsibilities, and the absence of fathers. In many countries traditional 'solutions' continue in domestic arrangements, but there is a growing recognition of the national politics of fatherhood, domestic responsibilities, and home–work reconciliation at least for some men. It is not surprising if there may be a degree of cultural uncertainty on men's place in the home and as fathers and a growing recognition of ambivalence, even when there is a strong familism. In many countries there are also counter and conflictual tendencies regarding men's position in families. Marriage is no longer a formal bar to women's employment, and, in that sense at least, men are not formally presumed to be the lifelong breadwinners. Yet in many countries, there is increasing emphasis on the privatised family. This may be connected to 'family values', right wing or gender equal status perspectives. In some cases this is being reinforced through new family ideologies within transformation processes after Soviet regimes, as in Latvia (Novikova, 2000a). On the other hand, there is a more demanding and more turbulent working life, with the imperative for all to work within 'third way' rhetoric. Through this men may be more absent. In Norway and elsewhere due to a post-parental-divorce system where most fathers lose contact with their children, higher work pressure and more work mobility, 'father absence' has probably become more widespread in real terms over the last ten years, as has the 'general absence of men' in children's environment, even if more positive trends can be seen (Holter and Olsvik, 2000).

Given the considerable difference that still exists between men's and women's earnings, it could be argued that it is not surprising that it is the woman who stays at home after the birth of a child. Since she is usually the person with the lower income, a couple do not need to be wholehearted advocates of traditional domestic ideology to opt for the traditional solution. On the other hand, this labour market difference is not in itself enough to explain the persistence of such patterns. Women's tendency to leave the labour force for childrearing, for varying amounts of time, has to be understood in terms of the diverse patterns across Europe. These patterns range from women's employment patterns being similar to men's to exit from employment at the birth of a first child at the other. Similarly, there are wide variations in the extent to which women with children and women without children have similar full-time employment patterns: these two rates are rather close for Finland; very far apart for the UK, where the difference is nearly 30% (Bertoud and Iacovou, 2002, Chart 12).

While generally greater provision of public childcare support and parental leave links with women's greater labour market participation, there are complications. Parental leave without public childcare support can reinforce the male breadwinner model, with or without women's part-time work. Men's unemployment can have clear and diverse effects on men's lives in families. There is also in some countries, such as Finland, growing interest in the reconciliation of work and home; and growing variety of ways of approaching this (Lammi-Taskula, 2000; see also Oakley and Rigby, 1998; Pringle, 1998a, 1998b, 1998c). When parental leave is left to negotiations between men and women, it is still mostly taken up by women, even though most people, men especially, say they want a more balanced situation (Lammi-Taskula, 1998; Holter and Olsvik, 2000). For example, in Sweden it is true that more men take parental leave than in most other European countries (Bergman and Hobson, 2001). However, women still take the overwhelming majority of such leave; indeed one reason why a 'daddy's month' of parental leave was introduced was because men's take-up was so slow (Bergman and Hobson 2001). In 2002, a second 'daddy's month', that could only be taken by fathers, was introduced because, although take-up had improved a little, it was still a relatively small increase. Men's parental leave take-up is also low in Denmark (Iovanni and Pringle, 2005a). The experience in Norway has been much more positive with the 'daddy's month' (Brandth and Kvande, 2003).

There are also the micro-politics of reconciliation strategies and practices within individual workplaces and families, including the impact of power relations between women and men in marriage and couple relationships. Recent research by Bekkengen (2002) suggests that the standard explanation for low take-up of parental leave by men (i.e. that labour market rigidities allegedly preventing many men from taking as much parental leave as they would like) have to be seriously questioned as sufficient in themselves. Her important qualitative study brings to light additional and crucial factors which quantitative studies have not been able to locate. In particular, Bekkengen's study indicates that the most crucial factor that the men in her study generally possessed much greater power to choose the extent of their involvement than did their female partners. Her research can be seen as part of that strand of Swedish research on fatherhood that focuses on *men as a problem* and the obstacles for implementation of gender equality. This contrasts with the strand, which has grown over the last ten years, in which the focus is more on *men's lives and experiences*. This perspective highlights both problems and obstacles for gender equal lives that men meet and men's experiences and new practices (Nordberg, 2006).

Men and indeed fathers are clearly not a homogeneous group. Men's unemployment can have clear and diverse effects on men's life in families. In Poland, for example, in research on unemployed men under 36 years of age, after they lost their jobs, 40% reported the loss of 'family leadership' to their working wives (Pielkowa, 1997). Finnish research suggests some unemployed men may have closer ties with children (Tigerstedt, 1994), and some UK research points in a similar direction (Kearney et al., 2000). Traditional men may not see any need to engage in balancing home and work, and may show more propensity and support for violence. 'Money' may be used to legitimate gender-specific divisions of responsibilities within families when traditional patriarchal models have to be justified; when the opposite is the case, the argument may not apply. A Swedish study on stepfathers shows class differences in men's relations to stepchildren (Bak and Bäck-Wiklund, 2003). While working class men tend to try to integrate the stepchild into one common family, middle class men tend to run a project of two families side by side. Italian researches have highlighted the complexity of family dynamics with more or less traditional fatherhood (Ventimiglia and Pitch, 2000).

Among men there has long been a contradiction between the ideas they profess and the way they actually live. In several countries, for example, Estonia (Kolga, 2000) the reasons for the discrepancies between men's values and men's actual behaviour in families remain unclear. The fact that men and women living together do not always give the same assessment of their relationship in general and the distribution of tasks between them in particular has become a much discussed in methodological debates. The paradoxical ways in which gender conflicts on the distribution of housework may be negotiated may be illustrated from German research: while in the early 1980s women living with men were generally more likely than men to claim that they did more of the work, some studies in the 1990s have shown the opposite. Men now tend to be the ones who claim they do relatively little housework, while women insist that the work is shared evenly (Frerichs and Steinrücke, 1994). It is almost as if the challenges that women face in living with and 'tolerating' a lack of equality in family and intimate relationships is now being expressed in an exaggerated assessment of the level of equality in those relationships (Müller, 2006).

The gender arrangements of work in the home and family impact on those on employed working life, and vice versa, and in turn mediated by state and market welfare provisions. For example, according to Holst and Spiess's (2004, 22) study of transitions from unemployment, education and housework to employment in 11 European countries, 'traditional gender roles and family status have a negative effect on female labour market participation. Family status . . . had negative effect for married females and those living with a partner, whereas a positive effect for the corresponding group of men. Further to this, the number of children has a negative effect for mothers but not for fathers.' In all the countries surveyed, the overall probabilities of transition to employment were better for men than women (p. 23).

Many gaps remain in our knowledge. A huge one exists with respect to the gender division of domestic labour and parenting in many countries. It would be interesting to see how and when, if ever, women and men form coalitions through a politics of reconciliation, and how gender constellations at home and work influence each other. It would be important to further research couples which experience labour market conditions, so that, for instance, the female partner is the main earner long term or working times are such that they do not allow traditional housework distribution.

Most research focuses on white heterosexual partners. There is a need for research on the intersections of men, the 'home' and the 'labour market' in its diverse configurations, including minority ethnic families and gay partnerships. This is a growing area of research attention in the UK (for example, Weeks et al., 2001). Relatively little research has generally been carried out on men as carers, though there is an established research tradition on this issue in the UK. Another research gap is the relationship between men's activities as carers and men's use of violence and abuse in families, whether violence against women or against children.

In seeking to make sense of the albeit limited increases in parental activity by some men in the home, there is the question of to what extent do these changes represent real social 'progress' or sometimes re-creations of patriarchal dominance in relatively novel forms. There is a need for much greater consideration of fatherhood in terms of cultural, sexual and other forms of diversity, and more inclusion of the 'voices' of women and children in studies of fatherhood.

Statistical sources

There is a very large amount of statistical data on men's relations to home and at work. Indeed this theme frequently constituted the major part of the national reports on the four key themes examined. There is also much more complexity in the variables and relations presented than for the other themes of violence, social exclusion and health. On the other hand, much of the data continues the tradition of dealing with home and work separately, so reinforcing the 'public/private' division.

In terms of the statistical sources on men 'at home', the general national systems of population and census statistics are clearly a useful starting point. These statistics need to be read in association with census and other statistical information on economic activity, employment and status. General demographic patterns include the higher mortality of men relative to women, and the larger numbers of women in the older population. There are also a variety of statistics on patterns of family formation, childbearing, separation and divorce. There has been a long-term increase in divorce, even if recent patterns are more uneven, including some downturns in some countries.

Many major patterns of change are identified. In some countries, for example Ireland, there has been a notable increase in women's employment in recent years, with associated effects on men. The main breadwinning is no longer the monopoly of men. Structural changes in the economy have been especially significant in the transitional countries, where they have brought major change for women and men at home and work. In Norway, there has been a slight decline of non-standard employment forms over the last years (LO-notat, 2000). In some cases, there is also the problem of a high rate of change in work and working place, with high amounts of layoffs. This has been very significant in the Baltic, Central and East European countries, but also in the UK and elsewhere. In Poland men aged 55–59 have been most affected by unemployment (Borowicz and Lapinska-Tyszka, 1993).

However, it is incorrect to consider all post-socialist countries in the same vein. Poland, Estonia and Russia are at different points of development, which may account for different forms of the social problem of men in these countries, and different patterns of occupational mobility for women and men. In Poland men aged 55–59 have been most affected by unemployment (Oleksy, 2001c). In some cases, notably Estonia and the Russian Federation, this has meant a decline in population, and the growth of the 'economically inactive' population and relatively high rate unemployment. In Estonia men, especially rural men, are the subjects of structural economic changes during the last ten years which appeared in the diminishing of the primary sector and the increasing of the tertiary sector in the economy.

In many countries there are twin problems of the unemployment of some or many men in certain social categories, and yet work overload and long working hours for other men. These can especially be a problem for young men and young fathers; they can affect both working class and middle class men as for example during economic recession. In working life, work organisations are becoming more time-hungry and less secure and predictable. On the other hand, it is necessary not to overstate the uniformity of this trend in all countries. In France working time has decreased with the 35 hour a week rule, but this national regulation was overturned in February 2005, despite trade union protests. In Germany, this is also the case but only for working time regulated by trade union–employer negotiations. The working time of people in high level positions has increased, and overtime continues at a relatively high rate.

Generally, the wage-earning working life of men has shrunk, because the training phase is becoming longer, careers start later, working life is shorter, and life expectancy (in some countries) is increasing. However, a quantitative time gain does not necessarily mean a qualitative gain, because the shortened working life has become more intensive, less tranquil and more uncertain. One of the most significant trends is the demand for productivity and an increasing pace of work. Work has also become mentally more wearing and uncertainty, competition and fixed-term employment contracts are more common (Sennett, 1998; Bunting, 2004).

As with the academic research, recurring themes in employment include men's occupational, working and wage gap over women, gender segregation at work, differences in patterns of working hours, many men's close associations with paid work. For example, Polish data show that more men worked full-time, in the private sector in particular, of all employees; part-time female employees dominate in both sectors. In all countries fathers are more employed than non-fathers. In Norway fathers with young children are 'the most stable labour power in the market' (Holter, 2001c). This applies especially to younger fathers in employment. Another important variable is the relation of women's salary to men's. There are also major national differences in class structure and the extent of variation in salaries between men who are in employment.

There has been a general lack of statistical studies on men as managers, policy-makers, owners and other power holders. There are now some studies of this in Finland. The change of women entering into senior management has been slow and the proportion of female senior staff and upper management has very much remained stable during the first half of the 1990s; 21% in 1990 and 22% in 1995 (Veikkola et al., 1997, 83). However, recent research in Finland appears to indicate that the proportion of women in top management and on the boards of the largest corporations is about 10% (Hearn et al., 2002). The salary of managers depends strongly on gender, but less so in case of lower level occupations.

Despite the long-term growth of divorces, the traditional family – officially married or cohabiting, with children – is the largest type of family in Estonia.

In Germany and elsewhere there is a trend toward smaller households. In Italy the process of decline of the marriage continues, even as cohabitations increase. This is also observable in Norway, where there has been a marked increase in cohabitation and, in that sense, decline in marriage. In the UK cohabitation has increased amongst young people. Similar changes in marriage patterns in Poland have meant growing numbers of single men (Oleksy, 2001c). Another important trend in practically all EU-15 countries since the 1980s is the rise in the age at which people get married. Increasing emphasis on gender equality in society might lead to a decrease in the age gap in marriage.

Housework is still mostly women's work, and this is clearly documented. There is much less statistical information on men's caring and associated activities at home, and on the interrelations of men's home and work, including the reconciliation of home and work life. For example, in Ireland government departments gather no data whatsoever on this and have been slow to commission research into this area. In many countries the option of a child-induced career disruption continues as the normal case for the mother and a special case for the father (Ferguson, 2001c).

In Finland educated men tend to have more children; men have been asked in a national survey for their views on state support to families. More men than women considered the support satisfactory; about 33% of men born in 1953–1957 and 1963–67 thought it was completely or somewhat insufficient, whereas more than half of the women of the same age groups considered it insufficient. The majority of men thought that a lower level of taxation would be the best way to support families, whereas women wanted more services (Nikander, 1995; also see Melkas, 1998).

There is a growing research and statistical literature on men's and women's differential take-up of various forms of state and occupational parental leave. This is an especially significant research area in both Germany and Norway (Müller, 2001b; Holter, 2001c; Brandth and Kvande, 2003). In the latter, cash support reform for families with small children has created a new trend where the mother cuts down on wage work while the father works as much, or more, than before. Indeed the number of fathers taking *long* parental leave has decreased.

There is a growing amount of statistical data on time use. In Poland from the point of view of the mean time of the duration of the activity, men devoted to their jobs twice as much time as women on the average. They also used mass media more frequently. They spent nearly twice as much time on sports and leisure activities. Women devoted almost three times as much time to housework, slightly more time than men to studying, as well as to religious practices. In the context of the mean time of the performance of the activity, professionally active men devoted to work more time than women by 33 minutes every day on the average (*Time Use Survey 1996*, 1998).

In Ireland men work an overall average of around 46 hours per week, with fathers tending to work slightly longer hours than non-fathers. A third of fathers (33%) work 50 hours per week or more compared to only a quarter of non-fathers (27%). Mothers, where they are employed, work an average of 31–32 hours per week outside the home, exactly 15 hours less than the number of hours worked outside the home by father. Non-mothers work longer hours in employment than mothers. It appears that fathers' work patterns are influenced by the employment status and earnings of their partners. Fathers whose partners are working outside the home spend less hours at work than fathers whose partners are not working. A further crucial variable is the time of the day or week when the work is done. A small proportion of fathers in Ireland do shift work, nearly half do evening work, a quarter do night work, two-thirds Saturday work and two-fifths Sunday work. Fathers are much more likely to work unsocial hours in employment than mothers. In Ireland the proportion of mothers in full-time employment is much lower than for fathers, with much higher proportions of women doing part-time work. Still, fathers were the exclusive breadwinners in only half of all families with dependent children (McKeown et al., 1998).

As a way of showing some of the variation in conditions, let us consider two very different countries in a little more detail. In the Czech Republic recent figures indicate that about 70 per cent of all Czech men in productive age (15+) are economically active. The proportion of employed women is high in the Czech Republic, 51%, and most people work full-time (part time jobs are held by 9% of women and 3% men). There were 20% of men self-employed (and 10% of women) (*Zeny a muzi v datech*, 2003).

Men earned 135% of the average women's wages and salaries in 1997 (or to put this conversely, women earned 73.4% of what men earned) (*Zeny a muzi v cislech*, 2000). The figure remains steady, with a gender pay gap of 26% in the 2001 Census. Education plays important role in the amount of money earned. University educated men have the highest salaries (but not those with academic training). The difference between men and women in earnings is low for secondary and technically educated people, and high for both uneducated and university educated. Relatively small differences in earnings in different segments of the labour market visible today trace back to the totalitarian times of 'equal distribution of wealth' – almost equal pay and living standard to anybody employed (and almost everybody was employed).

The level of unemployment remains low in the Czech Republic. It was 3% in 1996 and since 1997 has grown over 8% in 1999–2000 (Cermakova et al., 2000). The unemployment rate was 6% for men and 9% for women in 2002 (*Zeny a muzi v datech*, 2003). The figure is high for the youngest age group of men (for the age group of 15–19 men outnumber women since 1994) and men with lowest or no education (*Zeny a muzi v datech*, 2003, Cermakova et al., 2000).

The number of men staying at home to care for children has risen slowly from a statistical zero in 1990 to an estimate of 0.5–2% today, following the 1995 legislative act enabling men to take parental leave with financial assistance and officially become a caregiver (Marikova, 1999, 39). This is most common for fathers of older children. This view is supported also by figures of single parent households, where only 2% of children live with their fathers as sole parents at their age of 0–17, and dependent children at ages 18–24 live with their fathers in 3% of all cases according to the Census in 2001 (*Zeny a muzi v datech*, 2003). As far as custody over children after divorce is concerned, in 2002 only 7.2% of the cases were in favour of fathers custody (90.3% mothers and 2.1% joint or alternative custody) (*Zeny a muzi v datech*, 2003).

Sweden is well known as having a relatively strong welfare state and gender equality policies. However, it also has one of the most sex-segregated labour markets in Europe (Ohlsson and Sundgren Grinups, 1994). The segregation is both horizontal, men and women work in different areas, and hierarchical, men can more often be found in higher positions and have higher salaries than women. Women's wage level is about 80% of men's. The percentage of men in the workforce has declined since 1990, while the percentage of women has increased between 1970–1990 and then decreased. In 1970 there were 60% of the women and 90% of men in age between 20–64 years in the workforce. In the beginning of the 1990s the number of young men in the workforce decreased, but in 2001 the workforce percentage for men increased for all ages. In 2001 the percent was 79% for women and 84% for men. The percentage for men born in Europe was 84% and for men born outside Europe 78%, to be compared with 91% Swedish-born men being in the workforce. The statistics show that men with children under seven years of age are more often than men without children working full time, at least in ages under 34 and over 54. This points out that the male breadwinner model is still strong in Sweden. Women more often work part-time when having small children. In 2001 33% of the women worked part-time and only 8% of men. Men with children less than seven years old often work 40–50 hours per week. Part-time work is more common among elderly men than young fathers. It is also more common for women than men to working on temporary posts (SCB, 2002).

Most men work in the private sector and in traditional male work. In 2001 82% of the men were working in the private sector and 18% in the public sector (in 1970 21% were in the public sector). For women the statistics show a different movement – in 1970 42% of the women worked in the public sector, in 2001 50% were working there. In work considered to be gender equal – 40% of one sex and 60% of the other sex – only 12% of the men worked in 2001. Few men are working part-time; 74% work more than 34 h/week and only 5% work between 20–34 hours a week while 21% of the women do so. Unemployment was in 2001 highest for men born outside Europe, 13% to be compared with 4% for Swedish-born men (SCB, 2002).

The most male-dominated jobs are truck drivers (99% men) and house building. Only 2% of men work in female-dominated occupations in workplaces with less than 10% men. One per cent of women work in workplaces with less than 10% women (SCB, 2002). It seems easier for men to enter traditionally female-dominated areas than vice versa. Over the last decade the amount of men going into children, daycare and pre-school work has declined and is now about 2%–3%. There has been continuing public debate on the lack of men teachers in schools and boys' problems at school. There is also some debate in the media and policy circles on the uneven job prospects of women and men who recently immigrated to Sweden, alongside a growth in diversity discourse within Swedish management (Nordberg, 2006).

Law and policy

As we saw in Chapter 4, although there may not be a very large body of law and policy information specifically focused on men, the various historical and national traditions in the constructions of citizenship have large implications for the place of men in law and policy. These constructions of citizenship have often been presented as 'gender-neutral', even though they have clear historical gendering as 'male'. These constructions of citizenship have clear relevance for the formulation of law and policy on men in relation to home and work.

There is a general use of gender-neutral language in law and policy, and this has been reinforced in recent years through the ratification (or not) of a range of international agreements: the ILO Convention 100 on Equal Remuneration for Men and Women for Equal Work 1957, the ILO Convention 111 in Respect of Discrimination in Employment/Occupation 1957, the UN Declaration on Human Rights, the European Convention on Human Rights, the UN International Covenant on Civil and Political Rights, the International Covenant on Economic, Social and Cultural Rights, and the Convention on the Elimination of All forms of Discrimination Against Women (CEDAW). In all the countries there is some form of equality or anti-discrimination legislation, and in many there are a '(Gender) Equality Act', and some form of Equal Opportunities Office or Bureau of Gender Equality between Women and Men. Various forms of gender mainstreaming are also being increasingly promoted, in word at least, in government. In the EU, the main areas of activity include:

- equal pay;
- equal treatment for women and men at work and in access to employment;
- balanced distribution of work-related and family duties;
- training and informing of social partners on equality policy and norms in the EU;
- participation in EU equality framework programmes.

The general tradition in operation here is gender equality in treatment, opportunities and process rather than gender equality of outcome. There is also in EU countries the Directive on the restriction of working time, though again its practical implementation is varied. These and other formal 'gender-neutral' national and transnational apparatuses and objectives may contradict with both national historical tradition and contemporary legal and policy practice.

National governmental and constitutional frameworks intersect with the everyday patterns and realities of home and work. These variations in men's practices at home and work, and in state law and policy in relation to home and work, interact in complex ways. In all countries there are elements of the provider-breadwinner model, though the strength of this is variable. Taxation is sometimes and increasingly an untypical policy area, with moves to individualised taxation. Marriage and paternity law have been and remain basic ways of defining different men's statuses in law, with fatherhood generally assumed for men whose wives have children.

These have been and to varying extents are ways of defining men's relation to work as providers-breadwinners. In Ireland men have been constructed very much in terms of the good provider role at home rather than strictly as workers; the married father is the legitimate father, 'complementing' the recognition of motherhood in the national constitution (Ferguson, 2001a). In Italy there is support for maternity in law, alongside which fathers have rights in the case of the mother's illness or death (Ventimiglia, 2001a). In Poland paternity is assumed for the mother's husband, although it can be established differently by the court (Oleksy, 2001a). In Estonia men are generally not yet used to staying home to take care of children or to being single parents, and after divorce, as a rule, mothers raise the children.

In the Russian Federation the norms of the Family Code are mostly gender-neutral (Chernova, 2001a). At the same time a number of norms violate gender equality. Among them is the husband's rights in relation to divorce if his wife is pregnant and within a year after the birth of child, as well as the husband's duty to support his wife (his former wife) during her pregnancy and within three years after the birth of a child. There are also serious discrepancies between the legal stipulation of equal rights and the practical opportunities for their implementation, for example, in the field of women's property rights. These and other elements contrast with and complicate the gender-neutrality of most law and policy.

There are, however, major changes, complications and contradictions. There is growing politics around fathers' rights, some degree of shared care and parenthood, and leave for fathers and as parents. In the UK a recent ICM survey found a strong sympathy among young workers to balance family and work life responsibilities, in the shape of flexible working hours and other family-friendly work policies (Travis, 2004). In Latvia a husband-breadwinner model co-exists with an egalitarian family model reflecting a diversity of social attitudes towards the institution of the family. The model of a husband-breadwinner's family, however, is implicitly reconstructed in family politics and legislation targeted at women as childbearers and major childcarers. Two further tendencies are the growth of 'family sovereignty', on the one hand, and of 'family policies', on the other, as the family is stated to be an important institution of society in the draft document of the Family Act. A key issue, as always, is what is to be defined as 'a family' (Novikova, 2001a).

In all the nations reviewed, apart from the Russian Federation, there is some kind of parental or paternity leave, in part following the EU directive, but the conditions under which this operates are very variable. In Estonia an employer is required to grant parental leave to the mother at the time requested or the father raising a child up to three years of age, and a holiday at the time requested to a woman raising a child up to three years. A father's additional childcare leave is paid by the state. A 2001 legal amendment is a significant new right for fathers and acknowledges that both men and women have family responsibilities (The Holidays Act RT I 2001, 42, 233).

Policy development around men's parental and paternity leave and ideological support for fatherhood has been especially active in the Nordic countries. For example, supporting fatherhood is a central part of governmental policy in Finland (Ministry of Social Affairs and Health, 1996, 1997; see Hearn, 2001; Hearn et al., 2001a). In Sweden the benefits of heterosexual fatherhood and its positive models are stressed. Sometimes uncritically positive state propaganda on fathers is produced (The Swedish Institute, 2001), arguing that 'children need fathers, fathers need children'. In Finland and Sweden there is an emphasis on shared parenthood after divorce in law if not always in practice. In Norway a proposal from the Male Role Committee for the father's quota, or 'the daddy's month' (now two months) has been enacted (Holter, 2001a). Soon after its introduction in 1993, two-thirds of eligible fathers used the reform, which gave the father one month of paid leave (of a total of 10 months).

To illustrate the importance and specificity of national and cultural context, the Irish case is particularly instructive. The Irish case has involved a recent movement from a predominantly traditional, largely rural society towards increased political pressure to give fathers' equal rights as mothers, and increasing sharing of breadwinning between women and men. The 'family' in Irish law is the kinship group based on marriage, and the only legitimate 'father' is the married father. Despite the fact that 26% of all births in Ireland are now outside of marriage, unmarried fathers are not acknowledged as fathers under the Irish Constitution (whereas the mother is given automatic rights by virtue of being a mother). Unmarried fathers have to apply to the courts for guardianship of their children. The Irish State has come under increased pressure in recent years to give fathers equal rights as mothers to be a parent to their child. Yet there is little sign that this has led to a more explicit gendering of men in terms of legal reform or that fatherhood is being more actively addressed as a policy issue. Fathers have had no statutory entitlement to paternity leave, though the recent EU directive is likely to change this (Ferguson, 2001a).

Equal wage legislation on such grounds as an employee's sex, nationality, colour, race, native language, social origin, social status, previous activities and religion applies in some form in all countries. Yet equal pay for work of equal value is far from being realised. Clearly gendered policies and laws apply for the armed forces and conscription, and also for some other areas of work, such as religious workers and ministers. For example, in Finland the Lutheran church exercises legal self-government. In the workplace historical restrictions of work according to arduous and hazardous to health for women, and thus indirectly men, also continue. Definitions of unemployment and retirement age also vary for women and men, though EU requirements have meant in practice a levelling down of rates.

In many countries the increasing neo-liberal and market-oriented climate has brought a more individualist approach to gender. Various trends in the 1990s, such as 'turbo capitalism', globalisation, restructuring, more intense jobs, have ensured that absent fathers and the lack of men in care-giving roles remain as key issues. The result of a more laissez-faire political attitude and economic and working life developments is often an increase in the gender segregation in parts of society. There are, however, 'counter-trends' and increased positive engagement from men are 'intact' families, post-divorce childcare, and wage work. There is evidence from Norway that the provider model is strengthened in some sections of working life, especially at top levels, although ideological changes further down in the hierarchy, including middle management, seems to develop a pro-equality direction (Holter and Olsvik, 2000).

There are limited moves towards greater equality planning in workplaces, as in Finland, Sweden and Norway, where the 40% rule (as a minimum for women and men) operates, in theory but not always in practice, in public sector bodies and committees but not employment. In Germany a law on promoting gender equality in private enterprises was announced at the beginning of the former Red–Green government in 1999 and then postponed again (Müller, 2001a). A proposal for reform of the private sector, including company boards, along the lines of the 40% quota system, has been made in Norway, and the proposal for quotas similar to the public sector has been delayed. The Swedish gender equality minister has discussed the low amount of women (18%) among boards of directors and quotas have been suggested, but as yet not enacted. There is the beginning of such a debate in Finland.

Again, to illustrate some of the diversity throughout Europe, we turn to the Czech and Swedish cases. The totalitarian era brought an interesting phenomenon in the Czech Republic concerning the relation between home and work. The conventionally expected career of men was conditioned by their acceptance of the regime by becoming members of the communist party. The so-called 'grey zone', in the Czech context coded by Jirina Siklova (1996), resisted conformity to the regime by secluding themselves in their homes. People build their home fortresses (Mozny, 1991) as places of relative safety and wellbeing. This has also meant that most men spent much more time at their homes than is the case after 1989 with its stress on market economy and career success.

There is a strong pressure for reinforcement of conventional division of public–private spheres, from 'rational choice' within the family organisation of responsibilities. The pattern from the totalitarian era mingles with the now dominating pressure to conform to traditional gender images. At the same time, the latter is contested by other trends: high rate of women's employment, plural forms of intimate and family relationships, challenges to the traditional model by the problems caused – unemployment stressing masculine identity, health risks of workaholism. Also, preparations for EU accession brought new opportunities. For example, parental leave is available for both women and men since 1 January 2001 (men estimated as only 0.5–2% of all caregivers in 2002). The relatively low proportion nevertheless shows a limited progressive trend.

In Sweden in the 1990s the welfare system has been cut down and unemployment has risen to a higher level than earlier. The industrial sector has declined and many industries have moved to other countries where wages are lower. Daily one can read in the papers of men losing their jobs because of organisational reconstructions and new ownership. There has been a problem to get unemployed men into higher education. While women go into university studies men sometimes seams to be hard to convince that this is a useful career move. Men are now given a quota for nursing education and here the amount of men on the education has increased. There have also been quotas for men in pre-school education, but here the amount of men has not increased. Men and masculinity can be seen as a commodity being asked for and sold in the Swedish labour market directed to day care and school (Nordberg, 2002). There has been some research on gay men in workplaces recently showing marginalisation in the workplaces. It seems that homosexual men in women's work are more easily accepted than in the military and church (Forsberg et al., 2003).

Qualitative studies show that men have become more family and child orientated than earlier generations of men (Åström, 1990). In the research two lines can be found: one stressing that men in both work and family reproduce patriarchal benefits (for example, Bekkengen, 2002; Robertsson, 2002; Åberg, 2001); the other that men are marginalised with regard to fatherhood and in female occupations (Klinth, 2002; Havung, 2000; Plantin, 2001). Men take part of the household responsibilities, but it is still women who do the main part: during a week women average 28 hours, men 20 hours of unpaid work (SCB, 2002). Some researchers argue that men becoming more engaged in children are not always connected to becoming more gender equal (for example, Bekkengen, 2002). However many men find it important to spend more time with children and take a greater part in household responsibilities. Statistics show how 'female' coded household tasks are distributed, but there still is a lack of knowledge of how the 'male' coded household tasks. Divorce rates are still high in Sweden, but most children live with their biological father and mother. Parental leave has been directed to men in the form of two 'daddy's months' that cannot be used by the mother, who also has two months that cannot be used by the father. In 2001 Men used 14% of parental leave (SCB, 2002). Recent research showed that parents were satisfied with the mother taking 80 per cent of the parental leave.

Both the research and statistics on men, work and family are closely connected to the Swedish gender equality project. In official statistics men and women are compared to each other as groups, sometimes divided by age, place of birth (Swedish born compared to immigrants), and civil status. The 'good life' in the Swedish gender equality project is grounded in norm of two wage owners living in a heterosexual family. Men and their connection to the breadwinner model are not questioned so much. The gender equality project has been more directed to marginalisation of women and how to get women into the labour market and in higher positions. Men are mostly looked upon as an obstacle for gender equality in gender equality policies. The government states that it is important to get men engaged in gender equality work and to highlight and remove obstacles for men doing this (SCB, 2002).

Policy recommendations

One central recommendation is to encourage men to devote more time and priority to caring, housework, childcare, and the reconciliation of home and paid work. This is clearly an important and difficult goal for all countries, including the Nordic region that is often applauded for progress in this field. Indeed even there the changes in everyday practice have often not been very substantial. If major social policy inputs and governmental commitments to increasing men's actual parental leave can result in relatively modest results, then that suggests the need to reconsider carefully whether top-down policy initiatives are of themselves often sufficient for changing men's behaviours. In particular, a crucial factor is often the power relationship between men and women in relationships: specifically, the fact that men generally possess much greater power to choose the extent of their involvement than do their female partners.

Other recommendations include: removing men's advantages in paid work and work organisations, with the persistent gender wage, non-equal opportunities practices in appointment and promotion, and domination of top level jobs; developing policies on men in transnational organisations and their equality policies; encouraging men's positive contribution to gender equality; removing discriminations against men, such as conscription of men into the armed forces, and discriminations against gay men.

While there are growing governmental and related discourses about men at home and work, including the reconciliation of the demands of home and work, there is usually a lack of explicit focus on men, especially in clear and strong policy terms. There is also a lack of linkage between men as parents and governmental documentation on men, for example, as violent partners or violent parents.

7
Social Exclusion

Keith Pringle and Jeff Hearn, with Irina Novikova and Dimitar Kambourov

Introduction

Social exclusion has become a major focus of attention in both academic research and policy development in recent years, in both national and EU contexts.[1] In the course of the work of the Network that forms the basis for much of the material examined in this book, we systematically analysed different forms of available data (academic studies, official and semi-official statistical data, legal and governmental policy documentation, printed media). At each of those stages of analysis, social exclusion was the most difficult thematic concept to pre-define with considerable differences between the way each country in the study configured that concept. Moreover, these differences varied to some extent depending upon which forms of national and international data or evidence we were examining. For instance, what one country might define as social exclusion in terms of its academic outputs might differ to some extent from the definition in the same country in terms of what was found in legal and governmental documentation. Both forms of variability are interesting on several counts, and we explore some of these issues, among others, in this chapter.

We begin by looking at the way social exclusion and men's practices seem to be addressed across Europe in three forms of data: academic studies; statistical data; and legal and governmental policy documentation.[2] This includes a discussion of some implications arising from the transnational picture in terms of what forms of social exclusion are dealt with (or not dealt with) in various countries, and why. The next section considers how and why in some cases social exclusion seems to be defined differently in various forms of data from within the same country – and the possible implications of these patterns for the way academic outputs impact (or do not impact) on policy-making processes in relation to social exclusion. A third section considers the striking overlaps which seem to especially occur in the way the theme of social exclusion intersects with the other three key themes (home and work, violences, health). This includes a discussion about the potential usage of the data from the Men Network in further developing relatively new conceptual and theoretical frameworks for understanding the operation of various forms of power relations. Finally, arising from the foregoing analysis, the chapter summarises some key recommendations to policy-makers for challenging social exclusion in relation to men's practices.

Academic studies

First, let us consider the key forms of social exclusion identified within the academic data by our commentators in their national reports:

- Estonia – homelessness, social isolation, poor education, poverty.
- Finland – unemployment, homelessness and alcohol, links between social exclusion and health, criminal subculture, racing and car subculture, youth subculture, gay men, HIV/AIDS, ethnicity, ethnic minorities.
- Germany – unemployment of youth, juvenile delinquency, loosening social connections in old age, migrants, homosexuality.
- Ireland – unemployed, prisoners, excluded fathers (after divorce and unmarried fathers).
- Latvia – homosexuality.
- Norway – Sámi, new forms of marginalisation due to globalisation which leads to exclusion from labour market, men in non-traditional occupations.
- Poland – homosexuality.
- UK – intersection of gender, sexuality and cultural identities; older men.

Despite, and perhaps because of men's structural and societal power, there are clear issues of social exclusion of some men throughout all countries, albeit with important variations from one cultural location to another. They are especially important in the Baltic, Central and East European countries with post-socialist transformations of work and welfare bringing dire consequences for many men, as emphasised in the national reports from Estonia and Latvia (Kolga, 2000; Novikova, 2000a).

Even in Nordic countries, which are relatively egalitarian in class terms and have a relatively good social security system, new forms of problems have come to light. In Finland socially excluded men have been extensively studied through men's 'misery' and auto/biographical approaches, rather than through gendered studies of men (Kortteinen, 1982; Sulkunen et al., 1985). On the whole, Norwegian men have experienced relatively little unemployment, alcoholism and migration in recent years (Holter and Olsvik, 2000). However, in the last decade, new forms of marginalisation have developed there and elsewhere, with shifts from traditional industry to more post-industrialised society. Globalising processes may create new forms of work and marginalisation; some men find it difficult to accommodate to changes in the labour market and changed family structure. Instead of going into the care sector or getting more education, some young men become marginalised from work and family life. Working class men are considered the most vulnerable.

If we take Sweden as an example, in recent years some attention has been directed to the marginalisation of immigrants and gay men in the labour market (Nordberg, 2006). The diversity discourse has been positive in terms of getting immigrants into the labour market in recent years, but research findings points out that immigrant men from outside Europe are more marginalised in the labour market and are less integrated in the workplaces than immigrant women from these countries (Integrationsverket, 2002). As regards gay men, they are still marginalised in Sweden. At the same time that it has been easier and more accepted to 'come out' as a homosexual, violence to homosexual men is high and homophobia can be found in schools and workplaces (Forsberg et al., 2003). There is also marginalisation of men living in the countryside. Moreover, problems still occur in Sweden with persuading low-educated men to go into higher education. At the other end of the social scale, changes in the labour market with accompanying unemployment have also hit men in higher positions.

There is a lack of studies showing the variety of structures and processes that may lead to the marginalisation of men as groups or individuals, and what differences and similarities there are to women. For instance, does ethnicity in some respects override gender? In Italy, Estonia and the Czech Republic (Šmídová, 2006) and most other countries social exclusion is generally under-researched. More generally, the conceptual separation of 'the social problems which some men create' from 'the social problems which some men experience' is often simplistic and there is a need to study the intersections more carefully (Pringle, 2000). There is also a lack of attention to men engaged in creating and reproducing social exclusion, such as around racism. Furthermore, it is important to recognise that not only does the definition of social exclusion vary across cultural locations – so too does the extent of recognition of social exclusion itself as a concept. As Dimitar Kambourov comments (personal communication, 2004):

> It is telling that both Balkan academia and governments would never bother to think of problems like these. For example the crucial issue of huge number of men losing their jobs because of the imposed army dismissals or closed nuclear reactors, mines or whole industries, has never been overtly gendered. There is a cultural incapacity to identify the gender aspects in the phenomena of transition, especially if they affect men rather than women in particular regions. Thus it is important to recognise both the existence of such issues of social exclusion of men and the lacking interest towards their gender aspects in some countries and regions.

Regardless of recognition, though, the social exclusion of certain men links with unemployment of certain categories of men (such as less educated, more educated rural, ethnic minority, young, older), men's isolation within and separation from families, and associated social and health problems. Kambourov continues on this important issue:

> in the Balkans . . . the problem is . . . that good education excludes many men, forced by the capitalist re-establishment to look for paying jobs having nothing to do with their diplomas.

This highlights very clearly the way processes of social exclusion need to be carefully contextualised to understand their variability across Europe.

Statistical sources

National reports have identified statistical sources on social exclusion very differently, as follows:

- Estonia: education, ethnicity, drug addicts.
- Finland: poverty, homelessness, foreign nationals and ethnic minorities, prisoners, sexualities.
- Germany: wage gap between western and eastern Germany, unemployment, consolidated poverty (men with a low level of education, younger, under 40s age groups), immigrants.
- Ireland: educational disadvantage, disabilism, racism, long-term unemployment, prisoners, ethnicity.
- Italy: poverty.
- Latvia: poverty, unemployment, suicide.
- Norway: unemployment of certain groups, exclusion of non-Western immigrants, asylum applicants.
- Poland: homeless, ethnic minorities, homosexuality.
- Russian Federation: 'masculinity crisis', ill health.
- UK: Poverty (care system, unemployment, skills, age), ethnicity (criminal justice system, education, unemployment, health), disability.

The patterns of social exclusion of men in relation to unemployment are very similar to those noted above drawn from the academic data. Unemployment is also often higher for immigrant and minority ethnic men, as, for example, in the UK, Norway, Latvia and Sweden. Long-term unemployment is a problem for a relatively small but significant group of men in 'consolidated poverty' in many countries, including those that are more affluent, such as Germany (Müller, 2001c), and those that have gone through a recent economic boom, such as Ireland (Ferguson, 2001c). Research there has shown the factors associated with long-term unemployment for men of working age (20–59), giving up active job search and withdrawal from the labour force into the 'inactive' category: poor educational qualifications; living in local authority housing especially in larger cities; in the older age groups; sharing a household with other unemployed or economically inactive; being single or having a large family.

As with academic sources, the statistical sources make it clear that issues of social exclusion are fundamental in the Baltic, Central and East European countries. The pattern for the Nordic countries also bears strong similarities with that in the academic data. Statistical sources reveal that in Norway (Holter, 2001c) the job chances of non-Western immigrants are often much worse, perhaps 5–10 times so, than for Norwegians and Western immigrants. Discrimination seems to hit non-Western men especially. Similar patterns are found in the UK (Pringle et al., 2001). Again, there is a lack of attention to men engaged in creating and reproducing social exclusion.

Law and policy

Third, we turn to the how social exclusion of certain men figures in law and governmental policy, again from the national reports.

- Estonia – poor education, non-Estonian men's lower life expectancy, homophobia, drugs, AIDS, unemployment.
- Finland – poverty, unemployment, homelessness, alcohol and drugs, social exclusion and health, gay men and sexualities, ethnic minorities/immigrants, disabled.
- Germany – homosexuality.
- Ireland – travellers, asylum seekers, economic migrants, gay men, men in socially disadvantaged areas, personal development, fathers' rights, disabled.
- Italy – poverty, pensioners, benefit claimants.
- Latvia – not specified.
- Norway – class and ethnic divisions, welfare/benefits claimants, poverty, northern and poor municipalities, rural and urban youth.
- Poland – homosexuality, national/ethnic minorities, homeless, alcoholics, drug users, offenders, prostitutes.
- UK – neighbourhood renewal, gay men, sex and relationship education, young men, poor education.

Once again, the ways in which social exclusion figures seems to be rather different in the nations under review. However, even with this variation there is still frequently a lack of gendering of law and policy in relation to men: This is despite the fact that men often appear to make up the majority or vast majority of those in the socially excluded sub-categories. This also applies to the association of some forms of social exclusion with young men (see Chapter 4, this volume). If we take the Polish case (Oleksy, 2001a), social exclusion is not unequivocally reflected in legislation, except for a general anti-discrimination clause (Constitution of the Republic of Poland, Article 32.2), and with the exception of national and ethnic minorities referred to directly (Constitution of the Republic of Poland, Article 35, Clause 3.2). No differentiation on grounds of sex is made in these laws. Thus rather few laws and policies specifically address men in relation to social exclusion. In most countries many socially excluded citizens may often be discussed in politics and thus socially defined as men, yet the relevant laws and policies are not constructed in that way.

An important issue that needs attention is: why is it that some forms of social exclusion gain far more attention in some countries than others? Of course in many cases, it may well be that greater attention simply signals that certain forms of social exclusion are affecting more people more seriously in some countries than in others. However, it is clear that this is not always the case. For instance, it seems clear that the issue of alcohol and men is still given more attention in Finland (academically, statistically and in policy) than is the case in the UK. Although consumption *levels* do not by any means tell one everything about the issue of alcohol (for instance one might want to know more about consumption *patterns*), it is still surely significant that consumption of alcohol per head is greater in the UK than in Finland; and a similar argument could be made as regards Sweden (Pringle, 2003).

By the same token, in terms of academic research, statistical data and even governmental documentation, the UK has devoted far more attention to the issue of men's violences to women over a much longer period of time than is the case in either Finland or Sweden. Yet we know from relatively recent and very large surveys in both countries (Heiskanen and Piispa, 1998; Lundgren et al., 2001) that the levels of men's violence to women known is of a similar order as the levels reported in British surveys (for instance, Mooney, 1993). Several commentators have suggested that such a contrast between the common extent of the problem and the different amounts of attention it receives in Finland (Hearn, 2001), Sweden (see Pringle, 1998a, 2002) and the UK (see Pringle, 2000), must at least partly be attributed to cultural factors. This is a warning to all researchers and policy-makers that what gets researched and most policy attention may bear little relation to the extent of a social issue. Many mediating factors intervene – not least, in terms of research and policy on men, those patriarchal relations of power that permeate national research infrastructures and governments just as much any other social institutions.

Variations between data sources

As seen above, in the case of some, though not all, countries, the forms of social exclusion addressed within one institutional sphere differed to a certain extent from the forms addressed in another sphere within the same country. Typically this difference occurred between academic research, on the one hand, and government law and policy, on the other hand. The reasons for such a partial mismatch can be various and each mismatch has to be understood within its own specific cultural context. There is certainly scope within the data from the EU Network on Men for an exploration of these particular conjunctions by comparing in any one country the profiles of social exclusion to be found in the various sources of data.

To illustrate how such an analysis can be carried out, we provide one example: the UK. We will take each of three data sources (academic, statistical, governmental), and consider violence to women and children since we can regard such violence as a serious form of social exclusion for both those latter groups:

(a) In terms of academic outputs, in the previous ten years there has been a massive amount of critical research and scholarly activity in the UK devoted to men's practices including men's violences As regards the latter, this applies especially to men's violences to women but increasingly also to men's violences to children. This work on men's violences in the UK outstrips in extent virtually every other country in Europe and from a European perspective, represents one of the most distinctive and valuable contributions made by British researchers.

(b) In terms of statistical data, compared to most other European countries, there is considerable official statistical data-gathering in relation to gendered violences in the form of men's violences to women. However, this is less marked than is the case for academic outputs; at the same time men's violences to children is given far less attention than men's violences to women.

(c) In terms of legal and governmental documentation, the picture changes even more clearly. It is striking that men figure so little in an explicit way in governmental discourses compared to their prominence in much critical, and not so critical, academic literature in the UK over the past ten years. When men are addressed explicitly in government-produced material, this is far more likely to be in early-stage consultation documents or in enquiry reports than in hard recommendations, advanced consultative documents or (most of all) Acts of Parliament. Men as violent partners have been the focus of some attention in certain government discourses but far less than one might expect from the mass of UK research on this issue. Moreover, the topic of men as violent fathers, especially sexually violent fathers, is hardly on policy agendas at all compared to the growing mass of academic material on the subject.

No doubt there are many possible interpretations that could be made of this very specific picture in the UK. One is similar to the interpretation offered above regarding the processes that determine what gets researched and/or made subject to policy attention in different countries, i.e. that patriarchal relations of power have a deep influence on both research and governmental institutions. If this did apply to the case of the UK, then the question would be: why has so much research on men's violences been possible in British academia, compared to much of the rest of Europe, whilst UK government structures have not responded to anywhere near the same extent?

However, the main point being made here in using this example is not about the UK. Instead, it is to suggest that similar analyses can be made for every country by comparing how social exclusions are configured in each one in their various data sources. Of course the situations would vary from one national setting to another: but the process of analysis might well be useful in all cases in different ways.

Interconnections

There are massive interconnections between the forms of social exclusion across countries. After all, when we looked at statistical data on men in Chapter 3, we saw that there were strong interconnections across all four focus areas. This applied to both men's power and domination in each theme, and between some men's unemployment, social exclusion and ill health. Social exclusion applied to and intersected with the other themes: home and work, violences, health. Patterns of men's violence interconnected with all other themes to some extent and also cut across social divisions. Statistical data in this field, and more generally, tend to mainly focus on dyadic analysis, for example, poverty and gender, or poverty and ethnicity. Developing triadic statistical surveys and analyses of, say, poverty, gender and ethnicity is rarer, and a more complex, though necessary, task. We return to the topic of multi-dimensional analysis later; the need for it highlights a broader conceptual, and very practical, issue about social exclusion and ways of challenging it.

First though, we provide two specific examples of the kinds of thematic overlap we have been talking about, and these apply across all the forms of data that we have reviewed (i.e. academic, statistical, legal and governmental). One is the overlap that occurs between the themes of social exclusion and violences. The other is the overlap between social exclusion and health issues. Let us take the overlap with violences first. The social exclusion of certain men may often be associated with violence. This may be especially popular in media reporting of men's violence. In some situations social exclusion may indeed follow from violence, as in imprisonment. On the other hand, social exclusion may even be inhibited by some forms of violence, as when men show they are worthy of other men's support by the use or threat of violence. Social exclusion may also be seen as one of the causes or correlates of violence, but this explanation may only apply to certain kinds of violences, such as certain kinds of riots. The connections of social exclusion with interpersonal violence to known others are complicated. Deprivation may be associated to some extent and in some localities with some forms of men's violence, such as certain forms of property crime, violence between men, and the use of physical violence to women in marriage and similar partnerships. Such forms of violence are also typically strongly age-related, with their greater performance by younger men. On the other hand, men's violence and abuse to women and children in families crosses class boundaries. Generalisations on these connections thus need to be evaluated in the local situation. There is growing recognition of men and boys as victims of violence, albeit usually from other men.

As regards the second example of overlap – with health – obviously we can say that social exclusion is generally bad for one's health – and that socially excluded men are likely to be adversely affected in terms of their health. Moreover, physical and mental health and well-being may in some cases be resources for fighting against social exclusion. What then adds another level of complexity to this picture is if we combine the two examples we have given. For not only is there an overlap between social exclusion and both violences and health. There is also an overlap between men's violences and men's health issues: an overlap which is itself bound up with issues of social exclusion. For, as seen in Chapters 2–4, the major recurring health theme is men's relatively low life expectancy, poor health, accidents, suicide, morbidity. Generally men neglect their health and for some men at least their 'masculinity' is characterised by risk taking, especially for younger men (in terms of smoking, alcohol and drug taking, unsafe sexual practices, road accidents, lack of awareness of risk), an ignorance of their bodies, and reluctance to seek medical intervention for suspected health problems. In fact, to understand and respond to the health problems of some men, we may need to connect those problems to dominant and in certain cases oppressive ways of 'being a man': for instance, the risk-taking behaviour relevant to some injuries and addictions, unwillingness to take one's health problems seriously and seek medical help, or the marked violence in the ways some men commit suicide.

Nor should it be a surprise to us that there are multiple overlaps between the major themes that have run through this study. For, such an outcome is to be expected if we consider some of the more general theoretical and conceptual analyses of power and marginalisation that have emerged in the last few years from international sociological studies. Such studies suggest that we need to adopt far more complex ways of understanding what we are talking about if we wish to effectively address and challenge oppressive power relations in society that create social marginalisations. In particular, there is now a growing recognition internationally of the constant necessity to think about the complex ways in which various forms of power relations always inter-connect with one another, often in a somewhat contradictory fashion.

These issues are attracting major attention in the field of education, with studies of class, ethnicity and gender becoming more commonplace. In the UK case it has recently been reported that the mean gender gap (of girls over boys) in formal educational attainment increases between the ages of seven and 11, and is wider still at 14, but by then for poor pupils the gender gap is more than twice the average (Fitzgerald, 2005). In some cases such forms of interconnectedness is conceptualised as 'intersectionality' (see Brah, 2001; Lykke, 2003).

For others (see West and Fenstermaker, 1995; Pringle, 2004), it is easer to understand the processes concerned if they are conceptualised as the mutual constitution of various forms of power relations. This raises the question of the possible growing polarisation amongst men in some cases, with tendencies towards both greater marginalisation of the poor and greater accumulation for the rich. These tendencies may also apply to women at both ends of the spectrum of inequality, but for them be somewhat more muted.

In terms of our discussion in this chapter, the implications of these broader conceptual debates are clear: we should not expect to understand forms of social exclusion in terms of them ever being completely independent from one another. For, the social processes generating oppressive power relations associated with gender are always likely to also be generating oppressive power relations associated with, for instance, ethnicity and/or sexuality and/or age and/or class and/or dis(ability) – and vice versa. And, of course, the complexity of these processes of mutual constitution is frequently compounded by the fact that the relationships between them are just as likely to be contradictory as they are to be parallel. So, the fact that our study of social exclusion in terms of men's practices uncovered so many – and such complex – overlaps between various forms of social exclusion is totally consistent with those broader international debates about 'mutual constitution' and 'intersectionality'. Indeed, our data on social exclusion can be seen as a rather important avenue for further exploring those broader conceptual and theoretical issues – in terms of further developing theory from practice/praxis (Pringle, 2003; Hearn et al., 2004a).

Recommendations

The European Commission sought policy recommendations from the EU-funded Network on Men geared both to governmental structures at the national and trans-European levels. Consequently, the Network produced policy option papers for the governments of each country in the Network and a trans-European policy option paper, primarily aimed at the European Union. These policy option papers drew largely on the kinds of analysis presented in earlier sections of this chapter.

Some key issues in those recommendations included the following:

- reducing the social exclusion of men, especially young marginalised men, men suffering racism, and men suffering multiple social exclusions;
- reducing the effects of the social exclusion of men upon women and children;
- ameliorating the effects of rapid socio-economic change that increase the social exclusion of men;
- specifically addressing the transnational aspects of social exclusion of men, in, for example, transnational migration, and homosexual sexual relations;
- changing men's actions in creating and reproducing social exclusions.

With regard to the last point, two issues should be clear from the foregoing analysis. First, the relationship between the dynamics of racism and some dominant forms of masculinity has been both massively under-researched and largely ignored in terms of social policy initiatives. One model for the kind of analysis that is required can be found in Michael Kimmel's (2001) work on right-wing militias in the US. Secondly, we need to recognise that gendered violence to women and sexual violence to children are massive global, including European, problems that should be regarded as profound forms of social exclusion, and treated as such in social policy initiatives.

Conclusions

As shown in this and previous chapters, social exclusion is a most difficult concept to pre-define. There are considerable differences between the way each country configures it. Moreover, these differences vary to some extent depending upon which forms of national and international data one is examining: academic; statistical; legal/governmental. This variability in definition is highly interesting on several counts. For instance, again as we have seen in this chapter, it is necessary to determine in each national case how far the variations actually reflect levels of seriousness in relation to different forms of exclusion; and, how far they reflect different processes of social construction regarding what are the forms of exclusion to be researched or subjected to policy.

The fact that even in any one country there can be variations in definition depending upon which type of data is being used (i.e. academic research, official and semi-official statistics, or legal and governmental documentation) suggests that one should not underestimate the processes of social construction at work here. If that is so, then the question becomes why certain issues are sometimes constructed as exclusionary in one country rather than another; and also why, in any one country, people working in various institutional contexts (for instance, the universities or government) may well define social exclusion in somewhat different ways. One answer considered in this chapter is the influence of patriarchal relations of power which may well shape research and governmental institutions just as much as other social institutions in most, probably all, countries.

One of the major conclusions of this chapter flows from these questions. For, in order to effectively analyse and challenge forms of social exclusion associated with men and men's practices across Europe, it is necessary for these processes of social construction – operating differentially in various national milieux and in various institutional sectors (academia, government) – to be recognised and deconstructed. Because, otherwise, many marginalised groups in many countries will go unrecognised and their needs unaddressed in social policy.

The implications of this are manifold. However, we want to stress that some relationships between men's practices and social exclusion are particularly prone to non-identification across virtually all countries reviewed in this volume, especially at the level of government and social policy. Two of these major lacunae are: first, the need to recognise men's violence towards both children and women as major forms of social exclusion in all European societies; secondly, the need to recognise that there are important linkages between, on the one hand, social processes generating racism or ethnic discrimination and, on the other hand, dominant and dominating forms of masculinity. Both these issues relate to absolutely massive social problems confronting national and transnational governments in Europe.

It is within this context, that we identified the main themes of the policy recommendations made by the Network to national and trans-European governments, recommendations which the authors of this chapter continue to endorse to:

- reduce the social exclusion of men, especially young marginalised men, men suffering racism, and men suffering multiple social exclusions;
- reduce the effects of the social exclusion of men upon women and children;
- ameliorate the effects of rapid socio-economic change that increase the social exclusion of men;
- specifically address the transnational aspects of social exclusion of men, in, for example, transnational migration, and homosexual sexual relations;
- change men's actions in creating and reproducing social exclusions.

8
Violences

Jeff Hearn and Keith Pringle

Introduction

Men's use of violences, of various kinds and forms, is a clear social problem. This chapter begins by considering how violence and men's practices are addressed across Europe in academic studies, statistical sources, and law and policy. This includes a discussion of some implications arising from the transnational picture in terms of which forms of men's violences are dealt with, or not dealt with, in research, policy and practice in the various countries, and why this is so. We then consider the overlaps that seem to occur in the way the theme of violence intersects with the other three key themes of home and work, social exclusion, health. Finally, arising from the foregoing analysis, the chapter summarises some key recommendations to policy-makers for challenging violences in relation to men's practices.

Academic studies

The recurring theme in the academic research is the widespread nature of the problem of men's violences to women, children and other men, and in particular the growing public awareness of men's violence against women (Ferguson, 2000; Hearn and Lattu, 2000; Holter and Olsvik, 2000; Müller, 2000; Pringle, 2000). The social form of masculinity seems to be recognised as playing a significant role when violence against women is the explicit topic, but rather less so clearly recognised in men's violence to men. Men are over-represented among those who use violence, especially heavy violence. Men's violence is also age-related. The life course variation in violence with a more violence-prone youth phase has sometimes been connected to a number of social explanations, including increasing exposure to commercial violence and to other related social phenomena, but these connections are still rather unclear.

Violence against women by known men is becoming recognised as a major social problem in most of the fourteen countries in this European network.

The range of abusive behaviours perpetrated on victims include direct physical violence, isolation and control of movements, and abuse through the control of money. There has been a large amount of feminist research on women's experiences of violence from men, and the policy and practical consequences of that violence, including responses by state and welfare agencies, and some national representative surveys of women's experiences of violence.

There has for some years been considerable research literature on prison and clinical populations of violent men. There is also now the recent development of research in the UK and elsewhere on the accounts and understandings of violence to women by men living in the community, men's engagement with criminal justice and other agencies, and evaluation of men's programmes intervening with such men (Pringle, 1995; Brandes and Bullinger, 1996; Hearn, 1998; Lempert and Ölemann, 1998).

The gendered study of men's violence to women is a growing focus of funded research. There is, however, still considerable variation between European countries as regards the degree and depth of that research. The most extensive research in this field has taken place in the UK and Germany, with Finland instituting a national research programme in recent years. In other European countries, the topic has been far less researched. This relative neglect also includes other Nordic states, even though research on men more generally has been relatively intense in Norway and, to some extent, Sweden. Of the Nordic countries, Denmark has probably been the least active both in terms of research on men generally and specifically in relation to men's violences to women and children (Pringle, 2005a).

A significant recent development in the Nordic and Baltic regions has been the Gender and Violence Programme funded between 2000 and 2005 by the Nordic Council of Ministers. This Programme (2000–2005) funded by the Nordic Council of Ministers (Eriksson et al., 2002) is a significant step in the direction of increasing research knowledge about this field, as well as men's violences to women in the Nordic and Baltic regions. In addition, several recent publications suggest that a more critical research approach to men and children is developing in this region (see, for instance, Eriksson, 2003, Eriksson et al., 2005).

Child abuse, including physical abuse, sexual abuse and child neglect, is now being recognised as a major problem in many countries. Both its gendered nature and an appreciation of how service responses are themselves gendered are beginning to receive more critical attention, both in terms of perpetrators and victims/survivors. In Ireland there has been a series of clerical scandals particularly involving sexual child abuse by priests, some of whom were known to the Church hierarchy but not reported or brought to justice by them and moved onto another parish. Such a focus has resulted in playing down the significance of violences by hegemonic men and reluctance to problematise active married heterosexual masculinity and bring into question gender and age relations within the Irish family (Ferguson, 1995; also see Collier, 1995).

A very important, if still relatively unexplored, area of research is the relationship between men's violence to women and men's violence to children. There are both quantitative and qualitative connections between child and woman abuse. These are both direct connections and connections through children witnessing violence to their mothers or other close women relatives or friends. For example, Christensen's study of 394 women in crisis centres for women in Denmark found that 85 per cent of the women reported that their children had been in the same room witnessing the violence to themselves (Christensen, 1990). Another group reported that the children had been close by, and only 2 per cent reported that their children had not seen the violence to them. It was reported by the women that 25 per cent of the children had been abused in connection with the abuse of their mother, and that between 53 and 68 per cent had been subject to physical violence or physical punishment that their mother considered was too harsh.[1] In the more recent Swedish national survey of women's experiences of men's violence 'Fifty-four per cent of the women who have children and have been subjected to violence by a former husband/cohabitant partner state that their children have seen or heard the *former* husband/cohabitant partner employing violence toward them (the women)' (Lundgren et al., 2001, 37).

As for gaps in research knowledge, these are numerous. For instance, there is a striking lack of gender awareness in studies that understand themselves as dealing with 'general' issues around violence, for instance, racist violence. The question of traditional masculinity and its propensity for racist violence has not yet been even articulated in high budget studies. An aspect of men's violences that is rarely addressed in a gendered way is 'civil disorder'.

One example is a quantitative and qualitative study of 13 major recorded violent 'riots' in the UK in 1991–1992, where police clashed with young people in residential areas. The study found that in these areas: 'Concentrations of young people were much higher than . . . average. Boys and young men aged 10 to 30 were actively involved. Girls and young women played very little part.' 'All areas had a history of disorder with unusual levels of violence and law-breaking by young men, who saw causing trouble as a compensation for an inability to succeed in a "mainstream" way.' '(T)he vast majority of rioters were white and British-born.' Rioters and police officers saw the confrontations as chaotic street battles between these two groups of young men (Power and Tunstall, 1997).

In many countries relatively little academic literature exists on elder abuse and violence against men. Moreover, studies on the reasons for non-violent behaviour in men are lacking completely. Similarly, there is a lack of studies on connections between violence between men and men's violence against women.

Another area of growing interest is the relationship between visual or virtual violence and physically violent actions. There is some international evidence that people may tend to become temporarily more aggressive after playing violent video games, but this is not an absolute rule. Some young men who are *already* habitually aggressive may be liable to become even more so with repeated playing of such games. While some research suggests that aggressive and violent behaviour may be learnt by observing and modelling others' behaviour, this is dependent upon many factors. For most people exposure to aggression and violence as a passive spectator is probably of relatively minor significance in determining whether or not they will exhibit aggressive or violent behaviour themselves. There is, however, no evidence that playing violent video games leads to men and boys becoming *less violent*.

Other key research questions round violences that need more attention include (Hearn et al., 2003b, 2004a):

- How men's violent gendered practices intersect with other oppressive power relations around sexuality, cultural difference/ethnicity, age, disability and class, and the implications of such analyses for challenging those practices and assisting those abused. In Chapter 7 we discussed the concepts of intersectionality and the mutual constitution of different forms of power relations as regards the topic of social exclusion. The same considerations apply in relation to the topic of men's violences (see Pringle, 2005a).
- How different forms of men's violences interconnect. There are of course many interconnections. One of the most significant is the considerable degree of overlap which research has now established exists between men who are abusive to partners and men who are abusive to children (see Eriksson and Hester, 2001; Eriksson, 2005; Hester, 2005).
- How programmes against men's violences can be developed, particularly research into the promotion of successful initiatives at school, community and societal levels.
- Men's sexual violences to adult men.
- Men's violences to lesbians and gay men.
- Men's violences to ethnic minorities, migrants, people of colour, and older people.
- Intersections of men's violences and men's sexualities.

There has been a strong concern with the intersection of sexuality and violence in, for example, Italy (Ventimiglia, 1987; Castelli, 1990) and the UK (Pringle, 1998a, 2000, 2006), and this is likely to be an area of growing concern elsewhere. There is some research on men's sexual abuse of children but this is still an underdeveloped research focus in most countries, with a particular concentration in the UK (see Chapters 1 and 3, this volume). In some countries sexual abuse cases remain largely hidden in terms of research. To some extent, and rather surprisingly, this includes countries where other issues concerning men have received much research attention, such as Norway, Finland and Sweden (Pringle, 2004). Moreover, although levels of critical research have remained relatively low on child sexual abuse in these three Nordic countries, it is once again Denmark that is the least research-rich part of that region, and this is also the case with regard to the critical study of men more generally.

Statistical sources

In many respects, the picture regarding men's violences is similar to that for academic studies. The recurring theme is again the widespread nature of the problem of men's violences to women, children and other men, with men being strongly over-represented among those who use violence, especially heavy violence including homicide, sexual violence, racist violence, robberies, grievous bodily harm and drug offences. Similar patterns are found for accidents in general, accidents in the home, vehicle accidents and drunken driving. Suicide is discussed in the 'Health' theme.

Statistical sources confirm that violence is age-related. Most robberies and violent crimes are clearly committed by men between 21 and 40 years old. In Italy and elsewhere directly physically violent crime tends to involve violence by men to those whom are known whereas with property crimes victims tend to be directed more at strangers. There are gender differences in the crimes reported, for example, in Italy men report being victims of violent crimes, women more crimes against property.

In many countries there is a large amount of statistical data on crime, as a more general organising principle than violences. Official statistical information in many countries on men's violences is available primarily through crime statistics, in some cases supplemented by victim information based on reports to the police. For example, the problem of violence in Polish public statistics is limited to cases registered by the police and adjudicated in courts. There are no data for the whole country that specify types of violence used and data on non-registered cases. The source of data for the Chief Statistical Office is the information of the Chief Police Headquarters, which also present on their webpages the most important data on perpetrators of offences connected with domestic violence, rape, sexual abuse of children, infanticide and desertion; they do not, however, specify the sex of perpetrators or characterise the victim (Oleksy, 2001c). In Finland figures giving an overview of crime and the criminal justice system (*Rikollisuus ja seuraamusjärjestelmä tilastojen valossa*, 1997) were not separated by gender. This needs to be remedied in future. However, publications on homicide (Kivivuori, 1999) give gender-disaggregated data on victims and offenders. The national survey of women's experiences of violence (Heiskanen and Piispa, 1998) might be paralleled by statistical studies of men's use of and experiences of violence (Hearn et al., 2001c).

As with academic sources, a form of violence that is repeatedly highlighted in the national reports is men's violences to women. The range of abusive behaviours perpetrated on victims includes direct physical violence, isolation and control of movements, and abuse through the control of money. Estimates range from 10 to over 40 per cent of women experiencing such violations. There is now a vast international literature, in the form of official records, national crime statistics, dedicated domestic violence surveys, victim/survivor report studies, and so on that chronicles the extent and pervasiveness of men's violence to women and children worldwide (for example, Mullender, 1997; http://www.who.int/violence_injury_prevention/vaw/infopack.htm, *Domestic Violence . . .*, 2000). There are also a number of national surveys of such violence in European countries, based on self-reporting by women which indicates a much higher prevalence than official figures which because they depend on women's reporting to police and police recording of such violence tend to record a much lower prevalence (Hagemann-White, 2002).

A Council of Europe has reported that for women between 15 and 44 years old, 'domestic violence is thought to be the major cause of death and invalidity stating that 20 to 50 per cent of women in Europe are victims of conjugal violence'. The studies cited found that 1.35 million women were victims of domestic violence in 2001 in France alone – roughly close to 4 per cent of the female population. In Russia, 14,000 women are killed each year, most by their husbands or partners (Edwards, 2003). Given the enormity of the problem, the Council of Europe assembly has called on the member states to recognise domestic violence in national legislation as a criminal offence and to take the necessary measures to prevent, investigate and punish these acts in order to protect the victims.

Some estimates from recent British research suggest that between 10 and 25 per cent of British women have been a victim of violence from a male partner (Smith, 1989; Mirrlees-Black, 1994). A survey in Islington, London, found 27 per cent of women reported physical abuse by a partner and 23 per cent reported sexual abuse (Mooney, 1993, 1994). Even such estimates should be treated with caution, as they may not take full account of rape, sexual harassment, coercive sex and emotional, psychological and other abuses. Another survey in Hackney, London, reports:

- More than one in two women had been in psychologically abusive relationships during their lives;
- One in four women had been in psychologically abusive relationships in the past year;
- One in three women had suffered physical and sexual abuse requiring medical attention in their lives; and
- One in nine women had suffered physical and sexual abuse requiring medical attention in past year (Stanko et al., 1998).

A 1998 representative national survey of 4,955 women in Finland has reported as follows:

> 22 per cent of all married and cohabiting women have been victims of physical or sexual violence or threats of violence by their present partner, 9 per cent in the course of the past year . . .
>
> violence or threats by their ex-partner had been experienced by 50 per cent of all women who had lived in a relationship which had already terminated. (Heiskanen and Piispa, 1998, 3)

A 2001 representative national survey of 6,926 women in Sweden found that 46 per cent of women had been subjected to violence (physical violence, sexual violence or threats) by a man since their fifteenth birthday. Twenty-two per cent of women between 18–24 years old had been subjected to violence in the last year (Lundgren et al., 2001).

In Denmark only one national prevalence survey of violence to women has been conducted (Rigspolitichefen, 1998) specifically in the context of violence, and thus there is little statistical study of men's use of and experiences of violence. With the exception of the 1992 survey (Christensen and Koch-Nielsen, 1992), Denmark has until recently lacked a national prevalence survey on women's experiences of violence comparable to other countries. However, such a national study on violence against women was conducted in Denmark as part of the International Violence Against Women Survey (IVAWS) sponsored by the European Institute for Crime Prevention and Control affiliated with the United Nations (Balvig and Kyvsgaard, 2006). From a total survey of 6,862 women and a response rate of 55 per cent, interviews with 3,552 women aged 18 to 70 years old revealed that 50 per cent of the respondents had been exposed to at least one of twelve types of violence and abuse (threat [to hurt physically in such a way that frightened you], physical violence or sexual violence) by any man since age 16 and 5 per cent had experienced at least one of these in the last year.

In Germany, the national study of violence to women has been completed amongst 10,000 women. This concluded that 37 per cent of all interviewees had experienced at least one form of physical attack or violence since 16; 13 per cent of them had experienced some form of sexual violence, as defined narrowly as criminally forced sexual acts; and 25 per cent of all women resident in Germany have experienced physical or sexual abuse from their current or previous partners (Müller and Schröttle, 2004, 9).

National representative surveys of women's experiences of violence have tended to produce significantly higher reports than from general crime victim surveys. In turn, the latter tend to produce higher figures than police and criminal justice statistics. Thus some non-governmental sample surveys of the general population have produced higher figures than police and criminal justice statistics for levels of men's violences to women. For instance, a local study in North London (Mooney, 1993) suggested that a third of women will experience a form of 'domestic violence' in their lifetime and that just over 20% are raped by a husband or partner. Another local survey in Glasgow estimated that 40% of women have experienced rape or sexual assault (Glasgow Women's Support Project/Glasgow Evening Times, 1990).

However, few cases are reported and fewer still prosecuted. For England and Wales the British Crime Survey 2001 (p. 8) records that there are 4.5 times more crimes committed than those reported to police and estimates 499,000 cases of domestic violence (p. 28). There is no doubt of the disastrous effects of domestic violence and the risk to life. In the UK between a quarter and a third of victims of homicide are killed by a partner or former partner (*Justice for All*, 2002; see Edwards, 1996). In Portugal, roughly 60 women were killed at the hands of their partners last year, according to government statistics. Whilst in Spain approximately 40 female partners are said to be killed at the hands of male partners per year. These figures on domestic murder and the low level of reporting of domestic violence are evidence that across all member states we are failing women and children.

Child abuse, including physical abuse, sexual abuse and child neglect, is now being recognised as a prominent social problem in many countries. Both the gendered nature of these problems and an appreciation of how service responses are themselves gendered are beginning to receive more critical attention, both in terms of perpetrators and victims/survivors. A markedly 'male' offence is the sexual abuse of children, with a finding that around 90% of child sexual abusers are men being found in most surveys around the world (Pringle, 1998a, 2005a).

One Polish survey found that boys were physically or emotionally abused by their fathers and sexually abused by their relatives, teachers, friends of the family, neighbours and friends more often than girls (Kmiecik-Baran, 1999). However, girls contacting a Polish 'domestic violence' hotline reported being victims of violence twice as frequently as boys who contacted it (Oleksy, 2001c). In Ireland official statistics do not gather data on the gender of perpetrators of child abuse, a gap that is being filled to some extent by research (Ferguson, 2001c). The single Danish prevalence survey on child sexual abuse conducted with respondents at age 15 raises methodological questions (Helweg-Larsen and Larsen, 2002), as there is limited contextualisation of the data and there seems to be no additional work being done on the implications of what these data reveal.

Retrospective prevalence surveys within general adult populations always reveal far higher levels of child sexual abuse than official crime statistics. The most quoted retrospective British prevalence study amongst young people used successively narrower definitions of sexually abusive experiences in childhood to gauge the differences in reported prevalence levels. Using the broadest definition produced figures of 1:2 for females and 1:4 for males (Kelly et al., 1991; see Pringle, 1995).

Following the growing recognition of child abuse of boys, there is increasing interest in surveying men's experiences of violence, predominantly, but not only from other men. This is the subject of a recent survey of 266 men in Germany by way of 'largely standardized interviews that included some qualitative components', supplemented by some 32 guided interviews and 190 written questionnaires (Jungnitz et al., 2004). This found that up to two-thirds of physical violence reported in adult life took place in the public sphere or during leisure time, and that one in ten of the men studied had stated that he had had 'within the last five years at least once had the experience of someone seriously threatening to physically attack or injure him' (p. 7).

As with the academic sources, though perhaps to a slightly lesser extent, there is a considerable gap between European countries regarding the levels of statistical attention paid to both men's violences to women and to children – and the patterns are, broadly-speaking, similar to those we noted above in relation to academic sources (see Chapters 2 and 3, this volume).

Law and policy

Given what we have seen in terms of academic and statistical data, it is perhaps not surprising that the context set for law and social policy is the recurring theme of the widespread nature of the problem of men's violences to women, children and other men. While formal gender-neutrality operates in law in most respects, exceptions to this include in some cases the specification of sexual crimes, of which rape is a clear, though complex, example, with fine differences between countries. In Estonia the Criminal Code deals only with the rape of women, and the Code of Criminal Procedure does not distinguish between the sexes. In the latter Code, rape is included under private charges proceedings. This means unnecessary additional hindrances and inconveniences to the victim in criminal proceedings (Kolga, 2001a). In Poland provisions of the penal code do not refer to the rape victim's or the perpetrator's sex, even though men are almost exclusively perpetrators in these cases. In Latvia while there are legal acts and documents dealing with rape, only one woman has come to claim rape against her husband and nobody has come in connection of rape as a sexual and human rights violation. Recent UK legislation has made it an offence for a man to rape another man; rape became non-consensual sexual intercourse by a man either vaginally or anally. In Germany there have been reforms on the illegality of rape in marriage. In the Russian Federation gender asymmetry in criminal law manifests itself in defining the range of criminal offences, and in describing the formal elements of definition of a crime, i.e. in the establishment of criminal responsibility. There are also other national gendered differences in the definition and operation of law, for example, on the doctrine of self-defence and the doctrine of consent. Gender-neutrality and gender specificity intersect in complex ways.

The issue of violence against women is a relatively new topic for policy development for many countries. In many countries this is still constructed as 'family violence' rather than 'violence against women'. In Latvia (Novikova, 2001a) such violence is discussed in policy documents mainly as a problem of impoverished, less educated families with children. The family level remains a politically convenient target of governmental strategies and initiatives. In 1999, with the initiative of the Baltic-Nordic working group for gender equality co-operation the situation regarding 'family violence' and violence against women was mapped in Estonia (Kolga, 2001a). On the basis of the results of the survey, a national strategy to combat violence against women will be prepared. It was noted that due to the lack of information the general public, as well as health care specialists and police officers, do not fully realise the seriousness of the problem. In Italy public debate has led to new precautionary laws being developed, with a focus on orders of protection against family abuses; these are, however, not gendered (Ventimiglia, 2001a).

In the Irish case, the central organising ideology which dictates how men are governed in Ireland is the provider model and the hard-working 'good family man', so when evidence emerges that not all men are in fact 'good', a deficit in governance and services arises. Minimal attempts have been made to develop intervention programmes with men who are violent to their partners, while only a fraction of men who are sex offenders are actively worked with towards rehabilitation/stopping their offending. Masculinity politics with respect to violence are becoming more complex, with increasing pressure to recognise male victims of women's domestic violence.

In the UK 'domestic violence' has both received more attention and been more defined as a gendered crime in recent government guidance and legislation than any other form of men's violences. In Finland a national programme has been developed against violence, along with other initiatives against prostitution and trafficking (http://www.stakes.fi). There is also some change in terminology in Finland, UK and elsewhere from 'domestic violence' or 'family violence' to 'violence against women and children'.

Policy development in relation to men cannot be understood outside that for women. For the latter, there have been two linked trajectories in recent developments and debates: the provision of woman-centred services, and material support of women victims/survivors, including:

- provision of (more) women-centred services (such as women's refuges, rape crisis centres, incest survivors groups) in the state, community and voluntary sectors, and support of women victims/survivors;
- criminal justice system reforms, including enforcement of the law and protection of women victims/survivors;
- provision of safer housing and safer housing alternatives;
- income support for women and children;
- inter-agency policy development and co-ordination;

- education, training and publicity against the problem;
- recognition of differences in the experience of violence, and the need for particular services for black and ethnic minority women, and lesbians and women with disabilities which take account of those different needs;
- attempt to create safer public spaces for all women.

In most Western European countries there is some system of refuges for battered women but these are generally very much lacking in funding. In contrast, in Estonia there is no network of shelters for women or indeed consultation services to violent men. Overall in most countries there is little intervention work with men who are violent to women. In Norway and Denmark alternatives to violence projects for men are developed on a voluntary basis (Råkil, 2002; Helweg-Larsen and Kruse, 2004); in the UK some men's programmes are used in some localities on a statutory basis. In many countries concern with men's aggressive, abusive or violent behaviour is still regarded in traditional stereotypes and explained by impoverishment, anxiety, value crisis, alcohol and addiction.

Even with the rather uneven state of policy and practice responses to men's violence against women, it is important to consider that other forms of men's gendered violences have not received the same attention. For example, little recognition is afforded to the predominantly gendered nature of child sexual abuse in governmental documents and legislation despite the fact that this gendered profile of perpetrators is virtually commonplace as knowledge in research, practice and, to some extent, public domains. In the UK there have been many official enquiries into cases of child sexual abuse. Despite the fact that the UK possesses the most extensive research and statistical base in the whole of Europe for this topic, hardly any of them acknowledge one of the few relatively clear facts from research about this crime, namely that it is overwhelmingly committed by men or boys (Pringle, 1998a; Pringle, 2001). It is to be hoped that the studies by mainly feminist researchers, highlighting the very real linkages between 'domestic violence' and child abuse, may focus attention on child sexual abuse as a gendered crime (Eriksson and Hester, 2001; Eriksson et al., 2005). There has been also some attention to the implications of child sexual abuse vis-à-vis men employed in care work, in the UK, Denmark (Nielsen, 2003) and elsewhere.

Furthermore, in many countries there is often a lack of consistency regarding violence against women and governmental policy pressing for greater involvement of men in families and greater fathers' rights. In Germany there has also been policy attention to other diverse forms of men's violence, including in the army, sexual harassment, and violence in education. In addition, there are a wide range of other policy initiatives aimed more directly at men, with both the criminal justice system and the wider field of agency and social policy response. These include interventions by probation services social services, services for children and social work, housing and related issues, health and mental health agencies, education, schools and educational institutions, and inter-agency work.

Overall, there is generally a lack of attention in policy to the gendered quality of violences inherent in, for instance, pornography, prostitution, child sexual abuse, trafficking in people. There is also a need for more coherent government policies regarding men as child carers recognising *at the same time* both men's real potential as carers and the equally real problems of gendered violences by men against women and children (Pringle, 1998c; Hearn, 2001).

Men's programmes

Innovative policy for men has to supplement broad policy change, including consistent prosecution practice. There is increasing interest in policies seeking to stop men's violence through group-based programmes for men who have been violent to women. During the 1980s there has been a growth of group-based men's programmes specifically designed for men who have been violent to women. In North America, initial forms included shelter adjunct, mental health, and self-help programmes (Gondolf, 1985). There have also been related initiatives from anti-sexist men and feminist women, and within the criminal justice system itself, in particular Probation Services. There are major variations in philosophy, theoretical orientations and practical methods of men's programmes, including psychoanalytic, cognitive-behavioural, systemic, and profeminist (Dankwort, 1992–93). In profeminist models, the task is to educate men, sometimes didactically, on the inaccuracy and oppressiveness of their beliefs and actions – what has been called 'pro-feminist resocialisation' (Gondolf, 1993). There have been growing critiques of approaches that are narrowly psychological or focused on anger management (Gondolf and Russell, 1986), and instead a movement towards those based on 'power and control'. There are increasing arguments for court-mandated programmes, in which the man completes programme attendance as part of sentencing following conviction.

Typical methods involve the men describing and analysing their specific violence, abuse and controlling behaviour, and moving away from that power and control and towards more equal relationships. Techniques include cost–benefit analysis (of the gains and consequences of violent and abusive behaviour), safety plans (strategies for avoiding violence and abuse), and control logs (diary records of attempts to control partners). Some programmes are fixed length, say 25 weeks; others more open-ended. A major example of the feminist/profeminist approach is the Duluth 'Power and Control' model (Pence and Paymar, 1990, 1993; Shephard and Pence, 1999). In this, many aspects of men's power and control over women – physical, sexual, economic, emotional and so on – are confronted and, if possible, changed. The programme's aim is to educate, challenge and change the full range of men's behaviours, not only physical violence, and promote positive equal relationships.

The Council of Europe has recommended that '(m)ember states organise intervention programmes designed to encourage perpetrators of violence to adopt a violence-free pattern of behaviour by helping them to become aware of their acts and recognise their responsibility' (*Protection of Women Against Violence*, 2002, 12, 36). These are not intended as an alternative to sentencing, and it should be ensured that such intervention programmes be developed in co-operation and co-ordination with programmes dealing with the protection of women. In commenting on the COE recommendations, it is important to consider the long established international interest in and research on the evaluation of the effectiveness of men's programmes (Pirog-Good and Stets-Kealey, 1985; Edelson, 1990; Edelson and Syers, 1990). Evaluations of different curricula and approaches amongst programmes have shown uneven results. The longest evaluative research (Gondolf, 1998) found mixed results: nearly half (47 per cent) of the men (both completers and non-completers) used violence during the first 30 months; only 21 per cent of men were reported by their partner to have been neither verbally or physically abusive in that time. Tolman and Bennett (1990) found that 60 per cent of men who complete programmes were not physically assaultive of women after six months. However, with wide variations in methods and approaches, international evidence on their effectiveness is such that programmes cannot be evaluated or recommended in general.

A National Institute of Justice set of studies from the US published in 2003 have summarised the international evaluation research, as well as completing new evaluations of their own. The lead author, Shelly Jackson, writes:

> Early evaluations . . . consistently found small [men's] program effects; when more methodologically rigorous evaluations were undertaken, the results were inconsistent and disappointing. Most of the later studies found that treatment effects were limited to a small reduction in reoffending, although evidence indicates that for most participants (perhaps those already motivated to change), BIPs [batterer intervention programmes] may end the most violent and threatening behaviors. (Jackson, 2003, 3)

In their own research they found no significant differences between men who battered in the men's programme and the control group in one case. In the other case more complex findings indicated that men completing the 8-week programme showed no differences from the control, but men completing the 26-week programme had significantly fewer official complaints lodged against them than the control group, yet no significant change in attitudes towards domestic violence (Jackson et al., 2003).

Assessments of effectiveness *in general* thus need to be treated with great caution. Some evaluations have been methodologically limited, being made on men's self-assessments of change, rather than assessments by the woman, women or children concerned. Men's under-reporting of their own violence is well established in international research (for example, Heckert and Gondolf, 2003).[2] Some men enter programmes to rescue failing or failed relationships with a woman; stopping or reducing their violence, perhaps temporarily, seems to be a means to that end. For a substantial proportion, there appears to be a reduction or stopping of *physical* violence whilst in the group. For some men, programmes can be dangerous by increasing their knowledge of the particular violences and abuses experienced as most harmful or hurtful to particular women. Programmes need to screen out men with no interest in or capability of change in the short term at least, as well as recognising the differences between men more generally, for example, by ethnicity and relations to children in developing interventions.

Another key issue is cost effectiveness. Men's programmes may have relatively high per capita costs for the relatively low numbers of men who complete them. The number of men involved in men's programmes is much smaller than the number of men in contact with criminal justice agencies, and smaller still than the number of men in contact with other agencies, such as health and welfare. Beyond these larger numbers there is a greater number not in contact with any specific agency in relation to their violence. Thus it is important to evaluate the possible different uses of funds in relation to these various populations of men.

Priority measures that need to be addressed in developing programmes thus include:

- Ensuring, as the highest priority, the safety of women and children victims, through contact between the programme staff and the women and staff working with them; such professional contact with the women is especially important where the man is living with or in contact with the women;
- Not avoiding or diluting the legal consequences of criminal behaviour, so needing to link programmes to court-mandating, as groups do not replace legal sanctions;
- Working in co-operation and co-ordination with programmes dealing with the protection of women; this includes the central involvement of both women's programmes and women victims' assessments in evaluations of men's programmes;
- Need for clear principles in programmes, including the recognition in programmes that men's violence to women is largely about power and control, in contexts of men's dominance;
- Recognition that men are responsible for their violence within a gender power analysis;
- Examination of the effectiveness of programmes, and whether the degree of effectiveness justifies the cost; there is need to recognise problems in conducting comprehensive, long-term evaluations of new programmes;
- Resourcing of programmes must not divert funding from women's projects and services;

- Increase clarity on how to improve programmes, including co-leadership by women and men, full training of leaders, use of gender power analysis and retention of men in programmes;
- Give great attention to and caution in the risk assessment and selection process, as such group programmes are unlikely to be effective for the most dangerous men;
- Recognition of dangers in overstating effectiveness claims, especially in offering false hopes to partners, ex-partners and other interested and affected parties who may make plans on that basis (see Respect, 2000; Mullender and Burton, 2001; Hagemann-White and Kavemann, 2004, 24–6).

Inter-agency work

A crucial aspect of agency intervention is developing inter-agency, multi-agency and partnership work with men. Inter-agency work with women who have experienced violence from known men may lead to the recognition of the problem of what is appropriate work with men. Though inter-agency work with men is currently at an early stage of development, it is through such processes networks and nexuses that interventions can be enhanced. It involves identifying who has the key responsibility, both agencies and workers, for this work. In this inter-agency work, it is necessary to make men, men's power and men's violence explicit. Inter-agency work includes the development of local and regional domestic violence forums that include representatives from all relevant agencies and users.[3] Commitment and resources for such inter-agency initiatives is necessary from the highest levels (Hague, 2001; Mullender and Burton, 2001). A major recent German national research project on developing good collaborative practice for working together to combat 'domestic violence' has been completed (Hagemann-White and Kavemann, 2004). This both evaluated existing agency and inter-agency intervention projects and proposed its own guidelines for future practice.

Inter-agency work affects all relevant agencies, including legal and criminal justice agencies. For example, in police work, greater attention is needed to the interconnections between men's violence to women and child protection work, and greater liaison with other agencies. Similarly, interconnections between men's violence to known women and child protection work need to be considered in prosecution work – in understanding the full damage of men's violence, and prosecuting cases with maximum urgency. Depending on the particular national system, liaison of prosecution services with other agencies is often extensive, but primarily for compilation of evidence to inform prosecution or not. Such liaison is not, however, designed to assist victims/survivors or alleviate the situation. Liaison between agencies of criminal justice and civil law could be extended with this aim in mind, as prosecutors often have considerable knowledge of the problem.

Prosecution work would be eased by being able to obtain statements and other evidential information more speedily. This often relies on police who have their own demands and priorities. It may be possible in some systems to have specific police concerned with prosecution-related follow-up work.[4]

In addition, there are a range of more general agency policy developments, including promotion of campaigns against men's violence to women and children. Campaigns can be prompted by state, third sector and private sector organisations. They may be the outgrowth of men's anti-sexist activity, such as various Men Against Pornography campaigns; can accompany men's programmes, such as the 'Männer Gegen Männer Gewalt' public poster campaign in Hamburg in the 1980s; can be sponsored by local government, such as Edinburgh City Council's 'Zero Tolerance' campaign against men's violence using posters, stickers, T-shirts, exhibition and other materials, that circulated widely in the UK and elsewhere (Gillan and Samson, 2000). The tradition of special days or weeks or years against men's violence to women has been established in various towns, cities and countries.

Education

Another area for urgent policy development is education. The education of men and boys needs to be part of general policy development in state agencies, third sector agencies and indeed private sector organisations. This applies to both the education of men who work in those agencies and organisations, and their education of men in the community. Such developments have important implications for the devising of policies and practices that deal with men, and in particular education about and against violence (Hearn, 1999b; Hearn and Wessels, 2006; Ramberg, 2001a, 2001b).

Educating and changing men against violence to women, children and other men is a necessary element in reducing that violence which needs to be developed alongside political, policy and practical initiatives for women. Focusing on education is not to suggest that education alone can solve the problem; rather education is one key aspect of reducing men's violence. Education is a way of developing policy perspectives that cut across several significant divisions: family/state; prevention/intervention; men who are violent/men who are not violent; criminal justice system/non-criminal justice system; schooling/non-schooling; boys/men; perpetrators/professionals.

Education is about the production of changing and changed consciousness amongst boys and men in relation to violence, whereby non-violence and anti-violence are valued and valuable, rather than demeaned and non-valued. It is about developing understandings of what violence is; understandings of why violence occurs; understandings of the severely gendered nature of violence; and ways of working against violence. Schools and other educational institutions are very obvious arenas in which education of boys and thus men against violence to girls and women may be developed (Mullender, 2001). There are several ways of framing such interventions.

First, there are the attempts to produce non-violent educational environments, including actions against abuse of educational authority. Highlighting the importance of non-violence and anti-violence of schools and other educational institutions is both material and symbolic. It requires expertise and resources, not just increasing the workload and responsibilities of teachers, regardless of expertise.

Second, there have been increasing concerns with the operation of gender and sexual power relations in schools, and how these may include violence, abuse and harassment. This perspective often emphasises how the social production and reproduction of boys and young men in and around schools is a major part of the production and reproduction of adult men and masculinities, including men's violence to women. In order to reduce violence it is necessary to challenge and change the ways that boys are brought up and educated in schools and elsewhere. There is a huge range of possible interventions, exercises and practices that may be relevant to reducing boys' violence in the present and men's violence in the future: the school as a gendered institution, boys' sexualities, media education, language, the body, sport, learning to provide care for others, life stories, fathers and sons.[5] In each case practical exercises can be used for raising awareness and challenging sexism, usually drawing on boys' own experiences. Though these may not be directly focused on violence, they are designed to produce general change in boys', and thus men's, behaviours, so contributing to reducing violence.

Third, there is the problem of bullying and harassment in schools. This has attracted a great deal of attention in recent years. Bullying between boys can be understood as particular versions of boyhood that are enacted by some boys on other boys, and in turn different forms of boyhood encourage or discourage violence in adulthood. Norwegian research has found men's experience of being bullied, as boys, correlated with men's use of violence to women, as adults (Holter, 1989; see Råkil, 2002); this avenue deserves more attention in research and policy development. Anti-bullying polices and practices can be a central part of an educational environment in which violence, sexism and racism are not tolerated. They can re-examine the school's educational ethos, management style, relationship of bullying and learning.

Fourth, there are some specific attempts to introduce education on men's violence against women and children into the curriculum. This may be done as part of general education on peace and conflict resolution, personal and social development classes, or specific teaching on violence, gender equality or equal opportunities. Major areas covered include: defining abuse; understanding the myths and facts of domestic violence; comprehending social and psychological contributors to abuse; developing skills that provide alternatives to abuse, such as stress management, conflict resolution, assertion. These areas can be covered through a variety of brainstorming, discussion, role-play, and experiential activities. Educators may tailor the materials and activities to the particular needs of the audience (see, for example, *Education & Action*

Kit . . . , n.d.). Curricular innovation can range from the attempt to introduce this kind of material on men's violence across an entire state to individual talks and discussion from representatives of women's refuge organisations and criminal justice agencies. Such possibilities in schools are equally relevant for the (re)training of teachers and other personnel. Training for men teachers on gender awareness should include attention to issues of sexuality, violence and their interrelations.

Special attention needs to be given in curricular and related development in schools to the interconnections of sexuality and violence, including the persistence of homophobia, in developing sex education and elsewhere. There is increasing understanding that much sexual abuse of children and young people is enacted by young male adults. The educational arena is one where those who have abused or are abusing and have been or are being abused may become apparent. Thus, teachers and other educational personnel need their own education, training and support. There is also the question of responses to violence to staff. This perspective can be placed within the framework of increasing personal safety at work and the training necessary to achieve that (Cardy, 1992; see Hearn and Parkin, 2001, for a critical discussion).

Interconnections between violences and other spheres of men's practices

The work of the EU Network on Men has highlighted that there were numerous interconnections between findings in the four main fields of study: home and work, social exclusion, violences and health. In this section, we focus on a few of the most significant interconnections.

Home and work – violences

Much violence occurs in the home, in the form of men's violence to known women and men's child abuse, including child sexual abuse (and the co-occurrence of men's violences to women and children). The home is a major site of men's violence. There is increasing recognition of the scale of violence, including bullying and harassment, at work. Violence at home is clearly antagonistic to equality and care at home, and is detrimental to performance at work. Home and work both provide potential social support and networks, to both reproduce and counter men's violence.

Social exclusion – violences

The social exclusion of certain men may often be associated with violence. This may be especially popular in media reporting of men's violence. In some situations social exclusion may indeed follow from violence, as in imprisonment. On the other hand, social exclusion may even be inhibited by some forms of violence, as when men show they are worthy of other men's support by the use or threat of violence. Social exclusion may also be seen as one of the causes or correlates of violence, but this explanation may only apply to certain kinds of violences, such as certain kinds of riots. The connections of social exclusion with interpersonal violence to known others are complicated. Deprivation may be associated to some extent and in some localities with some forms of men's violence, such as certain forms of property crime, violence between men, and the use of physical violence to women in marriage and similar partnerships. Such forms of violence are also typically strongly age-related, with their greater performance by younger men. On the other hand, men's violence and abuse to women and children in families crosses class boundaries. Generalisations on these connections thus need to be evaluated in the local situation. There is growing recognition of men and boys as victims of violence, albeit usually from other men.

Two further significant but frequently overlooked points emerging from the work of the Research Network are: first, that men's violences to women, children and to some extent other men represent a massive forms of social exclusion themselves; and, second, men's violences, together with dominant and dominating ways of being a man, are intimately connected with the dynamics of racism – another profound form of social exclusion.

Health – violences

Men's violences and health connect in many ways. Violence is a graphic form of non-caring for others. Some forms of ill health, such as those induced by risk-taking, may also involve non-caring for the self. Risk-taking is especially significant for younger men, in, for example, smoking, alcohol and drug taking, unsafe sexual practices and road accidents. In this context it is interesting that some research finds that men are over-optimistic regarding their own health. Recent studies on men have often been concerned to show how men too are affected by health risks, violence and so on, without connecting the theses more systematically to societal context.

Recommendations and conclusions

The European Commission requested the Research Network to suggest policy recommendations. In this section, we summarise some of those key recommendations in relation to men's violences:

- stopping men's violence to women, children and other men, and assisting victims and survivors;
- enforcing the criminal law on clear physical violence that has historically often not been enforced in relation to men's violence to known women and children;
- making non-violence and anti-violence central public policy of all relevant institutions – including a focus on schools within extensive public education campaigns;

- assisting men who have been violent to stop their violence, such as men's programmes, should be subject to accountability, high professional standards, close evaluation, and not be funded from women's services; and recognising the part played by men in forms of other violence, including racist violence.

We also want to make a general point about social policy and men's violences to women and children (also see Chapter 4). If we look at welfare systems in Western Europe in terms of the extent to which they demonstrate awareness of these profound and extensive problems and a willingness to respond to them, then the transnational patterns that emerge in Europe are almost a reversal of the standard Esping-Andersen-type classifications (Esping-Andersen, 1990, 1996) for welfare system adequacy. The criteria that can be used for each country in this respect include:

- the levels of research carried out on men's violences;
- the extent to which the prevalence of men's violences has been researched and/or acknowledged publicly;
- the extent to which legal frameworks are focused on men's violences;
- the extent to which there are welfare initiatives aimed at dealing with the outcomes of men's violences;
- the extent to which welfare professionals are trained to address men's violences.

If such criteria are used, then, from this specific perspective, the UK and Germany emerge, perhaps rather surprisingly, as among the most advanced welfare systems in Europe, whilst some of the Nordic countries perform rather poorly or would only rate in the middle rank. In other words, on this important dimension of men's violences to women and to children, one of the relatively 'Neo-liberal' welfare systems in Europe performs much better than many of the 'Scandinavian' welfare systems – which is a reversal of the expectations that emerge from Esping-Andersen's analysis. Of course, on other measures of welfare performance, the Esping-Andersen pattern is confirmed to a greater or lesser extent with variations: not only in Esping-Andersen's own terms of financial benefits but also as regards other welfare criteria such as levels of day care and approaches to young people breaking the law (Pringle, 1998a).

However, it has been suggested that a similar reversal of Esping-Andersen assessments would occur if one assesses the differential responses of European welfare systems to issues of racism and ethnic discrimination in the lives of people from within ethnic minority groups (Pringle, 2005a). It has also been suggested that racism and ethnic discrimination can be defined as assaults on what we may call 'personal and bodily integrity' – and that violence to women and children and men may also be so designated. 'Personal and bodily integrity' can be defined as among the core requirements of citizens' welfare[6] – as also of course is the need for an adequate financial base (Pringle, 2005a). In many ways, mainstream Esping-Andersen style transnational analyses of welfare address the latter core welfare requirements – and as such are valuable. However, they largely ignore the former welfare needs of 'personal and bodily integrity' which are equally core.

Transnational welfare comparisons of men's violences to women and children, and indeed to other men, using this dimension of core welfare requirements produce a dramatic reversal of the analysis produced by a focus on financially-based core welfare requirements. This is significant for several reasons at various levels of policy analysis. First, it suggests that much needs to be done in the Nordic states to make their welfare responses in the field of 'personal and bodily integrity' as relatively comprehensive as they are in some other welfare fields. Secondly, it suggests that using Nordic welfare systems as models in social policy (which is often done in welfare fields) may be more hazardous than has generally been assumed: one has to choose *which* countries as models for *which* aspects of welfare. Finally, it suggests that social policy-makers should be wary of global welfare typologies more generally.

9
Health

Jeff Hearn and Voldemar Kolga

Introduction

Men's health has become a significant area of public debate in recent years. Indeed Rieder and Meryn (2001) go as far as suggesting, 'there seems to be a resurgence of men's health issues at the forefront, together with or in place of women's health policy and promotion'. The last ten years or so have seen a significant international expansion of gendered research and commentary on men's health (for example, Bruckenwell et al., 1995; Sabo and Gordon, 1995; Connell et al., 1998; Schmeiser-Rieder et al., 1999; Watson, 2000; Luck et al., 2000; WHO, 2000; Lee and Owens, 2002; White and Cash, 2003; Riska, 2004; Sabo, 2005), as well as the launching of two specialist journals: *International Journal of Men's Health*; and *The Journal of Men's Health and Gender*. Yet, having said that, until recently in many countries there has been relatively little focused academic work on men's health from a gendered perspective.

Research and policy in Europe and beyond on men's health has highlighted two contradictory elements. The life expectancy of men and thus men's ageing has increased markedly since the beginning of the 20th century, and the differences in mortality between men and women are generally decreasing. At the same time, the major recurring theme in research texts on men's health in Europe is men's relatively low life expectancy, poor health, accidents, suicide, morbidity. Men suffer and die more and at a younger age from cardiovascular diseases, cancer, respiratory diseases, accidents and violence than women. As Meryn and Jadad (2001, 1013) note, 'Despite having had most of the social determinants of **health** in their favour, men have higher mortality rates for all 15 leading causes of death[1] and a life expectancy about seven years shorter than women's' (bold in original).

The problem is especially acute in East Europe, and particularly so in the Russian Federation, where the gap in life expectancy between women and men is close to 10 years. Rieder and Meryn (2001) comment that: 'In 2000, the WHO report suggested a 77% increased risk of premature death for Russian men between 1987 and 1994. With life expectancy, the gap between the sexes generally decreases as average life expectancy increases. Russia has one of the lowest life expectancies and, therefore, the widest gaps between sexes in healthy life expectancy in the world (66·4 *vs* 56·1 years for men compared with women).'[2] Men are a high-risk group for premature death in this population.

Socio-economic factors, qualifications, social status, lifestyle, diet, smoking, drinking, hereditary factors, can all be important for morbidity and mortality. Gender differences in health also arise from how certain work done by men is in hazardous occupations. Generally men neglect their health, in terms of lifestyles and health care practices; many men are reluctant to seek medical intervention for suspected health problems.

Some studies see traditional masculinity as hazardous to health and, one could add, women's and children's health too. For some men at least their 'masculinity' is characterised by risk taking, especially for younger men – in terms of smoking, alcohol and drug taking, unsafe sexual practices, road accidents, lack of awareness of risk, and an ignorance of their bodies.[3] Men constitute the majority of drug abusers and far greater consumers of alcohol than women, though the gap may be decreasing among young people in several countries.[4]

In this chapter we begin by placing men's health within the broad context of work, home, social exclusion and violence, before focusing on, first, the impact of work and, then, the impact of home and family on men's health in more detail. This is followed by a review of law, policy and public debates from the work of the European Network, before concluding with some policy recommendations.

Putting men's health in context

There is a very large body of European research on 'gender and health'. Most of this has either focused on women or then, in an almost and strangely gender-neutral way, looked at 'gender differences' in health. For example, the contributions in Annandale and Hunt's edited collection, *Gender Inequalities in Health* (2001), do not generally raise the issue of men's health in an explicit way (*pace* Waldron, 2001).[5] In contrast, men's health, individually, nationally, collectively, is not to be seen as an isolated phenomenon, and cannot be understood outside of its social context.

Home and work can both be seen as sites affecting men's health positively or negatively. Men, especially men in positions of power or with access to power, are also able to affect the health of women, children and other men in their realm of power. This can apply to men as managers in, say, restructuring of workplaces, and to men as powerful actors in communities and families, as fathers, brothers, husbands, and so on. Men's health and indeed life expectancy is also often affected by relative material well-being arising from work, and by dangers and risks in specific occupations.

Social exclusion is generally bad for health. Socially excluded men are likely to be adversely affected in terms of their health. Physical and mental health and well-being may in some cases be resources for fighting against social exclusion. Men's violences and health also connect in many ways. Violence is a graphic form of non-caring for others. Some, but only some, forms of ill health, such as those induced by risk-taking, may also involve non-caring for the self.[6] Risk-taking is especially significant for younger men, in, for example, smoking, alcohol and drug taking, unsafe sexual practices and road accidents. In this context it is interesting that some research finds that men are over-optimistic regarding their own health. Recent studies on men have often been concerned to show how men too are affected by health risks, violence and so on, without connecting the theses more systematically to societal context.

Socio-economic factors, qualifications, social status, life style, diet, smoking, drinking, drug abuse, hereditary factors, as well as occupational hazards, seem to be important for variations in men's morbidity and mortality. In this section research on men's health problems associated with work and family is briefly reviewed. Men's working life and family life have been proposed as the central health factors. Education also appears to be relevant in many contexts. For example, Mayer et al. (2004) found that patients with higher education had lower global coronary risk than those with lower education. Significantly more patients with ischaemia had only primary education, in contrast with the remaining diagnostic groups. These authors suggest that this should be considered in clinical practice.

Other studies have focused on broad variations in cultural patterns. For example, different levels of depression have been studied in different countries or cultures, using identical measures. Arrindell et al. (2003) proposed that nations in which both women and men are offered more equal opportunities for the fulfilment of multiple social roles that are associated with good self-rated health would score significantly lower on national depression levels than tough or masculine societies in which such opportunities exist to a clearly lesser extent. Analyses of data collected in 14 European nations (N = 3,438 female, 2,091 male students; aged 17–30 yrs) demonstrated that higher scores on Hofstede's (1980) national 'masculinity index' and lower ones on national wealth were independent predictors of higher national depression levels. Interestingly, national traits on 'neuroticism' did not mediate the relationship between national 'masculinity' and national depression levels.

White and Cash (2003), have reviewed the state of men's health across seventeen West European countries, including subjective well-being and self-perception of health. This seems to be sensitive at the individual level as well on the national level (Table 9.1). Men perceive their health as 'good' more frequently than women in all these countries. The only exception to this is Finland where women estimate their health as 'good' slightly more frequently in the 25–64 age group. Men's health ratings seem to be contradictory, because

Table 9.1 Self-perception of health, for men and women aged 65+ and aged 25–64, 1998, for each country

	Men self-reporting as in 'good' health (%)		Men self-reporting as in 'bad' health (%)		Women self-reporting as in 'good' health (%)		Women self-reporting as in 'bad' health (%)		Ratio: 'good' % men to 'good' % women	
	65+	25–64	65+	25–64	65+	25–64	65+	25–64	65+	25–64
Sweden	60	80	9	5	52	79	12	5	1.15	1.01
Ireland	58	84	6	3	50	83	12	2	1.16	1.01
UK	57	74	14	8	53	70	17	10	1.08	1.06
Netherlands	56	80	6	3	44	74	11	4	1.27	1.08
Belgium	52	81	10	4	45	73	14	22	1.16	1.11
Denmark	50	80	18	4	47	80	16	5	1.06	1.00
Greece	41	87	25	4	31	81	28	6	1.32	1.07
Austria	38	78	19	4	34	77	25	5	1.12	1.01
Spain	37	74	25	7	26	72	35	9	1.15	1.03
France	30	63	22	5	24	59	22	8	1.25	1.07
Italy	26	70	33	6	20	60	38	8	1.30	1.17
Finland	23	66	19	6	22	68	28	6	1.05	0.97
Germany	21	53	30	16	19	47	40	17	1.11	1.13
Portugal	11	54	48	16	8	42	60	20	1.38	1.29

Source: White and Cash, 2003.

men die on average earlier than women. Why men estimate their health better than women do is unclear, and further research is needed to figure out the reason for this contradiction. There are striking differences between European countries in health perception, and what is intriguing is that the differences between countries are larger in the older people's sample. So, 60% of older age male Swedes perceive their health as 'good' compared with only 11% of Portuguese. Only 23% of older age male Finns and 21% of older age Germans viewed their health as 'good', even with their relative prosperity.

Insinga and Fryback (2003) have studied differences between self-ratings and population ratings for health. EuroQOL data were analysed from the 1993 measurement and valuation of health study. The representative sample comprised 2,997 members of the UK adult population sampled by age, gender and social class. Overall, mildly ill individuals provided lower self-rating, and moderately ill individuals higher self-ratings, than ratings for these states provided by the general population. Interestingly, socio-demographic characteristics did not explain differences between self-ratings and general population ratings. Rating differences related more closely to a lack of correspondence between health state descriptions and self-raters' actual health experiences. This means that caution is necessary in assuming doing statements about actual health in various countries on the bases of self-ratings of health.[7]

There are also striking differences in explanations of illness in women and men (Benrud and Reddy, 1998). As expected, when gender difference disadvantaged women it was primarily attributed to relatively uncontrollable, constitutional factors. In contrast, when the same gender difference disadvantaged men, participants attributed it primarily to relatively controllable, non-constitutional factors, such as behaviour.

The impact of work

Men are often defined rather by 'what they do' – their paid work in the public sphere – rather than by 'who they are'. A central tenet of many versions of hegemonic masculinity is the assumption that a 'real' man will have a full-time, permanent job – which supports his family financially (Price et al., 1998). However, there have been massive changes in employment patterns in the past few decades. Modern urban society is characterised by rapid changes in the labour market. Work organisations are becoming more time hungry, and less secure and predictable. Working life has become more intensive and more uncertain. It is very typical in East European countries where free market and weak trade unions are additional causes of psycho-social insecurity and stress. Men in the former communist states are under great pressure to cope with unstable working situations.

Gender differences in health arise partly from how certain work is done by men in hazardous occupations. One of the most controversial explanations of class inequalities in health is the health selection hypothesis or drift hypothesis which suggests there is a causal link between the health status of individuals and their chances of social mobility, both inter- and intra-generational. Cardano et al. (2004) tested this hypothesis, and tried to answer three related questions: (a) to what extent does health status influence the chances of intra-generational mobility of individuals? (b) what is the impact on health inequalities of the various kinds of social mobility (both mobility in the labour market and exit from employment) – do they increase or reduce inequalities? (c) to what extent does health-related intra-generational social mobility contribute to the production of health inequalities? The data analysed were drawn from the records of the Turin Longitudinal Study, which was set up to monitor health inequality of the Turin population by combining census data, population registry records and medical records. Occupational mobility was observed during 1981–1991. To evaluate the impact of the various processes of social mobility on health inequalities, mortality was observed over the period 1991–1999.

The study population consisted of men and women aged 25–49 at the beginning of mortality follow-up (1991), and registered as resident in Turin at both the 1981 and the 1991 censuses (N = 127,384). Health status was determined by observing hospital admission. For the purpose of the study healthy individuals were those with no hospital admissions during the period 1984–1986, while those admitted were classed as unhealthy.[8] The study found a weak relationship between health status and occupational mobility chances. Decidedly stronger was the impact on occupational mobility of gender, education and 'ethnicity' (being born in the South of Italy). The relationship between occupational mobility and health takes two different forms. Occupational mobility in the labour market decreased health inequalities; occupational mobility out of the labour market (early retirement, unemployment, housewife return) widens them. The maximum contribution health-related intra-generational social mobility can make towards health inequalities was estimated at about 13% for men.

Ribet et al. (2003) have studied the connections between job mobility and health indices in a large-scale French study at the French National Electricity and Gas Company (GAZEL cohort) of 11,447 male workers and 7,664 female workers. Longitudinally it was revealed that smokers and excessive alcohol drinkers in 1992 had a higher risk of non-mobility than, respectively, non-smokers and non-excessive alcohol drinkers. Non-mobile men in 1985–1992 had a higher risk of becoming smokers, excessive alcohol drinkers, and hypertensive in 1993–1999 than upwardly mobile men. These results suggest a complex relation between risk factors and occupational mobility. A high level of risk factors, particularly health behaviours, might account for a selection process reducing upward occupational mobility.

The association between low socio-economic status and poor health is well established. Kristenson et al. (2004) studied psycho-social factors that mediate socio-economic status and health variables. Psycho-biological responses to environmental challenges depend on acquired expectancies of the relations between responses and stimuli. Individuals with low socio-economic status report more environmental challenges and having less resources. This may lead to negative outcomes, loss of coping ability, strain, hopelessness and chronic stress. Kristenson et al. conclude that sustained activation and loss of capacity to respond to a novel stressor could be a cause of the higher risk of illness and disease found among people with lower socio-economic status. This conclusion is supported by Ribet et al.'s (2003) study above. Analyses revealed significant connections between psychological demands, decision latitude, social support, and physical demands, and self-reported health for both men and women. It was figured out that low decision authority for men, and low social support and high physical demands for women were predictive of poor self-reported health.

Forms and extent of control at work also seem to be significant for health outcomes. Ala-Mursula et al. (2004) found that women with a low level of worktime control had a 1.9 times (95% CI 1.4 to 2.5) higher odds ratio for poor self-rated health, a 1.4 times (95% CI 1.1 to 1.8) higher odds ratio for psychological distress, and a 1.5 times (95% CI 1.3 to 1.7) higher risk of medically certified sickness absences than women with a high level of worktime control. The health effects of worktime control were particularly evident among women with families. Among men, worktime control was not associated with self-rated health or distress, but it predicted sickness absences in two subgroups: those with dependent children and those with manual occupations. It was concluded that low level of worktime control increases the risk of future health problems. The risk is highest among women, especially those with families, and among manual workers. The results suggest that worktime control can help workers integrate their work and private lives successfully.

Elstad and Krokstad (2003) have examined how socio-economic inequalities in perceived health were reproduced as a cohort of adult men became 10 years older. They focused specifically on the role of social causation and health-selective mobility. A two-wave panel data set was collected by the Nord-Trøndelag Health Study (HUNT), Norway, based on a sample of 9,189 men aged 25–49 at baseline. Systematic socio-economic inequalities in perceived health were observed both at baseline and 10 years later when the sample was aged 35–59. Inequalities in perceived health widened during the study period, both among those who were continuously employed and between the employed and non-employed. Compared to higher white collar, changes in perceived health during the study period were more negative among medium-level and manual occupations, and even more negative among the non-employed. Mobility between occupational classes among those employed at both observation points was not selective for health, but transitions into and out of employment were strongly health-selective. It is argued that the transformation of the health inequality pattern among those continuously employed was solely due to social causation, i.e. to more negative changes in perceived health among medium status/manual occupations than among the white collar. The wider difference in perceived health between the employed and non-employed was, however, primarily a result of health-selective mobility into and out of the non-employed category.[9]

Occupational divisions also seem to be of importance for mental health. Sanne et al. (2003) examined if and how levels of anxiety and depression differed between occupations. The study encompassed 17,384 workers with occupations classified according to ISCO-88 (COM) from the population-based Hordaland Health Study. The relationship between skill levels and depression was equally strong. Elementary, low skill level occupations consistently showed higher-than-average depression scores. The strength of the associations between depression and skill levels are of clinical significance.

The impact of home and family

The influence of family life is crucial to women's and men's health. Willitts et al. (2004) have studied the mental health of men and women with differing histories of partnership transitions. Data were from nine waves of the British Household Panel Survey, a stratified general population sample with different partnership transition histories. Participants were 2,127 men and 2,303 women aged under 65 who provided full interviews at every survey wave. The main results were that enduring first partnerships were associated with good mental health. Partnership splits were associated with poorer mental health, although the reformation of partnerships partially reversed this. Cohabiting was more beneficial to men's mental health, whereas marriage was more beneficial to women's mental health. The more recently a partnership split had occurred the greater the negative outcome for mental health. Women seemed more adversely affected by multiple partnership transitions and to take longer to recover from partnership splits than men. Single women had good mental health relative to other women, but the same was not true for single men relative to other male partnership groups. The main conclusion was that partnership was protective of mental health. Mental health was worse immediately after partnership splits, and the negative outcomes for health were longer lasting in women. Future work should consider other factors that may mediate, confound, or jointly determine the relation between gender, partnership change and health (also see Lucht et al., 2003).

Wider ranging aspects of gender patterns of family–work relations have also been studied. For example, the purpose of Zamarripa et al.'s (2003) study was to determine whether the relationship between male gender role conflict variables and mental health generalises to women, along with investigating other aspects of gender roles and mental health. Men showed more restricted emotionality, more restricted affection, greater appropriate and inappropriate success, and more restricted affection, particularly for other men. There were, however, no gender differences related to the conflict between work and family, and this was the major predictor of depression and anxiety for men and women. For the most part these variables were related to depression and anxiety in similar ways in men and women.

Consideration of the psycho-social contributions to cardiovascular disease (CVD) remains an ongoing focus of research in the behavioural sciences, with a particular emphasis on the role of hostility (Consedine et al. 2004). There are, however, a number of inconsistent findings, and the generality of findings across genders remains a continuing concern. This article presents an emotions-theory perspective on the relation between personality and CVD and reports a test of the hypothesis that anxiety predicts CVD in women whereas hostility predicts CVD in men. Six hundred and eighty women and 415 men completed measures of traditional risk factors, emotion and cardiovascular disease. Structural equation analyses supported researchers' predictions. Data are interpreted in terms of their capacity to inform general psychosocial models of CVD.

Negative emotions, such as depression and anxiety, have been associated with the development of coronary heart disease (CHD). In multivariate models, negative emotions have predicted CHD outcomes, such as nonfatal myocardial infarction and CHD mortality (Todaro et al., 2003). Few studies, however, have investigated this relation while controlling for variables associated with the metabolic syndrome or those indicative of sympathetic nervous system activity. Negative emotion score, socio-demographic characteristics, health behaviours, components of the metabolic syndrome, and stress hormones were used to predict incident CHD over a 3-year follow-up period. After adjusting for potential covariates, negative emotions continued to predict the incidence of CHD. Patients with documented ischemic coronary heart disease have also been tested for the association of various measures of emotional distress (Ketterer et al., 2004). Females reported more depression and anxiety than males. However, spouses or friends reported more anger for males. Denial was greater in males for all three scales of anger, depression and anxiety.

There have been a number of attempts to assess connections between the possible changes in cancer risk and family status changes, such as widowhood and divorce. Hemminki and Li (2003) calculated standardised incidence ratios (SIRs) for cancer among 47,000 widows/widowers and 60,000 divorced people, based on the Swedish Family-Cancer Database. Persons were identified with the same family statuses (married, widowed, divorced) in the years 1960 and 1970; cancers were followed from 1971 to 1998. Both increased and decreased SIRs were found, and a consistent pattern emerged. The effects on the divorced were always stronger than those in widows/widowers, irrespective of the direction of the effect. The data suggest that the changes in lifestyle on the loss of a spouse impact on the incidence of almost every type of cancer. The effects were so large that a failure to consider marital status in epidemiological studies may be a source to bias.[10]

Against the background of increasing cancer rates in the mid-1980s, Europe Against Cancer launched an ambitious programme aiming to reduce cancer mortality by 15% by the year 2000. In accordance with Boyle et al.'s (2003) survey the target of a 15% reduction in the expected numbers of cancer deaths in the EU was not met, although the 10% reduction in number of deaths expected in men and 8% in women, along with a 11% reduction in risk of cancer death in men and a 10% reduction in women, was noteworthy. Only Austria and Finland achieved the 15% reductions in deaths amongst both men and women.

Levi et al. (2004) reported that in the EU total cancer mortality declined by 7% for both sexes during 1995–1999. The fall since the late 1980s was 10% in both sexes, corresponding to the avoidance of over 90,000 deaths per year, as compared to the rates of the late 1980s. For the first time, over the last few years, some levelling of mortality was reported also in the Russian Federation, the Czech Republic, Poland, Hungary and other Eastern European countries, although cancer rates in those areas remain exceedingly high. The overall favourable pattern of cancer mortality over recent years is largely driven by the decline of tobacco-related cancer mortality in men. However, important components of the trends are also the persistence of substantial falls in gastric cancer, mainly in Russia and Eastern Europe.

Taniguchi et al. (2003) studied 272 men and 252 women with cancer in terms of the impact of being married and the presence of spousal support on psychological distress and coping with cancer. All participants underwent a structured interview and completed the Profile of Mood States and the Mental Adjustment to Cancer scale. Multivariate analysis controlling for potentially confounding biomedical and psychosocial variables revealed that unmarried men had significantly higher levels of psychological distress and lower levels of fighting spirit than married men, and that men with spousal support showed higher levels of fighting spirit than men without spousal support. However, no such difference was observed between unmarried and married women or between women with and without spousal support. These findings suggest that being married may play an important role in reducing psychological distress and enhancing fighting spirit of men with cancer, and that being unmarried may be a risk factor for psychological distress and lower fighting spirit for men with cancer.

The objective of Artazcoz et al.'s (2004) study has been to analyse gender inequalities in the combination of job and family life, and their effects on health status and use of health care services. The data was derived from the Navarra Survey of Working Conditions from Spain carried out on a sample of 2,185 workers in 1997. The analysis was restricted to 881 men and 400 women, aged 25–64 years, who were married or cohabiting. Dependent variables were self-perceived health status, psychosomatic symptoms, and medical visits, all of them dichotomised. Independent variables were family demands and number of hours of paid work a week. The analysis was adjusted for age and occupational social class. Unexpectedly it was found that family demands were not associated with men's health whereas married women who lived in family units of more than three members had a higher risk of poor self-perceived health status. Among women, working more than 40 hours a week was also associated with both health indicators and, additionally, with a higher probability of medical visits.

This kind of study can be understood in relation to the role approach to gender and health. This has been an especially long-established concern in US studies, where research has often been directed towards analysis of women's multiple roles. There is also now some more nuanced research using this approach. For example, Roxburgh (2004) shows the gendered effects of time pressure but also that it is not the actual amount of pressure but the boring routine that is bad for health and harmful for women. It appears that the women surveyed can often tolerate much more time pressure than men while demeaning tasks are indeed stressful for them. In order to fully understand social determinants of workers' health, besides social class, gender inequalities in the distribution of family responsibilities should be considered.

Law and policy

What is particularly interesting is that the calls for more attention for men's health, particularly in policy development, are coming from a wide range of different, and sometimes contradictory, political interests, including governments (of left and right), health promotion and community health units, mainstream medical professionals, pharmaceutical companies, men's rightists and (pro)feminists.[11] It is important to contextualise policy development on men's health in relation to a number of very different institutional frameworks, political interests and discourses. For example, on one hand, there is what can be seen as a relatively benign public health approach to men's health. This may, however, often seek to reduce men's health to psychological concerns about their 'barriers' to using existing health services without explicitly raising the gendered aspect of men's health. On the other hand, pharmaceutical companies have discovered men as a relatively untapped and profitable market, as with the drug Viagra and some of the new anti-depressive drugs.

Men's morbidity and mortality are central topics of public discussions in some countries. In some countries, such as Estonia, this is argued to be the main social problem *of* men. In this context it is interesting that Estonian research finds that men are over-optimistic regarding their own health (Kolga, 2000a). In Latvia, there is public recognition that men fall ill and die with cardiovascular diseases more frequently than women, and life expectancy for males has decreased by four years, and two years for females. There has been attention to gendered health issues, with occupational health problems of work with asbestos, in chemico-pharmaceutical enterprises, and chronic lead poisoning, often mainly affecting men. There has also been a rapid decrease in fertility and growth of mortality, with a stress in public debate on the negative effects upon ethnic Latvians. The notion of depopulation is articulated in nationalist discourse. The most recent studies have shown that reproductive health in Latvia is characterised by: low birth rate; male life expectancy trends are downwards, and much lower than for women; male participation in the choice of contraception, family planning and child-raising is insufficient (Novikova, 2001a).

Despite this, law and policy on health is often non-gendered, or rather, is a mix of non-gendered and gendered elements. In many countries there are no specific policies regarding men's health. For example, there are no relevant provisions in Polish law exclusively on men's health. Men are referred to in individual provisions related to self-inflicted injuries or incapacitation of health carried out in order to evade compulsory military service (both of which are treated as offences). No data were found on Polish organisations that deal exclusively with problems of health, social welfare and suicides concerning men or on nationwide initiatives and programmes (they are mainly aimed at women and children). In Poland both men and women are entitled to social welfare and health care use on the grounds of being orphaned, homelessness, unemployment, disability, long-term illness, difficulties in parental and household matters (especially for single parent families and families with many children), alcohol and drug abuse, difficulties in readjusting to life following a release from a penitentiary institution, natural and ecological disasters, and, in the case of women, for the purposes of the protection of maternity (Oleksy, 2001a).

Similarly, in Latvia policy is directed towards the health of mother and child, and stress is put on the importance of women's health in terms of their reproductive health. There is no policy statement or mention on men's (reproductive) health. In general, the family is marked as an integrated unit out of which a woman is singled out in terms of her childbearing functions. In Germany the state is now withdrawing partly from health insurance and this will impact upon gendered health outcomes. In the Russian Federation there are, as of August 2004, planned reforms that threaten the health of women and men. These include replacing the system of social benefits, inherited from the former political system, and including housing subsidies, free public transport, discounts on prescription medication, artificial limbs and spa treatment, with cash payments. These led in summer 2004 to noisy demonstrations, the first such reactions since President Putin came to power in 2000 (Wheeler, 2004).

At the same time, there are counter tendencies. In several countries there are now national health education programmes that include aspects directed towards men. In Germany, the Federal Bureau for Health Education has been focusing men's health since some years in a rather comprehensive perspective. The relation that boys develop to their bodies, men's procreative behaviour, men's experiences of violence, knowledge about procreation in juveniles with migrant backgrounds are some of the issues (www.bzga.de; www.maennerleben.de). There are the beginnings of health education in Ireland, though the construction of health is mainly in physical terms. Sometimes health programmes, as in Estonia, focus especially on children and youth. In Norway a number of health campaigns and measures are related to men's health, like attempts to reduce the proportion of smokers, but masculinity is not a main focus. Some research on men's health is ongoing or planned, but it cannot be described as a coherent research field. It is only recently that women's health has achieved this status. In many areas of health prevention, like reducing smoking, the problem patterns persist. There is a need to try new perspectives and methods, including a focus on masculinity and negative 'semiautomatic' life style habits among boys and men. Similarly, in Estonia, national programmes for the prevention of alcoholism and drug-use, tuberculosis, and HIV/AIDS and other sexually transmitted diseases, are all relevant for men.

Men's suicide rates are higher than women's; this especially applies to young men's suicide in the Baltic countries, Finland, Poland, Russia. In these countries there is also a high difference in life expectancy between men and women. In Ireland, Italy and Norway, men perform suicide about three times as often as women; in Poland the ratio is over 5:1. In Italy over the last 10 years there has been a clear prevalence of men relative to women, while regards suicide attempts, the trend is reversed, with over half by women.

There is growing policy concern with young men's suicide and health more generally in a number of countries. Much needs to be done on men's and young men's suicide, and on the very high level of deaths from accidents (especially road traffic accidents) for young men. UK reports have noted how class factors intersect with gender regarding suicide rates for the highest risk age group (under 44 years), thus linking with some men's social exclusion. Ireland has one of the highest differences internationally between young male and female suicides (7:1) for 15–24 year olds, and with an overall male rate of 18.4 per 100,000 in 2003 Ireland is, however, still relatively high in the World Health Organisation table of 100 countries (http://www.who.int/mental_health/prevention/suicide/suiciderates/en/). Finland has one of the highest figures, with a rate of 34.6, higher than Czech Republic and Poland, though this still much lower than Estonia with 45.8, Latvia 56.6, Russian Federation 70.6 per 100,000. There is a very low level of take up of services by young male suicides prior to their deaths: 'this group does not see the services, as presently structured and delivered, as being relevant to them' (Ferguson, 2001a). Suicide rates have generally fallen across the UK over the last 15 years, except among young men aged 15–44; suicide rates for Scotland are considerably higher than other UK countries. Local areas where suicide rates were significantly high tended to be those characterised as having high 'deprivation' levels.

The health of men is just beginning to be recognised as a health promotion issue in Ireland, in the context of growing awareness of generally poor outcomes in health for men compared with women and generally lower resource allocation to men's health. The Irish government published its second health promotion strategy in 2001 including a short section on men (*National Health Promotion Strategy*, 2001) and has stated for the first time that a specific section on men's health will appear. Health is still tending to be conceptualised in physical terms, with a neglect of psychological well-being. While increases in male suicide, especially by young men, are increasingly the focus of public concern, there has been little attempt to develop gender specific policies and programmes which can help men to cope with their vulnerability and despair.

The UK Government has also supported the movement towards improving men's health. Since 1997 it has assisted The Men's Health Forum (founded 1994) in several ways, such as setting up its website. Previously the Men's Health Forum has argued that the government has relied too much on general health policies, hoping that men would be included in these via the general health structures, even though men often do not access these structures as much as women. In January 2001 an All Party Group on Men's Health was set up to raise awareness and co-ordinate policies. The governmental Health Development Agency has appointed its first men's officer. One aim is to encourage local surgeries to open at times more convenient to men and make health promotion material more accessible to men.

What is almost wholly absent from national governmental policy discourses, as opposed to some research, in relation to men's health is any recognition that high levels of accidental and suicidal death might link with more critical approaches to men's practices, such as risk-taking, self-violence, problems in emotional communication, being 'hard'. Overall there is little consideration of how problems of men's health link with a critical analysis of men's oppressive social practices more broadly.

Policy recommendations

Finally, several policy recommendations follow from this review.[12] They include most obviously: to improve men's health and reduce unnecessary illness. This involves facilitating men's improved health (or 'illth') practices, including use of health services. Men's relative lack of use of health services, delaying of use or use only after appointments have been made by women are examples of health practices with vital implications for medical and other professional intervention (Bond, 2001; Mansfield et al., 2003; White and Banks, 2004).

More generally, there is the need to connect men's health to forms of masculinity, such as risk-taking and 'unhealthy' behaviour. As regards the last point, the outcomes from the Network suggest that to fully understand, and deal with, the dynamics around the health problems of at least some men we may need to connect those problems to dominant, or even in some cases oppressive, ways of 'being a man': for instance, risk-taking behaviour relevant to some injuries and addictions; or an almost 'macho' unwillingness to take one's health problems seriously and seek medical help; or the marked violence which enters into the methods which a number of men seem to use to commit suicide. There is also a need to focus on the negative effects of men's health problems upon women and children; to ensure that focusing on men's health does not reduce resources for women's and children's health.

These points are also good examples of a more general conclusion arising from the Network outcomes which is highly relevant for policy-makers, namely that in designing policy interventions, one must seek to bridge the central divide which has previously existed in much research on men, i.e. the splitting of studies which focus on 'problems which some experience' from those which explore 'the problems which some create'.

Acknowledgement

We would like to thank all the members of the CROME collective who contributed to the gathering of information on men's health in their respective countries, and especially thank Elianne Riska for detailed comments on an earlier draft of this chapter.

10
Configurations of Europe

Jeff Hearn, Keith Pringle, Harry Ferguson, Voldemar Kolga, Emmi Lattu, Ursula Müller, Irina Novikova, Elżbieta H. Oleksy, Teemu Tallberg, Dimitar Kambourov, Marie Nordberg, Iva Šmídová, Joanna Kazik and Hertta Niemi

Introduction

This book has sought to gender men in Europe by drawing on various sources of information and in relation to key themes and policy arenas. In this final chapter, we consider some broad issues concerning the position and impact of men in the context of changing configurations of Europe, including, but not only, in relation to the EU. There are many ways in which the more explicit gendering of men raises new sets of questions about the EU and the changing definitions of 'Europe'.

We begin by exploring how men's gendered power relations are played out at the supranational European level and the way they are implicated in the processes – often oppressive processes – by which dominant definitions are constructed about who is 'European' and who is 'more European'. In considering these, it is important to rectify the relative neglect and yet gradually growing analysis of gendered economic, political, cultural, welfare and state regimes in Central and Eastern Europe, including gendering the impacts of and upon men.

This is followed by a more focused discussion of variations and contradictions between and within the regions of Europe, before some final concluding remarks on the contemporary picture. The variations noted are of several kinds: regional, cultural, national, local. One key implication of explicitly gendering men, masculinities and men's practices concerns analysis of gendered welfare regimes, and state regimes more generally, and indeed vice versa. This involves a critique of most previous attempts to categorise and classify variations in European welfare state regimes, which in practice has often meant Western European regimes.

Yet, even these variations are not the whole story, for there are a number of major complications and contractions that need to be spelt out. One set of contradictions concerns the conclusion that the division of research and policy development between the problems that some men endure as a result of patriarchal relations in society; and the problems that men create for women and/or children and/or other men and/or themselves, is not tenable in scholarly terms. This applies at local, national, supranational and transnational levels.

Writing transnationally – across national, cultural and other boundaries – is a challenge. In so doing, we need to recognise and yet decentre the nation and nations, in both their variety and their historical contingency. At the same time, while specific nations may come and go, be formed and reformed, the notions of 'nation' and moreover nationalism seem resilient in this particular historical period.

Europe and the EU

There are many complex ways in which gendered power relations associated with dominant forms of masculinity are entering centrally into the hegemonic processes whereby the EU, its member states and associated countries are seeking to redefine what is 'Europe' and what it is to be 'European'. Moreover, the part played by gender relations, and specifically those associated with masculinities, within these processes has largely been kept invisible, in both policy and academia.

Currently, there is an imbalance of research attention towards 'the problems that men endure' in the countries of northern, southern and western parts of Europe compared to the attention devoted to 'the problems that men create'; and this imbalance needs to be contextualised more broadly. In much of Central and Eastern Europe, profound transformations in gendered power relations are occurring as a result of the social and economic upheavals since the late 1980s and due to the strong links being forged with countries of 'the West', not least the accession of many of these countries to the EU in 2004. Interestingly, the EU's own research and policy approach to men's practices has largely mirrored the imbalance noted above that exists among the pre-2004 members. Hence, the EU itself as an institution has tended to concern itself far more with issues such as reducing limitations on men as carers, men's working conditions, and men's health, rather than on topics such as men's violences to women and children.

While there are signs that some shift is beginning to occur in the EU's approach to these matters, EU policy and research priorities overall still remain tilted very much in favour of the 'problems that men endure'. For instance, even the very considerable concern of the EU with child prostitution, pornography and the sexual exploitation of children betrays this order of priorities. In the past that concern largely focused on the activities of EU citizens (mainly men) *outside* the territory of the EU – typically in parts of Central and Eastern Europe, South Asia and East Asia (Pringle, 1998a). This emphasis has to a large extent not paid sufficient attention to the systematic abuse and exploitation of children *within* the confines of the pre-2004 EU (Pringle, 2003, 2004). The development of EU policy on these issues, as some countries in Central and Eastern Europe are now themselves EU members, is of considerable interest.

An obvious illustration of EU priorities on men's practices is 'trafficking' of women. In recent years this has come relatively high on EU agendas, particularly in relation to women from central and eastern parts of Europe. Whilst this may seem to contradict the previous argument, the context of the EU's interest in trafficking in fact supports it. EU interest has been framed to a considerable extent in terms of the fight against crime associated with migration into the EU from outside, rather than primarily from concern with women's well-being (Pringle, 1998a). This is one of the motivations behind the Schengen/Fortess Europe approach.

Furthermore, this has been made much more complex by the huge growth in use of information and communication technologies in the sex trade (Hearn and Parkin, 2001; Jyrkinen, 2005). EU anti-crime initiatives on trafficking have largely ignored the male users of trafficked women, many of whom are citizens of the EU-15. Yet there are clearly a considerable number of such men whose activities fuel trafficking. The relative invisibility of users within the EU's approach to trafficking persists despite actions in the Swedish EU presidency, a country which led the way on anti-prostitution policy at the national level, by urging prosecution of buyers of sex rather than the women (Månsson, 2001; Månsson and Söderlind, 2004). The focus of EU concern has not primarily been on its own citizens who create trafficking, but rather on inward migrants and their countries of origin outside the EU, or formerly the EU-15. Given the inclusion of some of these states in the EU, once again the development of EU policy will be important.

This outward focus, also seen in relation to the commercial sexual exploitation of children, is a clear example of hegemonic definitions of 'otherness' to which we alluded above. The commercial sexual exploitation of children and the trafficking of women are intensely gendered and direct outcomes of practices associated with dominant forms of masculinity. In both cases, the reaction of the EU and most of its existing members has been to divert attention to outside Europe or to the citizens of allegedly 'problematic' European nation states, all of them outside the EU until 2004. The implication is that they have been defined as less civilised, less 'European' than the pre-2004 EU members to whom they supposedly posed 'threats' from outside. It is important to consider how EU policies and practices in relation to such gendered issues will develop now that some of those stigmatised 'others' are member states, and what 'messages' regarding gender have been, and are being, received and constructed in the newly acceding countries (Modood and Werbner, 1997). In other words, how will gendered 'otherness' be dealt with by both the EU-15 and the post-2004 EU members?

In the past, the EU and its member states have separated the issue of trafficking women from prostitution and pornography, and conflated it with inward migration. This, along with the allied topic of racism, offers another example of how power relations associated with dominant forms of masculinity enter into the processes by which the idea and practice of 'Europe' is being constructed. Racism, in one guise or another, seems to be very widespread in virtually all the countries of Europe, even if its precise configuration varies from one cultural context to another. Social exclusion and processes of social marginalisation are often defined and constituted differently in the various European countries. The issue of hegemonic masculinity is remarkably absent in debates on racism in northern, southern and western Europe; the relative silence about men's practices and racism in European academic and policy debate is particularly strange.

Often central to the issues of racism in Europe and how EU member states treat migrants are questions about what is 'Europe', who is 'European' and who is 'more European' – who is 'other'? Such questions may often be partly about 'whose masculinity' is 'purer' or 'superior'. Yet both the pre-2004 member states of the EU and the European Commission itself have largely avoided confronting those highly gendered issues in their policies to combat racism and to address the issue of migration. The part played by power relations associated with hegemonic forms of masculinity in the processes of 'Europe creation' has been disguised and ignored. We need to ask ourselves what impact this state of affairs is having on conceptions and practices of gender across the countries within the central and eastern parts of Europe, many of which have been defined by the processes above as 'other'. This is especially so given their growing economic, social and cultural dependence on the states of northern, southern and western Europe including the accession of some to the EU.

The notion of Europeanisation (or perhaps 'European Union-isation') does not have a single definition. It suggests several ongoing processes including Europe's transformation into a single political formation, as well as facilitation of institutions of governance as a means of balancing European unity and national diversity. Europeanisation has also involved western capitalist expansion(ism) and transnational labour practices and markets of transnational labour migrants from 'access' societies.[1] With the move from the EU-15 to the EU-25, some countries have joined the EU as a form of legitimated entry into European, transnational globalised capital (Novikova et al., 2005). But some have not so entered, either into the EU or into this new economic world. At the cultural level, Europeanisation usually implies reference to 'something else' outside itself (Hobsbawm, 1998).

In debates on Europe and Europeanisation there is of course a huge historical and cultural set of legacies, not least from past and present empires in, around and beyond Europe – including those from classical and mediaeval periods, through the early modern empires such as France and Sweden to the 'great (colonial) powers' of the nineteenth century, the massive movements of various Russian empires, and, in a different guise, the contemporary US empire. Even the Nordic region, which is sometimes assumed to be outside many of such influences has been subject to the historical impacts of the Danish and Swedish, and more recently German and Russian empires, in ways that continue to affect the constructions of nation, value, 'others' and gender relations. Imperial and post-imperial histories continue to contribute to constructions of included/excluded, men/women and different masculinities/ femininities.

Thus to speak of Europe and Europeanisation necessarily raises the question of who is included, and who is excluded, and what kinds of men and women are so included or excluded. In recent years the place of Moslems has appeared to become especially problematic for many in the Christian, white, western supposed 'centre(s)' – even though Moslems comprise a vary large and long established set of communities in some parts of the geomorphological area called 'Europe'. Significantly, as with other taken-for-granted dominant 'centres' (Hearn, 1996a), Europe or Europeans rarely stop to deconstruct themselves, in the face of and by reference to the all too obvious discourses of 'elsewhere' further east: the Orient, Asia, Africa, and so on. Rather this is usually left unspoken or asserted. Having said that, there may be some growing articulation of transnational collective memories on a European scale, whether in terms of the Holocaust, the EU as a legal entity, 'parliamentary democracy' or difference from other powers and continents. Paradoxically, at the cultural level, even within the self-affirmations of Europe in relation to 'others' noted above, complex blurrings of 'east' and 'west' are probably increasingly in process.

Such a situation in which the states of Central and Eastern Europe are gravitating economically, socially, culturally and politically towards their neighbours in the west raises important issues about complex forms of masculinity in both the 'Western' and 'Eastern' segments of Europe, and the relationships between those segments. One way of opening up some of those issues may be by considering how men's practices have been conceptualised transnationally. In analysing the interactions between processes of masculinity formation in the 'Eastern' and 'Western' parts of Europe, Connell's (1998) model of changing historical forms of 'globalising masculinities' offers assistance here. Although his thesis may be critiqued in detail for an over-reliance on Western-oriented globalisation theories (Pease and Pringle, 2001; Hearn, 2003b), his contention of the ongoing development of 'global business masculinity' is important. Certain dominant forms of masculinities have now been globalised and shaped by global forces. To understand masculinities in specific local contexts, we need to think in global terms at least to some extent (Pease and Pringle, 2001). The main axis that Connell identifies for 'global business masculinity' is the 'metropolitan societies', particularly those of the North Atlantic (Connell, 1998). This concept has proved useful for analysing some developments in Western Europe, for instance, the recent history of masculinity formation in Ireland (Ferguson, 2006). It may also be relevant to a range of broader issues across Europe, for example, job insecurity, unemployment and long working hours.

Indeed, one highly under-researched issue across Europe is that of men in positions of corporate power. It is true that dominant and diverse genderings of mainstream business and governmental organisations have been subject to research and analysis. Feminist and feminist-influenced studies have spelt out the explicit and implicit genderings of business organisations and management (Collinson and Hearn, 1994, 1996; Ferguson, 1984; Powell, 1988; Acker, 1990; Mills and Tancred, 1992; Hearn and Parkin, 1983, 1995). Nevertheless, much research on gender relations in organisations has not considered the gendering of women and men in organisations equally thoroughly. This is even though an explicit gendered focus on men in organisations is important in several ways, including analysis of national and transnational managers and managements. This relative silence may attest to the critical importance of dominant and transnationalising forms of masculinity, not least those associated with global capital, multinational corporations and diffusion of information and communication technologies (Hearn, 2004b).

For present purposes, it is useful to address 'global business masculinity' in relation to the pre-2004 EU. On one hand, this configuration of 'masculinity' seems consonant with a 'neo-liberal' welfare model, as promoted by certain European Commission neo-liberal economic and social policies (as in prescribing budget stringency). The 2000 Lisbon Agenda social goal of the EU was 'to become the most competitive and dynamic knowledge-based economy in the world capable of sustainable economic growth with more and better jobs and greater social cohesion' by 2010. Six years on, achieving this seems unlikely. Indeed Europe overall has a marked lower economic growth rate than the China, India or the US. On the other hand, the European Commission's (1994) first 'White Chapter' on Social Policy, entitled 'The Way Forward', includes a rather confused and confusing mélange of statements. Many clearly espouse a form of neo-liberalism; however, more unexpectedly, a significant number derive from more socially responsible Conservative Corporatist or Social Democratic ideologies (Pringle, 1998a). Also, the Lisbon Agenda aimed to make 'a decisive impact on the eradication of poverty' by 2010. Likewise, the now defunct EU 'European Constitution' stated, somewhat idealistically, and in contradiction to neo-liberal practices, that 'Equality between women and men must be ensured in all areas, including employment, work and pay' (Treaty establishing a Constitution for Europe, 2004, Article II-83). Moreover, it is important to remember that 'neo-liberalism' harbours more divergence than often acknowledged (Gibson-Graham, 1996; Edwards and Elger, 1999; Waddington, 1999; Kite, 2004).

A mixed picture also emerges regarding mainstream pre-2004 EU policies towards Central and Eastern Europe. On one hand, a heavily neo-liberal agenda has often been apparent. The EU criteria for states seeking accession have had and have strong neo-liberal overtones. The approach is similar to the often socially regressive criteria set by the World Bank and the International Monetary Fund whereby some Central and Eastern Europe states were given financial support in the 1990s (Pringle, 1998a). The message being sent by the EU to these regions has been, and still is, that highly capitalist values (which appear consonant with 'global business masculinity') are to be prized and promoted. What is the impact of such an approach on those countries in Central and Eastern Europe already seeking to cope with major social and economic transformations? In particular, what is the impact on gender relations that have been undergoing various forms of transformation in those various countries? On the other hand, the pre-2004 EU placed policies in a central position that have clearly not been consonant with the values of 'global business masculinity'. An obvious example is the EU's emphasis on gender equality mainstreaming for acceding states as well as existing members. What might be the consequences of such policies for gendered power relations in those states that have just acceded and those waiting to do so?

With post-socialist changes of the 1990s, many countries of East-Central Europe, the Baltic region and the New Independent Commonwealth faced economic challenges, in terms of employment rates; reliance on agriculture and heavy industry; and transformations in public services and effectiveness of their delivery. The lead-up to the accession of eight Central and Eastern European states to the EU in May 2004 highlighted fears within the EU-15 that their economic performance would damage the enlarged EU's overall economic performance. Considerable attention was devoted to the promotion of their economic restructuring and 're-skilling' towards a more competitive service-orientated 'European' economy, as part of the Lisbon Agenda of 2000 for Europe (that is, the EU). However, in May 2005 the *Financial Times* reported that the GDP of the ten new EU members rose 5% in 2004, from 3.7% in 2003, and some overall economic growth forecasts are over twice those of the EU-15. Meanwhile, governments are under pressure to cut public spending to meet borrowing limits for joining the Eurozone (Wagstyl, 2005).[2] Such socio-economic conditions have created new variations and contradictions for post-Soviet gender inequalities.

Variations, complications and contradictions within Europe: from East to West?

Variations

Within these changing and gendered configurations of Europe there are multiple variations, and moreover complications and contradictions. They take many forms and representations. In considering societal variations in Europe, it has become popular to rely on analyses of welfare provision and welfare states, and specifically the work of Esping-Andersen and various subsequent derivatives. Such approaches have been critiqued in several ways, including in terms of their neglect of gender relations, ethnicity, race and racism, and violence. Attempts to establish such regional variations have generally not addressed men, masculinities and men's practices, at least not in an explicitly gendered way. They have also usually focused on Western, Northern and sometimes Southern Europe, to the neglect of Central and

Eastern Europe. And additionally, some of the contradictions within societal welfare systems have been underplayed. So, how do we move from this situation towards an analysis that takes fuller account of these neglected features?

Throughout this book we have stressed both the enduring consistencies across Europe and yet, at the same time, the marked variations and differences between and within regions and countries. For example, in business, particularly big business, state and religion, men are characteristically still very much the predominant and dominating social category across Europe. Also, throughout these countries men also continue to create problems for others, and indeed in a different way for themselves, with continuing men's violence to known women, now recognised as occurring at higher levels than formerly, and usually, assumed. At the same time, certain groups of men remain subject to forms of disadvantage and social exclusion, in terms of ethnicity, health, sexuality, and so on.

Meanwhile, the clear differences between regions and nations need to be acknowledged and analysed. As discussed in this and other publications (for example, Pringle et al., 2006), there are some clear differences in recent political history between the countries of the EU-15 (Denmark, Finland, Germany, Ireland, Italy, Sweden, the UK), in this context along with Norway, and those countries that have joined the EU-25 (Czech Republic, Estonia, Latvia, Poland), together with Bulgaria and the Russian Federation. The profound societal differences include perhaps most obviously the historical form of the nation-state and the state, and their relations to civil societies in forming and re-forming different men, masculinities and men's practices. Other variations persist by region, nation, culture, political economy, and so on, from south to north, as well as from east to west. One notable set of variations is in terms of men's relation to the formal economy. For example, as previously noted, men in Ireland and Italy have significantly greater earned income (2.55, 2.22 greater respectively) and economic activity rates (1.89, 1.69 respectively) compared with women, in a way that contrasts markedly with all the other twelve countries reviewed in this book (see Tables 2.1 and 2.2).

Thus, some broad contrasts can be seen across the different regions of Europe – comparing, say, the diverse political transformations of the transitional nations of the former Soviet bloc to the situations in relatively well developed 'welfare societies' of the Nordic countries. In the former, there has been much change in men's gendered positioning and gender relations more generally, but the form it takes has varied hugely for different men, different localities, and different nation-states. Regarding the latter, a recent World Economic Forum Report (Lopez-Claros and Zahidi, 2005) concluded that the five Nordic countries lead in woman's empowerment, in terms of economic, political, educational, and health and well-being measures. Thus, there is often both a persistence of relatively less gender inequality, but at the same time major dominations of men persist in these countries, for example, in business, violence, the military, academia and religion.

Complications

With this in mind, there is a danger of simplifying and over-generalising about men's practices within the complex context of political, economic and social restructurings. Moreover, in considering regional comparisons, it is important not to proceed by way of seeing Western European nation-states or welfare states as *the* reference point, against which to compare experiences and outcomes elsewhere in Europe. It is necessary to seek to avoid, or at least minimise, 'Western European-centrism'. As such, there are dangers of moving, in any simple way, either from a focus on 'the West' to one on 'the East', or vice versa, as if this represented some 'natural' progression. Indeed there are clear variations in the extent to which the former East–West boundary makes sense empirically.

Apart from the obvious complication presented by the unification of Germany across the former frontier, it has been observed that the Czech Republic is a particularly interesting case. Šmídová (2006) writes as follows:

> In recent years Czech society is becoming stabilised and is coming closer to Western patterns of societal structure. . . . Yet due to the lack of public debate and political concern, almost no attention is directed to gendered structure of society and to the structures of masculine domination. The impetus for political concern about gender comes largely from the European Union.

Somewhat similarly, Kolga (2006), though writing in the Baltic context in Estonia, says:

> in considering men, and indeed gender relations more generally, there is need to avoid stereotypical thinking that divides countries into 'west as developed' and 'east as developing' countries. This is because these groupings do not all share the same specific characteristics. Estonia is similar to Russia in terms of a high divorce rate, but different in the relation to the structure of economy, that is indeed closer to Ireland's.
>
> Another example is that Estonian men earn about 25% more than women, and a similar gender relation of salaries has been revealed in many developed Western countries, excluding Finland. This means that Estonia is in the same group with the Western countries on the basis of this one characteristic and yet closer to many post-socialist countries on the basis of some other dimensions.

Contradictions

A major barrier to generalisation is the persistence of various contradictions, which add further complexity to any attempt to summarise variations across Europe. Cross-cutting variations, whereby different trajectories exist in, say, economic or religious or cultural power, are part of the reason for the production of not just complications but rather contradictions in gender relations and of men and masculinities. Gender relations, both dominant and subordinated gender relations, may intersect and contradict social relations of other forms.

A first set of contradictions, and indeed a further antagonism to over-generalisation, concerns the multiple and complex impacts of social changes from beyond societies. Analysis of gender, men and women requires a long-term comparative historical analysis of how cultural meanings of gender have been and are constituted, stabilised and destabilised in specific settings. National histories represent extremely rich, yet still under-researched potential archives for the investigation of the construction of men's relations to gender orders (Yuval-Davis, 1997; Blom et al., 2002; Novikova et al., 2003, 2005). Dominance remains a key dimension of social structures in previously subject European countries whose gender relations have historically been part of European imperial configurations often with associated large-scale inequalities. This sets the larger framework for men's diverse practices, cultural forms and identifications.

There are huge historical and cultural legacies in Europe, from past and present empires – classical, mediaeval, early modern, nineteenth and twentieth century, and contemporary – and the various uneven experiences of colonialism and postcolonialism. For example, taking a broad historical view, most states and cultures of Central and Eastern Europe, together with their perceived European identity, have been historically shaped by forces of exclusion and marginalisation, as well as by shared peripherality to German, Russian, British, Austro-Hungarian and Ottoman empires. This is the case, even if it is also true that recently there has been a return to a more central political position by some regions which played an important part in seventeenth-century and eighteenth-century European History – such as the present Czech Republic, Hungary and Poland.

Over the last fifteen years or more, labour and gender inequalities have been restructured across Europe. We have seen the heavy interplay and contradiction of quite different political economic systems – most obviously, the previously socialist or Soviet system, and the developing capitalist, often neo-liberal system. This has involved changing forms of transnational economic restructurings, labour migration and domestic service, across altered borders, with gender hierarchies produced and maintained in relation to transnational circuits of labour mobilisation and capital accumulation. Transnational (trans-European) labour migration, with its gender hierarchies, confronts welfare policies. These have been the contexts for producing gender equality policies and gender mainstreaming within national and supranational agendas of Europe and the EU. In Central and Eastern Europe, they intersect with and may contradict post-socialist reformist agendas, with national machineries defusing gender challenges. These issues of men and masculinities in East-Central Europe, the Baltic states and the countries of New Independent Commonwealth need to be contextualised within such regional and national developments, and how the gendering of cultures and nations have 'organised' variable routes into modern formations of nation-state and citizenship. In such postcolonial contexts some categories of men have clearly benefited markedly, whether through a reinforcement of traditional family authority or economic success, while others, for example, ex-military, minority ethnic, and unemployed men, have experienced major changes in their lives, with which they may not have coped easily in many cases.

Accordingly, and as discussed earlier in this book, in many other countries of Eastern and Central Europe, men's low life expectancy is a major health problem. In some countries, men's life expectancy has dropped, and the life span gender gap varies from 10 to 15 years, with stress as a gender-related process and cardiovascular heart disease common among middle-aged men. What Kolga (2006) writes of Estonia could well apply across much of Central and Eastern Europe:

> The permanent societal instability and unceasing transitions has transformed Estonia into a real life laboratory of social experiments. ... During the last fifteen years Estonia has passed through tremendous changes in all parts of life, and this may be experienced as a feeling of the acceleration of time. It is also expressed in people's subjective inability to predict life events and the consequent stress, especially in the early 1990s. Several social indices – life expectancy, and rate of divorces – indicate that the 1994–1995 period was the worst time in the recent post-socialist era in Estonia. It is necessary to attend to this in analyses of men and men's social problems.

Another case is Poland. There, the number of suicide attempts registered by the Militia in the 1980s went down from 4.7 per thousand in 1980 to 3.7 per thousand in 1989 (*Statistical Yearbook 1990*, Table 32(90), p. 56), with men making up almost 80% of them. The number of suicides increased greatly in the 1990s in comparison with the 1980s, and men were still more numerous in this population at 81%. Increasing unemployment, especially among men, may be connected with crime committed by men in Poland, also domestic violence, deterioration of the condition of health of Poles, an increase in suicide committed due to hardship following a job loss and inability to find new employment (Oleksy, 2001c; Oleksy and Rydzewska, 2006).

A specific and urgent issue is the intersection of gender and ethnicity. The Latvian case is especially instructive here:

> Latvia has chosen the political route of excluding those who moved to its territory after 1940 (as well as their offspring) from enjoying political rights. There are, however, several visible components of social exclusion in the Latvian society. In *political* terms the discriminating Citizenship Law stigmatized a fourth part of the population who are in the category

> of 'aliens'. It was lifted after international pressure. However, it did not radically transform the situation as regards social and gender exclusion. In the transitional society and economy of Latvia a *socially* excluded people range across radical political, social and gender divisions from violation of previously acquired social positions to a complete loss of social ties with society. (Novikova, 2006)

It is extremely important to look at political, economic and social developments in a way that seeks to integrate gender analysis of processes of men's social and cultural self-identifications. For example, Papic (2003, 1) states that:

> the most influential concept in post-communist state-building was the patriarchal nation-state concept, the ideology of state and ethnic nationalism based on patriarchal principles inevitably became the most dominant building force. Various forms of ethnic nationalism, national separatism, chauvinist and racist exclusion or marginalisation of old and new minority groups are, as a rule, closely connected with patriarchal, discriminatory and violent politics against women, and their civil and social rights, previously guaranteed under the old communist order. (see also Watson, 1996)

A key question is the diverse constructions of men, in contrast with essentialist notions of the reclaimed nation-state and nationhood that have excluded or marginalised some men in the formal structures of national economies, politics and cultures. Part of this concerns how forms of citizenship inspired by neo-liberal economics are likely to transform gender relations of men and women, and among men in their private and public practices. Novikova et al. (2005, 152–3) discuss this in the context of Central and Eastern Europe as follows:

> With economic restructuring and the development of social forms of gender related to the nonmonetary economic sector, the deterioration of the former welfare system brings the 'welfare' function of women (taking care of children and the elderly) into the family. A woman takes back her 'natural' functions in the family, with the collapse of social care and health care. . . . In Latvia, for example, it is not unusual to have urban families involved in monetary economic sectors of the national economy spend large amounts of time in the countryside in the planting, growing, and harvesting seasons, thus organizing their gendered time use accordingly. Postsocialist women may also be invited into the service sector of a transitional economy, as an 'offspring' of their family functions. (also see Eley, 1998)

A complex relationship between local, traditional and transitional gender systems and the production of men in socialist mythology of hegemonic masculinities has been contested, reworked, and reaffirmed as a relationship between residual (traditional and socialist) and emergent (neo-liberal) institutions, practices and ideologies. Accession processes into the EU created the necessity to attend to gender as a category of social analysis within national labour markets, but its longer-term effect is much harder to detect. EU demands to harmonise accession countries' national legislations with pre-existing EU gender policies does not in itself overcome difficulties in economic and social development.

These conditions may actually reduce the recognition that women's and men's economic and social situation in Central and Eastern European countries radically worsened in post-socialist liberalisations of national markets. Such changes also often restricted opportunities for women's movements in the democratic processes of the late 1980–early 1990s (Papic, 2003; Novikova, 2006), even with some renewed and proactive organising by women, often against huge opposition in some of the countries of Central and Eastern Europe (Gal, 1996; Smejklová, 1996; Acsády, 1999; Feminist Review Collective, 2005).

Another geopolitical set of contradictions takes us back to the point made at the beginning of this chapter about the inadequacies of some academically-dominant models of comparative welfare analysis such as the early versions of Esping-Andersen (Esping-Andersen, 1990, 1996) and also some later developments of these models (Esping-Andersen, 1999, 2002). Our entry point here to these inadequacies and contradictions is that the division between, on the one hand, the problems that some men endure as a result of patriarchal relations in society, and – on the other hand – the problems that men create for women and/or children and/or other men and/or themselves – is not tenable in scholarly terms. The exact ways in which the relations of, and connections between, the problems men create and the problems men experience vary considerably in different countries of Europe. This relation cuts across the themes of home and work, social exclusion, violences and health. Instead, the close analytic interconnections of 'the problems which men endure' and 'the problems which men create' follows from men's individual and collective practices, and thus needs to be recognised in both policy and research.

For example, one cannot adequately address the issue of men's health without in various ways considering the linkages with men's violences more broadly, in terms of accidents, mortality rates, drug/alcohol abuse, and indeed inattention to self-health care and various forms of violence to the self. Similarly, one cannot adequately analyse either the promotion of men as carers or men's violences without a mutual consideration of their interconnections. In different countries there have also been considerable differences in the extent of attention between these two emphases on the problems that men create, as against the problems that men experience. Even though men's violences are beginning to be addressed more fully, most research on masculinities in these parts of Europe has – as we have previously noted – focused considerably more on the problems that men endure than on those that men create. The partial exceptions to this pattern are the UK and, to some extent, Germany.

The focus of research in Finland, for example, tends to have been on 'the misfortune or misery of some men' as regards such issues as mortality, unemployment and alcohol abuse. By contrast, the emphasis of critical research on men in the UK has been more on the problems that some men create for women, children and, to a lesser extent, men (Pringle 1995, 1998a; Hearn, 1998b), particularly in the form of violence. The amount of research on men and violence is not in proportion to the actual amount of violence in different societies (Hearn, 2001). Such differences of emphasis do not simply represent differences in the size of social problems. For instance, the issue of men's violences to women in Finland, a Nordic welfare system, is large (Heiskanen and Piispa, 1998), with levels of such violence comparable to community-based studies in the UK (for instance, Mooney, 1993). A similar point could be made in relation to Sweden, following the survey of the experiences of 7,000 women (Lundgren et al., 2001). That study provided provisional evidence of high levels of child sexual abuse in Sweden committed primarily by men against children, another issue which has been researched and addressed in the UK to a greater extent than elsewhere in Europe (Pringle, 1998a; Hearn et al., 2002b).[3]

These differential patterns in research on men's violences can also to some extent be translated to similar patterns regarding law, policy and practice in relation to men. This overall picture has important implications for how we view the dominant models that are often used to analyse welfare systems transnationally, especially the model developed by Esping-Andersen (1990, 1996). His original welfare analysis was largely premised on the rather narrow bases of cash transfers, de-commodification in the labour market and class stratification. This model tended to identify some of the most progressive European welfare systems as those in the Nordic region (approximating to his 'Scandinavian' welfare regime ideal-type) and one of the least progressive as the UK (approximating to his 'neo-Liberal' welfare regime ideal-type). Moreover, his later work (Esping-Andersen, 1999, 2002) and indeed the gendered typologies that provided the critique have in some respects not massively altered the patterns originally suggested by him. Even in the more gendered typologies – which to a considerable extent focus on issues of labour in the home and outside – many of the Nordic countries still emerge rather positively in a relative sense.

However, in looking at European welfare systems in terms of the extent to which they demonstrate an awareness of men's violence to women and/or children and their relative willingness to respond to these issues, then the patterns even in Western Europe differ significantly from standard Esping-Andersen-type classifications (see pp. 168–9). This is important for several reasons at various policy levels (see Balkmar and Pringle, 2005a; Iovanni and Pringle, 2005a; Pringle, 2005): first, much needs to be done in the Nordic states to make welfare responses in this field as relatively comprehensive as they are in some other welfare fields; second, using Nordic welfare systems as models in social policy, as is often done, may be more hazardous than has generally been assumed, even if, on some other dimensions of welfare, their positive reputation is more well-deserved.

In learning from international experience one needs to look widely for inspiration depending on which aspect of welfare is focused on – rather than identifying one welfare system as uniformly positive for all dimensions of welfare. Social policy-makers should be wary of global 'welfare typologies'.

Thus men and masculinities in these various regions are differentiated in contradictory ways. They display patriarchal processes, tendencies and structures of men's individual and collective practices, institutions and identifications.

Concluding remarks

This final chapter has examined the underlying, often hidden, gender processes which permeate the current (re)creation of 'Europe'. The Network has brought together women and men researchers in developing research on men in Europe. The inclusion of scholars from Bulgaria, the Czech Republic, Estonia, Latvia, Poland and the Russian Federation has been an excellent opportunity for collaboration, mutual learning, and promotion of comparative methodologies and disciplinary developments in research on men in national and regional settings. The Network's activity points to the urgent necessity for researchers to address these issues, especially in terms of which models of differential welfare and economic regimes are being constructed in East-Central Europe, the Baltic states and the Russian Federation. This in the context of the EU enlargement and EU demands upon new member and accession countries to harmonise their legislation with *acquis communataire*.

With analysis of distinctions and contrasts amongst welfare regimes of Western Europe well established, the countries of Central and Eastern Europe also need to be subjected to extended comparative analysis. In so doing, it should be borne in mind that these latter countries have been, and still are, undergoing dynamic social changes beyond anything experienced in Western Europe for decades. Such comparative analysis involves examining the historical trajectories of gender orders and state regimes in these regions, as well as how the ongoing gendering of these nation-states incorporates and transforms these trajectories. Gender analysis of welfare and indeed economic regimes needs to attend critically to the gendering of men's practices and relations thereto, including their interaction with men's dominant cultural practices and traditional views upon men and masculinities.

The 're-creation' of 'Europe' and the so-called 'New Europe' centrally involves gendered and gendering processes. These cannot be fully understood without considering the complex interaction of oppressive power relations between a dominant 'West' (partly through such institutions as the EU and NATO) and the countries of Central and Eastern Europe. Many socio-economic problems persist; most recently, since the accession of eight Central and Eastern European states to the EU in May 2004 there are some reports of limited economic benefits for at least some sectors of society, together with massive social, economic and political challenges.

Along with many other political and cultural upheavals, societal situations of great gender uncertainty and contradictions continue. The pattern of alliances around the Iraq War and debates on the European Constitution and the EU budget may suggest new cleavages between East and West, 'Old Europe' and 'New Europe', and even possible delays in Turkey's EU application process. Possible inter-societal divisions may be accompanied by growing polarisation amongst men within some national societies, with tendencies towards greater marginalisation of the poor and greater accumulation for the rich. How far dominant power relations can be subverted in transformation by the rapidly changing societies of Central and Eastern Europe will be crucial for the well-being of all living there, especially women and children, but also men.

Even more complex questions apply to the changing, sometimes rapidly changing, economic, political, cultural and gendered configurations of Turkey, the Balkans, the Middle East, the huge Asian expanses of the Russian Federation, and the Central Asian Republics, and their often ambiguous relations to 'Europe' or the rest of Europe.[4] There are also growing political economic attempts to redefine Europe, in different ways, in relation to China and Africa. Meanwhile, intersections of national and international state militarism and non-state terrorism, both heavily dominated by men, are not only being brought to the streets and subways of Europe – Moscow, Madrid, London, elsewhere – but are also ways of defining 'the West'/'Europe' and 'the East', and producing 'Europe' as a new collective actor in foreign policy, as well as the ongoing production of 'others'.[5]

This book has sought to address some of these complex gendered processes and explicitly link them with the social production, reproduction and diverse, yet frequently dominating, constructions of men and men's practices in what has come to be called 'Europe'.

Notes

Chapter 1

1 The position or strategy of absent presence is very widespread in men's relations to men (Hearn, 1998a). This can also be understood as part of broader questions of silence and silencing in gender relations (for example, Stanley and Wise, 1983).
2 Kimmel (1987) provides an interesting discussion of such earlier challenges to dominant forms of masculinity, prompted by women's agency in social change in Elizabethan England and First Wave feminism.
3 This question of characterising Europe and European culture (even civilisation) has taken a recent political urgency with discussions of the proposed, but for the time being defunct, EU constitution. For example, a number of national governments, led by Italy, sought in 2004 to enshrine Christianity in the constitution. This is despite the very large numbers of non-Christian groups, especially Moslems, in many countries, as well as the very strong secular aspects of culture in much of Europe.
4 On its own website, the EU is described as:

> . . . *a family of democratic European countries, committed to working together for peace and prosperity*. It is not a State intended to replace existing states, but it is more than any other international organisation. The EU is, in fact, unique. Its Member States have set up common institutions to which they delegate some of their sovereignty so that decisions on specific matters of joint interest can be made democratically at European level. This pooling of sovereignty is also called 'European integration'. (emphasis in original) (http://europa.eu.int/abc/index_en.htm)

5 The EU-15 comprised Austria, Belgium, Denmark, Finland, France, Germany, Greece, Ireland, Italy, Netherlands, Portugal, Spain, Sweden and United Kingdom. The accession countries to the EU-25 are: Cyprus, Czech Republic, Estonia, Hungary, Latvia, Lithuania, Malta, Poland, Slovakia and Slovenia. The applicant countries are: Bulgaria, Croatia, Romania and Turkey.
6 Present members of Schengen are: Austria, Belgium, Denmark, Finland, France, Germany, Iceland, Italy, Greece, Luxembourg, Netherlands, Norway, Portugal, Spain and Sweden. Switzerland voted by referendum to join in June 2005.
7 In June 2005, with crises over the proposed European Constitution and the EU budget, it was strongly being suggested, in much of the European media at least, that these timetables for new accessions may be delayed or even abandoned.
8 As embodied in Article 34 of the Charter of Fundamental Rights of the European Union, which states the right to social security, the right to social and housing assistance, and the ambition of combating social exclusion (EU, 2000). Also see Roche and van Berkel (1997), and Steinert and Pilgram (2002).
9 Room (1999, cited in Giertz, 2004, 13) provides five advantages of the shift from the concept of poverty to that of social exclusion:

from financial to multi-dimensional disadvantage;
from static to dynamic analysis;
from focus on resources of individuals or households to concern also with those of the local community;

from distributional to relational dimensions of stratification and disadvantage; and from a continuum of inequality to catastrophic rupture.

Chapter 2

1 The national reports are available at: http://www.cromenet.org (also see Hearn et al., 2002a, 2003b, 2004b).
2 For a comparison of Australian, Nordic, UK and US studies on men, see Hearn (2000/2002).
3 These three features parallel the three influences set out in Chapter 1; they also have some resonance with Messner's (1997) three-way framing of 'men's politics', in terms of focusing on patriarchal privilege (as in much feminist analysis), differences between men (as in gay perspectives and those of men of colour), and men's rights (as in furthering even more the 'voices' of men).
4 We are grateful to LeeAnn Iovanni for work on Danish academic sources (see Iovanni and Pringle, 2005a).
5 As such it is distinct from the 'crisis of masculinity' that has been discussed in the US and elsewhere, usually as a more positive re-evaluation of the 'male sex role'.

Chapter 3

1 The national reports are available at: http://www.cromenet.org (also see Hearn et al., 2002c).
2 We have previously assembled baseline measures for the initial ten nations in the Network in terms of: i. demographic measures: population size, life expectancy; ii. working life and labour market: economic structure, economic activity, unemployment, and decision-making; iii. social exclusion: poverty, imprisonment, ethnicity; iv. violence: homicide and suicide (Hearn et al., 2002c).
3 We are grateful to LeeAnn Iovanni for work on Danish statistical sources.

Chapter 4

1 A number of very informative documents on the challenges facing men in different parts of the world that were part of this preparation are available online (Division for the Advancement of Women, 2003a). These should be read in association with the subsequent Report to the Secretary-General on 'the role of men and boys in achieving gender equality' (Division for the Advancement of Women, 2003b).

Chapter 5

1 The review of these three Russian newspapers was from Tartakovskaya (2000), in which she examines gender representations in January–February 1984 and the same months in 1997. These are the three most well-known Russian newspapers, rather than those that would be chosen strictly on the criteria set out (*Russian Federation . . .*, 2001).
2 A major reason for difficulties in classification is that the thematic categories are of different characters: social exclusion is a sociological category, while violences, home and work, and health are categories of the participants themselves, specifically

the authors of articles. On the other hand, this structure maintains the possibility of comparing how these four broad themes have been treated across research, statistical, and law and policy, as well as newspaper media. Indeed, research, statistical, and law and policy can themselves be understood as *forms of media and representation*, with their own diverse traditions, interests and genres. For further discussion of methodology, see Hearn et al., 2003c.

Chapter 7

1 This a major policy plank of the European Union, as in Article 34 of the Charter of Fundamental Rights of the European Union (EU, 2000), that has also become part of national policy agendas. In some cases this has been proactive, often reactive. The concept of social exclusion is also widely debated in more academic circles.
2 The information reviewed derived from data sources in Hearn et al. (2004a), together with additions for Bulgaria (Kambourov, 2005), Czech Republic (Šmídová, 2006) and Sweden (Nordberg, 2006).

Chapter 8

1 Also see Morley and Mullender, 1994; Hester et al., 1998; Hester, 2000 for research reviews.
2 It should be noted that some women victims also under-report violence, appearing to do so primarily to preserve the relationship (Heckert and Gondolf, 2000a).
3 For example, the Finnish National Programme for the Prevention of Prostitution and Violence Against Women (1998–2002) established 12 multi-professional working groups and seven regional forums.
4 Susan Edwards has noted that there are in the UK some examples of good practice in developing a co-ordinated approach to domestic violence prosecutions under the Crime and Disorder Act (1998) where the Crime Reduction Unit and the Violence Against Women Initiative of the Home Office have funded several projects involving police, prosecutors and other agencies (Edwards and Hearn, 2005).
5 An excellent review of theory and practice for working with boys around these issues is provided by Salisbury and Jackson (1995).
6 Keith Pringle is grateful to Maria Eriksson for discussions on the concept of 'personal and bodily integrity'.

Chapter 9

1 Citing Mathers et al., 2001.
2 Ibid.
3 Several of these social tendencies can be linked or associated with the long established debate on men's 'emotional inexpressivity' (cf. Sattel, 1976; Heikell and Riska, 2004), even though any simple equation of men, masculinity and lack of emotion is very questionable (Hearn, 1993; Riska, 2004).
4 Green et al. (2001) have studied use of alcohol and social support connections in a randomly selected, representative sample of 3,074 male and 3,947 females. Statistical analyses indicate that social support is associated with alcohol consumption in similar ways for both genders. However, men with fewer role limits due to physical health drank more, while women with better psychological well-being

drank less. Men with few functional limitations and good health may be a risk factor for increased alcohol use among men.

5 Such a gender-neutral perspective on gender and health is to be found amongst a wide range of European sociological and public health researchers on social inequality in health. This approach (for example, Lahelma et al., 1999, 2002, 2003; Mackenbach et al., 1999) has had substantial impact on public health policies on social inequalities in health in Nordic countries. Lahelma et al. (1999) draw on 1986 and 1994 Finnish data on women's and men's self-measured symptoms and perceptions of their own health and ill-health, to suggest that this does not confirm gendered patterns. Interestingly, gender differences in ill-health were resistant to the deep labour market crisis in the early 1990s. For most health indicators women had slightly poorer health than men. Gender differences have remained stable over the period studied. Observed gender differences appeared surprisingly immune to the possible additional impact of education, employment status, region, social relations, marital and parental status. Although such studies raise the issue of gender, they are largely class-focused, so that men's health remains under-theorised. We are grateful to Elianne Riska for alerting us this issue.

6 Romanov et al. (1994) have studied 'Self-reported hostility and suicidal acts, accidents, and accidental deaths' in a prospective study of 21,443 adults aged 25 to 59. Based on a representative sample, this suggests that the association between self-reported hostility and accident-prone behaviour in males is significant and not restricted to either specific populations or specific tests.

7 An example of comparative analysis of self-reported health is that by Szaflarski et al. (2004) on Poland and the US. This revealed that Polish people showed more rapid decline in health for people over 60 than those from the US. In Poland, women report worse health than do men, while the opposite is found for the US, as well as the pre-2004 accession EU-15 states. However, crucially the relationships between education, income and health were stronger in the US than in Poland. The authors concluded that age, gender, and socio-economic status may operate differently in the two countries because of a gap in social development between the West and the former Eastern Europe.

8 Social mobility in the labour market was measured via an interval data index of upward and downward movements on a scale of social desirability of occupations, designed for the Italian labour force from an earlier empirical study (de Lillo and Schizzerotto, 1985). Movement out of the labour market was described by a discrete variable with four conditions: employed, unemployed, early retired and women returning from work to housewife status. Health inequalities were measured by the ratio of standardised mortality rates in the unskilled working class and the upper middle class.

9 Social role researchers (for example, Janzen and Muhajarine, 2003) are increasingly going beyond simply asking whether role occupancy is associated with health status to clarifying the context in which particular social role-health relationships emerge. Building on this perspective, Mustard et al. (2003) have investigated the relationship between social role occupancy and health status over time in a sample of employed Canadian men and women who vary by family role occupancy, life stage, and income. While family role occupancies were not as strongly related to the health status of men or women, one exception emerged: for older men, single and double role occupants reported significantly poorer self-rated health status than triple role men (defined as those who are married, have children living at home and are in the workforce). This study also examined the extent to which position in the occupational hierarchy is predictive of decline in perceived health status over a 48-month period

in a representative sample of the labour force. They hypothesised that the proportion of workers reporting decline in health status would be greater among persons in lower position in the occupational hierarchy, and that these differences in risk would primarily be explained by characteristics of the psychosocial work environment and secondarily by the baseline prevalence of adverse health behaviours.

There was no association between position in the occupational hierarchy and the prospective risk of health status decline for women. For men, the association between position in the occupational hierarchy and decline in perceived health status was moderately reduced but remained statistically significant following adjustment for baseline health, health behaviours and psychosocial work exposures. Adjustment for household income did not alter these findings. When stratified by gender, position in the occupational hierarchy was associated with the prospective risk of health status decline for men but not women. Among men, the collective influence of health behaviours and psychosocial work exposures explained a moderate component of the decline in perceived health status.

10 Every significant SIR for a cancer site for widows and widowers was accompanied by a more deviant and significant SIR than for the divorced. SIRs between divorced men and women ($r = 0.83$, $P < 0.0001$) and between widows and divorcees correlated ($r = 0.70$, $P < 0.0001$). The overall cancer risk for the divorced was 0.92–0.94, and this was a balance between increased risks at tobacco-, alcohol-, and human papilloma virus-related sites, and decreased risks at most other sites.

11 The first World Congress on Men's Health was held in Vienna in November 2001, along with the launch of the International Society for Men's Health (http://www.ismh.org/ismh/index.htm) and the European Men's Health Forum (http://www.emhf.org/) (see Baker, 2001).

12 The Institute of Social Medicine in Vienna reported in 1999 to the Austrian government on men's health – specifically, how to provide a basis on which to identify focal points on men's health issues (Schmeiser-Rieder et al., 1999). The report concluded both that men need to be specifically addressed as a target group for prevention campaigns, and that their health can be significantly improved. To do this will involve not only appropriate primary and secondary prevention measures, but support for gender-specific research and dissemination and greater translation of results into health care practice.

Chapter 10

1 Interestingly and contrary to some media reports, of the 133,000 East European migrant workers who have registered with the British government's register of migrants from May 2004 to March 2005, 21 have signed on as unemployed, according to the UK Home Office (Jeffries, 2005).

2 According to Merrill Lynch and Eurostat data, the highest growth rates in Europe in 2004–2005 are in Greece, the Baltics, Slovakia and Ireland, yet all but the last have unemployment at over 10% and in the case of Slovakia as high as 18% (Seager, 2005).

3 More generally, qualitative analysis of the Swedish welfare system suggests that dominant discourses within it (in terms of research, policy documents and public media) routinely downplay forms of oppression perpetrated by men upon women and children, especially where they are mainly perpetrated by men from within the white ethnic majority (Balkmar and Pringle 2005a; Pringle, 2002a, 2005). There is also a tendency within the Swedish research infrastructure to avoid topics and

research methodologies that might bring such forms of oppression by men into clearer view (Balkmar and Pringle, 2005a). This situation can be contrasted with that in the UK where such forms of oppression towards women and children have been more problematised publicly, professionally and within the research community. An earlier qualitative research study of the Danish welfare system suggests a pattern in Denmark similar to those for Finland and Sweden (Pringle and Harder, 1999). 'Mainstream' Danish society there may be even more resistant to recognising men's violences, especially those by majority ethnic group men, than is so in Finland or Sweden (Iovanni and Pringle, 2005a, 2005b, 2005c).

4 With the Amato Commission (International Commission on the Balkans, 2005), setting out pathways for Balkan membership of the EU, it has been commented that: 'With [Bulgaria, Romania,] Croatia, Turkey and the rest of the Balkans, this would mean that in just 10 years' time the European Union would contain some 35 member states and perhaps 600 million people, of whom nearly one in six would be Muslim. And that's not counting east European aspirants, such as Ukraine after its orange revolution, and Belarus and Moldova . . . Nor does it include any of the successor states of the Ottoman Empire in the Near East or North Africa, although Morocco has in the past asked if it could apply' (Garton Ash, 2005).

5 There is indeed a growing and urgently needed body of critical research on men in the fields of international relations, foreign policy, war and peace, militarism, and transnational state violence and terrorism. For examples of recent contributions, see, for example, Zalewski and Palpart, 1998; Eduards, 2004; Higate, 2002; http://www.socialsciences.manchester.ac.uk/gipp/events/hmc.htm). Much remains to be done in developing this critical expertise and intervention in what are literally matters of life and death for millions.

References

Åberg, B. (2001) *Samarbet på könsblanade arbetsplatser. En könsteoretisk analys av arbetsdelningen mellan kvinnor och män i två yrken: akutsjuksköterskor och ordningspoliser*, Örebro: Studies in Sociology 1, Örebro Universitet.

Acker, J. (1990) 'Hierarchies, jobs, bodies: a theory of gendered organizations', *Gender and Society*, 4(2), 139–58.

Acsády, J. (1999) 'Chances for feminism in Eastern Europe', *Women's Studies International Forum*, 22(4): 405–09.

Adams, R. and Savran, D. (eds) (2002) *The Masculinity Studies Reader*, Malden, Mass.: Blackwell.

Ala-Mursula, L., Vahtera, J., Pentti, J. and Kivimaki, M. (2004) 'Effect of Employee Worktime Control on Health: A Prospective Cohort Study', *Occupational and Environmental Medicine*, 61(3), 254–61.

Alasuutari, P. and Siltari, J. (1983) *Miehisen vapauden valtakunta. Tutkimus lähiöravintolan tikkakulttuurista.* Tampereen yliopisto sarja B 37.

Alber, J. (1995) 'A Framework for the Comparative Study of Social Services', *Journal of European Social Policy*, 5, 131–49.

Alimo-Metcalfe, B. (1993) 'Women in Management: Organisational Socialisation and Assessment Practices that Prevent Career Advancement', *International Journal of Assessment and Selection*, 1(2), 68–83.

Andersen, J. and Larsen, J.E. (1998) 'Gender, Poverty and Empowerment', *Critical Social Policy*, 18(2), 241–58.

Andersson, S. (2003) *Ordnande praktiker. En studie av status, homosocialitet och manligheter utifrån två närpolisorganisationer*, Stockholm: Stockholms universitet, Pedagogiska institutionen.

Annandale, E. and Hunt, K. (eds) (2001) *Gender Inequalities in Health*, Buckingham and Philadelphia: Open University Press.

Anthias, F. and Yuval-Davis, N. (1992) *Racialized Boundaries: Race, Nation, Gender, Colour and Class and the Anti-racist Struggle*, London: Routledge.

Anttila, J. and Ylöstalo, P. (1999) *Working Life Barometer in the Baltic Countries.* Helsinki: Ministry of Labour, Labour Policy Studies, No. 214.

Anttonen, A. and Sipilä, J. (1996) 'European Social Care Services: Is It Possible to Identify Models?', *Journal of European Social Policy*, 6, 87–100.

Aronson, A. and Kimmel, M. (2001) 'The Saviors and the Saved. Masculine Redemption in Contemporary Films', in Lehman, P. (ed.) *Masculinity. Bodies, Movies, Culture*, New York and London: Routledge, 43–50.

Arrindell, W.A., Steptoe, A. and Wardle, J. (2003) 'Higher Levels of State Depression in Masculine than in Feminine Nations', *Behaviour Research & Therapy*, 41(7), 809–17.

Artazcoz, L., Artieda, L., Borrell, C., Cortes, I., Benach, J. and Garcia, V. (2004) 'Combining Job and Family Demands and Being Healthy – What are the Differences between Men and Women?', *European Journal of Public Health*, 14(1), 43–8.

Askew, S. and Ross, C. (1988) *Boys Don't Cry: Boys and Sexism in Education*, Milton Keynes: Open University Press.

Aslanbeigu, N., Predssman, S. and Summerfield, G. (1994) *Women in the Age of Economic Transformation: Gender Impact of Reform in Post-Socialist and Developing Countries*, London: Routledge.

Åström, L. (1990) *Fäder och söner. Bland svenska män i tre generationer*, Stockholm: Carlsson.
Bak, M. and Bäck-Wiklund, M. (2003) 'Den gode stedfar. Om stedfædre og omsorg', in Hjort, K. and Nielsen, S.B. (eds) *Mænd og omsorg*, København: Hans Reitzel, 203–27.
Baker, P. (2001) 'The International Men's Health Movement', *British Medical Journal*, 3 November 323, 1014–15.
Balkmar, D. and Pringle, K. (2005a) *A Review of Academic Studies Relating to Men's Practices in Sweden*, Critical Research on Men in Europe at: http://www.cromenet.org
Balkmar, D. and Pringle, K. (2005b) *A Review of Official Statistical Data Relating to Men's Practices in Sweden*, Critical Research on Men in Europe at: http://www.cromenet.org
Balvig, F. and Kyvsgaard, B. (2006) 'Vold og overgreb mod kvinder. Dansk rapport vedrørende deltagelse i International Violence Against Women Survey (IVAWS).' [Violence and abuse against women. The Danish report on participation in the International Violence Against Women Survey (IVAWS)]. Copenhagen: University of Copenhagen and the Ministry of Justice Research Unit. February 2006. Retrieved 24 February 2006 from: http://www.jm.dk/wimpdoc.asp?page=dept&objno=44803
Bauman, Z. (1998) 'Europe of Strangers'. Available at: http://www.transcomm.ox.ac.uk/working%20papers/bauman.pdf
Bebbington, P. (1996) 'The Origins of Sex Differences in Depressive Disorder: Bridging the Gap', *International Review of Psychiatry*, 8(4), 295–332.
Bekkengen, L. (2002) *Man får välja. Om föräldraskap och familjeledighet i arbetsliv och familjeliv*, Malmö: Liber.
Bengtsson, M. and Frykman, J. (1987) *Om Maskulinitet. Mannen som forskningsobjekt* [On Masculinity. The Man as an Object of Research], Stockholm: JÄMFO rapport no. 11.
Benrud, L.M. and Reddy, D.M. (1998) 'Differential Explanations of Illness in Women and Men', *Sex Roles. A Journal of Research*, 38(5–6), 375–86.
Bergman, H. and Hobson, B. (2001) 'Compulsory Fatherhood: the Coding of Fatherhood in the Swedish Welfare State', in Hobson, B. (ed.) *Making Men into Fathers: Men, Masculinities and the Social Politics of Fatherhood*, Cambridge: Cambridge University Press, 92–124.
Berthoud, R. and Iacovou, M. (2002) *Diverse Europe: Mapping Patterns of Social Change Across the EU*, Report produced for the ESRC Conference in London, October.
Bhabha, H.K. (1995) 'Are You a Man or a Mouse?', in Berger, M., Wallis, B., Watson, S. and Weems, C. (eds) *Constructing Masculinity*, New York: Routledge.
Binnie, J. (2005) 'Queering Hegemonic Masculinities: Sexual Citizenship and the Queer Politics of Transnational Activism', Conference Paper, Hegemonic Masculinities in International Relations Conference, University of Manchester, 5–6 May.
Black, I. (2002) 'How the Sun Cast a Two-faced Shadow on the Eurozone. Tabloid's View of New Currency Suffered an Irish Sea Change', *Guardian*, 8 January.
Blom, I., Hagemann, K. and Hall, C. (eds) (2002) *Gendered Nations. Nationalism and Gender Order in the Long Nineteenth Century*, Oxford and New York: Berg Publishers.
Bond, M. (2001) 'Men's Experiences of Health Problems and Services in North Derbyshire', *Research Policy and Planning*, 17(2). Available at: http://www.elsc.org.uk/socialcareresource/rpp/articles/1731999art2.htm
Böröcz, J. and Sarkar, M. (2005) 'What is the EU?', *International Sociology*, 20(2): 153–73.
Borowicz, R. and Lapinska-Tyszka, K. (1993) *Syndrom bezrobocia*, Warszawa: Polish Academy of Science.
Bose, C.E. (1987) 'Dual Spheres', in Hess, B.B. and Ferree, M.M. (eds) *Analyzing Gender. A Handbook of Social Science Research*, Newbury Park, Ca.: Sage, 267–85.

Boyle, P., d'Onofrio, A., Maisonneuve, P., Severi, G., Robertson, C., Tubiana, M. and Veronesi, U. (2003) 'Measuring Progress against Cancer in Europe: Has the 15% Decline Targeted for 2000 Come About?', *Annals of Oncology*, 14(8), 1312–25.

Brah, A. (2001) 'Re-framing Europe: Gendered Racisms, Ethnicities and Nationalisms in Contemporary Western Europe', in Fink, J., Lewis, G. and Clarke, J. (eds) *Rethinking European Welfare: Transformations of Europe and Social Policy*, London: Sage.

Brandes, H. and Bullinger, H. (eds) (1996) *Handbuch Männerarbeit* [Manual for working with men], Weinheim: Psychology of Publishing House Union.

Brandth, B. and Kvande, E. (2003) *Fleksible fedre*, Oslo: Universitetsforlaget.

Breines, I., Connell, R.W. and Eide, I. (eds) (2000) *Male Roles, Masculinities and Violence: A Culture of Peace Perspective*, Paris: UNESCO Publishing.

British Crime Survey (2001) Research Development and Statistics Directorate. Home Office Statistical Bulletin 18/01.

Brittan, A. (1989) *Masculinity and Power*, Oxford: Blackwell.

Brod, H. (ed.) (1987) *The Making of Masculinities: The New Men's Studies*, London and Boston: Unwin Hyman.

Brod, H. and Kaufman, M. (eds) (1994) *Theorizing Masculinities*, Newbury Park, Ca.: Sage.

Brown, A. and Caddick, B. (eds) (1993) *Groupwork with Offenders*, London: Whiting & Birch.

Brown, C. (1981) 'Mothers, Fathers, and Children: From Private to Public Patriarchy', in Sargent, L. (ed.) *Women and Revolution. The Unhappy Marriage of Marxism and Feminism*, New York: Maple; London: Pluto.

Bruckenwell, P., Jackson, D., Luck, M., Wallace, J. and Watts, J. (1995) *The Crisis in Men's Health*, Bath: Community Health UK.

Bruggemann, B.R. and Haltenhof, H. (2002) 'Socio-cultural Factors in Understanding Gender Differences regarding Depressive Disorders', *Zeitschrift für Klinische Psychiatrie und Psychotherapie*, 50(1), 101–32.

Bulmer, S. (1998) 'The Protection of Pregnant Women at the Workplace', in Armstrong, K. and Bulmer, S. (eds) *The Governance of the Single European Market*, Manchester: Manchester University Press.

Bunting, M. (2004) *Willing Slaves: How the Overwork Culture is Ruling Our Lives*, London: HarperCollins.

Busch, G., Hess-Diebaecker, D. and Stein-Hilbers, M. (1988) *Den Männern die Hälfte der Familie, den Frauen mehr Chancen im Beruf*, Weinheim: Deutcher Studienverlag.

Cardano, M., Costa, G. and Demaria, M. (2004) 'Social Mobility and Health in the Turin Longitudinal Study', *Social Science and Medicine*, 58(8), 1563–74.

Cardy, C. (1992) *Training for Personal Safety at Work*, Aldershot: Gower.

Carrigan, T., Connell, R.W. and Lee, J. (1985) 'Towards a New Sociology of Masculinity', *Theory and Society*, 14(5), 551–604.

Castelli, C. (1990) *Sesso e aggressività. Alle radici della violenza sessuale*, Milano: Angeli.

Cermakova, M., Haskova, H., Krizkova, A., Linkova, M., Marikova, H., and Musilova, M. (2000) *Souvislosti a zmeny genderovych diferenci v ceske spolecnosti v 90. letech.* [Conditions of and changes of gender differences in Czech society of the 1990s], Praha: Sociologicky ustav – Czech Academy of Sciences.

Cervinkova, H. (2003) *We're Not Playing at Being Soldiers. An Ethnographic Study of the Czech Military And Its Changing Relationship with the State and Society in the Period of Post-Socialist Transformation*, Doctoral thesis. Graduate Faculty, New School for Social Research, New York.

Chant, S. and Gutmann, M.C. (eds) (2000) *Mainstreaming Men into Gender and Development: Development Debates, Reflections and Experiences*, Oxford: Oxfam.

Chapman, R. and Rutherford, J. (eds) (1988) *Unwrapping Masculinity*, London: Lawrence & Wishart.

Chernova, J. (2000) *Russian Federation National Report on Research on Men's Practices. Workpackage 1*, EU FPV Thematic Network: The Social Problem of Men and Societal Problematisation of Men and Masculinities. Available at: http://www.cromenet.org

Chernova, J. (2001a) *Russia National Report on Law and Policy Addressing Men's Practices. Workpackage 3*, EU FP5 Thematic Network: The Social Problem and Societal Problematisation of Men and Masculinities. Available at: http://www.cromenet.org

Chernova, J. (2001b) *Russia National Report on Statistical Information on Men's Practices. Workpackage 2*, EU FP5 Thematic Network: The Social Problem of Men and Societal Problematisation of Men and Masculinities. Available at: http://www.cromenet.org

Christensen, E. (1990) *Børnekår. En undersøgelse af omsorgssvigt i relation til børn og unge i familier med hustrumishandling*, Copenhagen: Akademisk Forlag, Nordisk Psykologi's monografiserie, nr. 31.

Christensen, E. and Koch-Nielsen, I. (1992) *Vold ude og hjemme – en undersøgelse af fysisk vold mod kvinder og mænd* [Violence in and out of the home: an investigation of physical violence against women and men], Copenhagen: Danish National Institute of Social Research, 92:4.

Cleaver, F. (ed.) (2002) *Masculinities Matter! Men, Gender and Development*, London and New York: Zed.

Cockburn, C. (1983) *Brothers: Male Dominance and Technological Change*, London: Pluto.

Cockburn, C. (1991) *In the Way of Women: Men's Resistance to Sex Equality in Organizations*, London: Macmillan – now Palgrave Macmillan.

Collier, R. (1995) *Masculinity, Law and the Family*, London and New York, Routledge.

Collins, P.H. (1990) *Black Feminist Thought*, Boston and London: Unwin Hyman.

Collinson, D.L. (1992) *Managing the Shopfloor: Subjectivity, Masculinity and Workplace Culture*, Berlin: Walter de Gruyter.

Collinson, D.L. and Hearn, J. (1994) 'Naming Men as Men: Implications for Work, Organizations and Management', *Gender, Work and Organization*, 1(1), 2–22.

Collinson, D.L. and Hearn, J. (eds) (1996) *Men as Managers, Managers as Men. Critical Perspectives on Men, Masculinities and Managements*, London: Sage.

Collinson, D.L. and Hearn, J. (2005) 'Men and Masculinities in Work, Organizations and Management', in Kimmel, M., Hearn, J. and Connell, R.W. (eds), *Handbook of Studies on Men and Masculinities*, Thousand Oaks, Ca.: Sage, 289–310.

Communication from the Commission to the Council, the European Parliament, the Economic and Social Committee and the Committee of the Regions (2000) Brussels, 28.6.2000 COM (2000) 379 final.

Connell, R.W. (1987) *Gender and Power: Society, The Person and Sexual Politics*, Cambridge: Polity.

Connell, R.W. (1993) 'The Big Picture: Masculinities in Recent World History', *Theory and Society*, 22(5), 597–623.

Connell, R.W. (1995) *Masculinities*, Cambridge: Polity.

Connell, R.W. (1996) 'Teaching the Boys: New Research on Masculinity, and Gender Strategies for Schools', *Teachers College Record* (USA), 98(2), 206–35.

Connell, R.W. (1998) 'Men in the World: Masculinities and Globalization', *Men and Masculinities*, 1(1), 3–23.

Connell, R.W. (2002) *Gender: An Introduction*, Cambridge: Polity.

Connell, R.W., Hearn, J., and Kimmel, M. (2005) 'Introduction', in Kimmel, M., Hearn, J. and Connell, R.W. (eds) *Handbook of Studies on Men and Masculinities*, Thousand Oaks, Ca.: Sage, 1–12.

Connell, R.W., Schofield, T., Walker, L., Wood, J., Butland, D.L., Fisher, J. and Bowyer, J. (1998) *Men's Health: a Research Agenda and Background Report*, Commonwealth Dept of Family and Community Services, Australia.

Consedine, N.S., Magai, C. and Chin, S. (2004) 'Hostility and Anxiety Differentially Predict Cardiovascular Disease in Men and Women', *Sex Roles*, 50(1–2), 63–75.

Cornwall, A. and White, S.C. (eds) (2000) Special Issue. Men, Masculinities and Development: Politics, Policies and Practice. *IDS Bulletin*, 31(2).

Courtenay, W.H. (2000) 'Constructions of Masculinity and their Influence on Men's Well-being: A Theory of Gender and Health', *Social Science and Medicine*, 50, 1385–401.

Craib, I. (1987) 'Masculinity and Male Dominance', *Sociological Review*, 34(3), 721–43.

Craig, S. (ed.) (1992) *Men, Masculinity and the Media*. Newbury Park. Ca.: Sage.

CVVM (2003) http://www.cvvm.cz/index.php?disp=zpravy&r=1&shw=100172

Dankwort, J. (1992–93) 'Violence against Women: Varying Perceptions and Intervention Practices with Woman Abusers', *Intervention* (Quebec), 92, 34–49.

Davidson, M. and Burke, R. (eds) (2000) *Women in Management: Current Research Issues II*, London: Sage.

Davidson, M.J. and Cooper, C.L. (1984) 'She Needs a Wife: Problems of Women Managers', *Leadership and Organization Development Journal*, 5(3), 3–30.

de Lillo, A. and Schizzerotto, A. (1985) *La valutazione sociale delle occupazioni. Una scala di stratificazione occupazionale per l'Italia contemporanea*, Bologna: II Mulino.

Dicks, B., Waddington, D. and Critcher, C. (1998) 'Redundant Men and Overburdened Women: Local Service Providers and the Construction of Gender in Ex-mining Communities', in Popay, J., Hearn, J. and Edwards, J. (eds) *Men, Gender Divisions and Welfare*, London: Routledge, 287–311.

Digby, T. (ed.) (1998) *Men Doing Feminism*, New York: Routledge.

Division for the Advancement of Women, United Nations. (2003a) 'The role of men and boys in achieving gender equality'. Expert Group Meeting, Organized by DAW. In collaboration with UNDP, ILO and UNAIDS, 21–24 October 2003, Brasilia, Brazil. Retrieved 20 May 2004, from: http://www.un.org/womenwatch/daw/egm/men-boys2003/documents.html

Division for the Advancement of Women, United Nations. (2003b) 'The role of men and boys in achieving gender equality'. Thematic issue before the Commission: The role of men and boys in achieving gender equality. Report to the Secretary-General. Retrieved 20 May 2004, from: http://www.un.org/womenwatch/daw/csw/csw48/Thematic1.html

Domestic Violence against Women and Girls (2000) Innocenti Digest No. 6, Florence: UNICEF.

Dominelli, L. (1991) *Women Across Continents: Feminist Comparative Social Policy*, Hemel Hempstead: Harvester Wheatsheaf.

Donaldson, M. (1993) 'What is Hegemonic Masculinity?', *Theory and Society*, 22(5), 643–57.

Duncan, S. (1995) 'Theorizing European Gender Systems', *Journal of European Social Policy*, 5(4), 263–84.

Duncan, S. (2001) 'Introduction. Theorising Comparative Gender Inequality', in Duncan, S. and Pfau-Effinger, B. (eds) *Gender, Work and Culture in the European Union*, London and New York: Routledge, 1–23.

Duncan, S. and Pfau-Effinger, B. (eds) (2001) *Gender, Work and Culture in the European Union*, London/New York: Routledge.

Eckermann, L. (2000) 'Gendering Indicators of Health and Well-being: Is Quality of Life Gender Neutral?', *Social Indicators Research*, 52(1), 29–54.

Edleson, J.L. (1990) 'Judging the Success of Interventions with Men who Batter', in Besharov, D. (ed.) *Family Violence: Research and Public Policy Issues*, American Enterprise Institute, Washington, DC, 130–45.

Edleson, J.L. and Syers, M. (1990) 'The Relative Effectiveness of Group Treatment with Men who Batter', *Social Work Research and Abstracts*, 26, 10–17.
Edley, N. and Wetherell, M. (1995) *Men in Perspective*, Hemel Hempstead: Harvester Wheatsheaf.
Eduards, M. (2004) 'September 11 and MALE VIOLENCE', *NIKK Magazine*, 3: 25–8.
Education & Action Kit. Men Working To End Men's Violence Against Women (n.d.) Toronto: White Ribbon Campaign. Available at: http://www.whiteribbon.ca/educational_materials/#edkit
Edwards, P. and Elger, T. (eds) (1999) *The Global Economy, National States, and the Regulation of Labour*, London: Mansell.
Edwards, S.S.M. (1996) *Sex and Gender in the Legal Process*, London: Blackstone.
Edwards, S.S.M. (2003) *'Gender Based Violence in the UK'*, Paper presented to Moscow Conference, 26–27, May, organised by AIDOS and FOCUS, for European Commission Tacis Programme.
Edwards, S.S.M. and Hearn, J. (2005) *Working Against Men's 'Domestic Violence': Priority Policies and Practices for Men in Intervention, Prevention and Societal Change*, Strasbourg: Council of Europe.
Edwards, T. (1990) *Erotics and Politics*, London: Unwin Hyman/Routledge.
Edwards, T. (1997) *Men in the Mirror*, London: Cassell.
Eichler, M. (1980) *The Double Standard: A Feminist Critique of Feminist Social Science*, London: Croom Helm.
Ekenstam, C., Frykman, J., Johansson, T., Kuosmanen, J., Ljunggren, J. and Nilsson, A. (eds) (1998) *Rädd att falla. Studier i manlighet*. Hedemora: Gidlund.
Ekenstam, C., Johansson, T. and Kuosmanen, J. (eds) (2001) *Sprickor i fasaden. Manligheter i förändring*. Hedemora: Gidlund.
Eley, G. (1998) 'From Welfare Politics to Welfare States: Women and the Socialist Question', in Gruber, H. and Graves, P. (eds) *Women and Socialism. Socialism and Women. Europe between the Two World Wars*, New York and Oxford: Berghan Books, 516–46
Elstad, J.I. and Krokstad, S. (2003) 'Social Causation, Health-selective Mobility, and the Reproduction of Socioeconomic Health Inequalities over Time: Panel Study of Adult Men', *Social Science and Medicine*, 57(8), 1475–89.
Enloe, C. (1990) *Bananas, Beaches, and Bases: Making Feminist Sense of International Relations*, London: Pluto; Berkeley: University of California Press.
Equal Opportunities to Everybody in Latvia (2001) Draft document, The Ministry of Welfare. Latvia.
Eriksson, M. (2003) *I skuggan av Pappa.* [In the shadow of Daddy. Family law and the handling of fathers' violence], Stehag: Förlags AB Gondolin.
Eriksson, M. (2005) 'A Visible or Invisible Child? Professionals' Approaches to Children whose Father is Violent to the Mother', in Eriksson, M., Hester, M., Keskinen, S. and Pringle, K. (eds) *Tackling Men's Violence in Families – Nordic Issues and Dilemmas*, Bristol: Policy Press.
Eriksson, M. and Hester, M. (2001) 'Violent Men as Good-enough Fathers? A Look at England and Sweden', *Violence Against Women*, 7(7), 779–98.
Eriksson, M., Hester, M., Keskinen, S. and Pringle, K. (eds) (2005) *Tackling Men's Violence in Families – Nordic Issues and Dilemmas*, Bristol: Policy Press.
Eriksson, M., Nenola, A. and Nilsen, M.M. (eds) (2002) *Gender and Violence in the Nordic Countries*, Copenhagen: Nordic Council of Ministers, TemaNord.
Ernst, C. and Angst, J. (1992) 'The Zurich Study. 12. Sex-differences in Depression – Evidence from Longitudinal Epidemiologic Data', *European Archives of Psychiatry and Clinical Neuroscience*, 241(4), 222–30.

Ervø, S. and Johansson, T. (eds) (2003a) *Among Men: Moulding Masculinities Volume 1*, Aldershot: Ashgate.
Ervø, S. and Johansson, T. (eds) (2003b) *Bending Bodies: Moulding Masculinities Volume 2*, Aldershot: Ashgate.
Esping-Andersen, G. (1990) *The Three Worlds of Welfare Capitalism*, Cambridge: Polity Press.
Esping-Andersen, G. (ed.) (1996) *Welfare States in Transition*, London: Sage.
Esping-Andersen, G. (1999) *Social Foundations of Post-industrial Economies*, Oxford: Oxford University Press.
Esping-Andersen, G. with Gallie, D., Hemerijck, A. and Myles, J. (2002) *Why We Need A New Welfare State*, Oxford: Oxford University Press.
EU (2000) Charter of Fundamental Rights of the European Union, *Official Journal of the European Communities* C 364.
European Business Survey (1996) *Proportion of SMEs with No Women in Management*, cited in Vinnicombe, S. (2000) 'The position of women in management in Europe', in Davidson, M.J. and Burke, R.J. (eds), *Women in Management: Current Research Issues: Volume II*, London: Sage, 9–25.
European Business Survey 2002 – 10 Years of a Single European Market . . . (2002) Hong Kong: Grant Thornton. Available at: http://www.grantthornton.com/downloads/GT EBS 2002 New 61637.pdf
European Commission (1994) 'The Way Forward . . .', Brussels: European Commission.
Eurostat (2002) *The Life of Women and Men in Europe. A Statistical Portrait. Data 1980–2000*, Luxembourg: Eurostat/European Commission.
Eurostat: http://www.europa.org/
Feldberg, R.L. and Glenn, E.N. (1979) 'Male and Female: Job versus Gender Models in the Sociology of Work', *Social Problems*, 26(5), 524–38.
Feminist Review Collective (ed.) (2005) *Feminist Review: Post-Communism Issue 76: Women's Lives in Transition*, Basingstoke: Palgrave Macmillan.
Ferguson, H. (1995) 'The Paedophile Priest: A Deconstruction', *Studies*, 84 (335), 247–56.
Ferguson, H. (2000) *Ireland National Report on Research on Men's Practices. Workpackage 1*, EU FPV Thematic Network: The Social Problem of Men and Societal Problematisation of Men and Masculinities. Available at: http://www.cromenet.org
Ferguson, H. (2001a) *Ireland National Report on Law and Policy Addressing Men's Practices. Workpackage 3*, EU FP5 Thematic Network: The Social Problem and Societal Problematisation of Men and Masculinities. Available at: http://www.cromenet.org
Ferguson, H. with the assistance of C. Mackinnon (2001b) *Ireland National Report on Newspaper Representations on Men and Men's Practices. Workpackage 4*, EU FP5 Thematic Network: The Social Problem and Societal Problematisation of Men and Masculinities. Available at: http://www.cromenet.org
Ferguson, H. (2001c) *Ireland National Report on Statistical Information on Men's Practices. Workpackage 2*, EU FP5 Thematic Network: The Social Problem of Men and Societal Problematisation of Men and Masculinities. Available at: http://www.cromenet.org
Ferguson, H. (2006) 'Ireland: Men and Masculinities in a Late-Modern Society', in Pringle, K., Hearn, J., Ferguson, H., Kambourov, D., Kolga, V., Lattu, E., Müller, U., Nordberg, M., Novikova, I., Oleksy, E., Rydzewska, J., Šmídová, I., Tallberg, T. and Niemi, N. *Men and Masculinities in Europe*, London: Whiting & Birch.
Ferguson, H., Hearn, J., Holter, Ø.G., Jalmert, L., Kimmel, M., Lang, J., Morrell, R. and de Vylders, S. (2004) *Ending Gender-based Violence: A Call for Global Action to Involve Men*, Stockholm: SIDA. Available at: http://www.sida.se/content/1/c6/02/47/27/SVI34602.pdf
Ferguson, K. (1984) *The Feminist Case Against Bureaucracy*, Philadelphia, Pa.: Temple University Press.

FitzGerald, M. (2005) 'White boys fail too', *Guardian*, 1 June: 15.

Forsberg, G., Jakobsen, L. and Smirthwaite, G. (2003) *Homosexuellas vilkor i arbetslivet.* Karlstad: Karlstads universitet, jämställdhetscentrum, ämnet Genusvetenskap, Arbetsrapport.

Fossato, F. and Kachkaeva, A. (1998) 'Media Empires IV'. Available at: http://www.rferl.org/nca/special/rumedia4/

Fraser, N. (1989) *Unruly Practices: Power, Discourse and Gender in Contemporary Social Theory*, Cambridge: Polity Press.

Frerichs, P. and Steinrücke, M. (1994) 'Sie tun nur das, was sie sollen, und auch das nicht immer . . .', *Arbeit*, 3, 203–19.

Friedman, S. and Sarah, E. (eds) (1982) *On the Problem of Men*, London: Women's Press.

Gal, S. (1996) 'Feminsísm and civil society', *Replika*, Special Issue 'Feminism', 75–81.

Gardiner, J.K. (ed.) (2002) *Masculinity Studies and Feminist Theory*, New York: Columbia University Press.

Garton Ash, T. (2005) 'For a Pax Europeana', *Guardian*, 14 April. Available at: http://www.guardian.co.uk/Kosovo/Story/0,2763,1459169,00.html

Gibson-Graham, J.K. (1999) *The End of Capitalism (as we knew it)*, Cambridge, Mass: Blackwell.

Giertz, A. (2004) *Making the Poor Work: Social Assistance and Activation Programs in Sweden*, Lund: Lund Dissertations in Social Work, No. 19.

Gillan, E. and Samson, E. (2000) 'The Zero Tolerance Campaigns', in Hanmer, J. and Itzin, C. (eds) *Home Truths about Domestic Violence*, London: Routledge, 340–55.

Glasgow Women's Support Project/Glasgow Evening Times (1990) *Violence Against Women Survey*, Glasgow: Glasgow Women's Support Project.

Glucksmann, M. (1995) 'Why "Work"? Gender and the "Total Social Organization of Labour" ', *Gender, Work and Organization*, 2(2), 63–75.

Gondolf, E.W. (1985) *Men Who Batter: An Integrated Approach for Stopping Wife Abuse*, Holmes Beach, FL.: Learning Publications.

Gondolf, E.W. (1993) 'Male Batterers', in Hampton, R.L. (ed.) *Family Violence: Prevention and Treatment*, Newbury Park, Ca.: Sage, 230–57.

Gondolf, E.W. (1998) 'Multi-site evaluation of batterer intervention systems', Paper at Program Evaluation and Family Violence Research Conference, Durham, NH, cited in Mullender and Burton (2001).

Gondolf, E.W. and Russell, D. (1986) 'The Case against Anger Control Treatment Programs for Batterers', *Response*, 9(3), 2–5.

Green, C.A., Freeborn, D.K. and Polen, M.R. (2001) 'Gender and Alcohol Use: The Roles of Social Support, Chronic Illness, and Psychological Well-being', *Journal of Behavioral Medicine*, 24(4), 383–99.

Greig, A., Kimmel, M. and Lang, J. (2000) *Men, Masculinities and Development: Broadening Our Work Towards Gender Equality*, New York: UNDP, Gender in Development Monograph Series #10. Available at: http://www.undp.org/gender/resources/UNDP_Men_and_Masculinities.pdf

Habermas, J. (1984) *The Theory of Communicative Action. Reason and Rationalization of Society. Vol. 1*, Boston: Beacon.

Habermas, J. (1987) *The Theory of Communicative Action. System and Lifeworld: A Critique of Functionalist Reason. Vol. 2*, Boston: Beacon.

Hagemann-White, C. (2002) 'Violence against Women in the European Context: Histories, Prevalences, Theories', in Griffin, G. and Braidotti, R. (eds) *Thinking Differently: A Reader in European Women's Studies*, London: Zed, 239–51.

Hague, G. (2001) 'Multi-agency Initiatives', in Taylor-Browne, J. (ed.) *What Works in Reducing Domestic Violence?*, London: Whiting and Birch, 275–306.

Hall, S. (ed.) (1997) *Representation. Cultural Representations and Signifying Practices*, London: Sage/Open University Press.
Hankin, B.L., Abramson, L.Y., Moffitt, T.E., Silva, P.A., McGee, R. and Angell, K.E. (1998) 'Development of Depression from Preadolescence to Young Adulthood: Emerging Gender Differences in a 10-year Longitudinal Study', *Journal of Abnormal Psychology*, 107(1), 128–40.
Hanmer, J. (1990) 'Men, Power and the Exploitation of Women', in Hearn, J. and Morgan, D. (eds) *Men, Masculinities and Social Theory*, London and New York: Unwin Hyman/Routledge, 21–42.
Hanmer, J. and Hearn, J. (1999) 'Gender and Welfare Research', in Williams, F., Popay, J. and Oakley, A. (eds) *Welfare Research: A Critical Review*, London: UCL Press, 106–30.
Harcourt, W. (ed.) (2001) Special Issue 'Violence Against Women and the Culture of Masculinity', *Development: the Journal of the Society for International Development*, 44(3).
Harder, M. and Pringle, K. (eds) (1997) *Protecting Children in Europe: Towards a New Millennium*, Aalborg: Aalborg University Press.
Haugen, T., Hammer, G. and Helle, M. (1998) *Den Norske Mannen 1998 (The Nordic Man 1998)*, Oslo: MMI Tabellrapport 23.9.
Havung, M. (2000) *Anpassning till rådande ordning. En studie av manliga förskollärare i förskoleverksamhet.* Lärarhögskolan i Malmö: Institutionen för pedagogik.no. 145.
Hearn, J. (1983) *Birth and Afterbirth: A Materialist Account*, London: Achilles Heel.
Hearn, J. (1987) *The Gender of Oppression: Men, Masculinity and the Critique of Marxism*, Brighton: Wheatsheaf; New York: St. Martin's.
Hearn, J. (1992) *Men in the Public Eye: the Construction and Deconstruction of Public Men and Public Patriarchies*, London and New York: Routledge.
Hearn, J. (1993) 'Emotive Subjects: Organizational men, Organizational Masculinities and the (De)construction of "Emotions"', in Fineman, S. (ed.) *Emotion in Organizations*, London and Newbury Park, Ca.: Sage, 148–66.
Hearn, J. (1996a) 'Deconstructing the Dominant: Making the One(s) the Other(s)', *Organization*, 3(4), 611–26.
Hearn, J. (1996b) 'Is Masculinity Dead? A Critique of the Concept of Masculinity/Masculinities', in Mac an Ghaill, M. (ed.) *Understanding Masculinities*, Buckingham: Open University Press, 202–17.
Hearn, J. (1997) 'The Implications of Critical Studies on Men', *NORA. Nordic Journal of Women's Studies*, 5(1), 48–60.
Hearn, J. (1998a) 'Theorizing Men and Men's Theorizing: Men's Discursive Practices in Theorizing Men', *Theory and Society*, 27(6): 781–816.
Hearn, J. (1998b) *The Violences of Men: How Men Talk About and How Agencies Respond to Men's Violence to Women*, London: Sage.
Hearn, J. (1999a) 'A Crisis in Masculinity, or New Agendas for Men', in Walby, S. (ed.) *New Agendas for Women*, Basingstoke: Macmillan – now Palgrave Macmillan.
Hearn, J. (1999b) 'Educating Men against Violence to Women', *Women's Studies Quarterly*, 27(1–2), 140–51.
Hearn, J. (2000) 'Forskning om maend I fire dele af verden: USA, Australia, England og Norden', *NIKK Magasin*, 1, 7–9; http://www.nikk.uio.no/publikasjoner/nikkmagasin/magasin/mag20001.pdf. Reprinted in English as 'Critical Studies on Men in Four Parts of the World', *NIKK Magasin*, No. 3, 2002, 12–15. Also available at: http://www.nikk.uio.no/publikasjoner/ nikkmagasin/magasin/mag20013.pdf
Hearn, J. (2001) 'Nation, State and Welfare: The Cases of Finland and the UK', in Pease, B. and Pringle, K. (eds) *A Man's World? Changing Men's Practices in a Globalised World*. London: Zed Books, 85–102.

Hearn, J. (2003a) 'Epistemologies for Studying Men', in *Developing Studies on Men in the Nordic Context. A Report on Men's Cultures and Networks Conference. 4th October 2002*, Finnish Council for Equality between Women and Men, Helsinki/Nordic Institute for Women's Studies and Gender Research, Oslo, 53–65. Available at: http://www.tasa-arvo.fi/ta-neuv/developing_studies_on_men_4_10_02.doc

Hearn, J. (2003b) 'Men: power, challenges of power and the "big picture" of globalisation', in Novikova, I. and Kambourov, D. (eds) *Men and Masculinities in the Global World: Integrating Postsocialist Perspectives*, Helsinki: Kikimora Publishers, Aleksantteri Institute, 45–74.

Hearn, J. (2004a) 'From Hegemonic Masculinity to the Hegemony of Men', *Feminist Theory*, 5(1), 97–120.

Hearn, J. (2004b) 'Tracking "the Transnational": Studying Transnational Organizations and Managements, and the Management of Cohesion', *Culture and Organization*, 10(4), 273–90.

Hearn, J. and Collinson, D.L. (1994) 'Theorizing Unities and Differences Between Men and Between Masculinities', in Brod, H. and Kaufman, M. (eds) *Theorizing Masculinities*, Newbury Park, Ca.: Sage, 97–118.

Hearn, J. and Lattu, E. (2000) *Finland National Report on Research on Men's Practices. Workpackage 1*, EU FPV Thematic Network: The Social Problem of Men and Societal Problematisation of Men and Masculinities. Available at: http://www.cromenet.org

Hearn, J. and Lattu, E. (2002) 'The Recent Development of Finnish Studies on Men: A Selective Review and a Critique of a Neglected Area', *NORA: Nordic Journal of Women's Studies*, 10(1), 49–60. Available at: http://www.uta.fi/laitokset/naistutkimus/miestutkimus/

Hearn, J., Kovalainen, A. and Tallberg, T. (2002a) *Gender Divisions and Gender Policies in Top Finnish Corporations*, Helsinki: Swedish School of Economics and Business Administration.

Hearn, J., Lattu, E. and Tallberg, T. (2001a) *Finland National Report on Law and Policy Addressing Men's Practices. Workpackage 3*, EU FP5 Thematic Network: The Social Problem and Societal Problematisation of Men and Masculinities. Available at: http://www.cromenet.org

Hearn, J., Lattu, E. and Tallberg, T. (2001b) *Finland National Report on Newspaper Representations on Men and Men's Practices. Workpackage 4*, EU FP5 Thematic Network: The Social Problem and Societal Problematisation of Men and Masculinities. Available at: http://www.cromenet.org

Hearn, J., Lattu, E. and Tallberg, T. (2001c) *Finland National Report on Statistical Information on Men's Practices. Workpackage 2*, EU FPV Thematic Network: The Social Problem of Men and Societal Problematisation of Men and Masculinities. Available at: http://www.cromenet.org

Hearn, J., Lattu, E. and Tallberg, T. (2003a) 'Minne mies menossa? Miehiä koskevan tutkimuksen kehitys Suomessa' [How's it going, man? The development of studies on men in Finland], *Naistutkimus/Kvinnoforskning* [Women's Studies], 16(1), 6–28.

Hearn, J., Lattu, E., Tallberg, T. and Niemi, H. (2006) 'Finland: Gender Dominance, Gender Equality and Gender-Neutrality', in Pringle, K., Hearn, J., Ferguson, H., Kambourov, D., Kolga, V., Lattu, E., Müller, U., Nordberg, M., Novikova, I., Oleksy, E., Rydzewska, J., Šmídová, I., Tallberg, T. and Niemi, N. *Men and Masculinities in Europe*, London: Whiting & Birch.

Hearn, J. and Morgan, D. (eds) (1990) *Men, Masculinities and Social Theory*, London: Unwin Hyman/Routledge.

Hearn, J., Müller, U., Oleksy, E., Pringle, K., Chernova, J., Ferguson, H., Holter, Ø.G., Kolga, V., Novikova, I. Ventimiglia, C., Lattu, E., Tallberg, T. and Olsvik, E. (2004a)

The European Research Network on Men in Europe: The Social Problem and Societal Problematisation of Men and Masculinities. Volumes 1 and 2, Brussels: European Commission. Available at: http://improving-ser.jrc.it/default/show.gx?Object.object_id=TSER----000000000000121D&_app.page=show-TSR.html

Hearn, J. and Niemi, H. (2005) 'Researching the "Man Problem" in National and Transnational Contexts: men, policy and organisational practices in six EU countries', Hegemonic Masculinities in International Politics Conference, University of Manchester, 5–6 May.

Hearn, J., Oleksy, E. and Pringle, K. (2004b) *The Concept of 'Intersectionality' in Relation to Men's Violences: Developing a Trans-European Analysis and Methodological Framework*, Paper at Nordic Sociology Congress, Malmo, 7 August.

Hearn, J. and Parkin, W. (1983) 'Gender and Organizations: A Selective Review and a Critique of a Neglected Area', *Organisation Studies*, 4(3), 210–42.

Hearn, J. and Parkin, W. (1995) *'Sex' at 'Work'. The Power and Paradox of Organisation Sexuality, Revised and Updated*, Hemel Hempstead: Harvester Wheatsheaf/Prentice Hall; New York: St. Martin's Press.

Hearn, J. and Parkin, W. (2001) *Gender, Sexuality and Violence in Organizations: the Unspoken Forces of Organization Violations*, London: Sage.

Hearn, J., Pringle, K., Müller, U., Oleksy, E., Lattu, E., Chernova, J., Ferguson, H., Holter, Ø.G., Kolga, V., Novikova, I., Pitch, T., Ventimiglia, C., Olsvik, E. and Tallberg, T. (2002b) 'Critical Studies on Men in Ten European Countries: (1) The State of Academic Research,' *Men and Masculinities*, 4(4), 380–408.

Hearn, J., Pringle, K., Müller, U., Oleksy, E., Lattu, E., Chernova, J., Ferguson, H., Holter, Ø.G., Kolga, V., Novikova, I., Ventimiglia, C., Olsvik, E. and Tallberg, T. (2002c) 'Critical Studies on Men in Ten European Countries (2): The State of Statistical Information', *Men and Masculinities*, 5(1), 5–31.

Hearn, J., Pringle, K., Müller, U., Oleksy, E., Lattu, E., Tallberg, T., Chernova, J., Ferguson, H., Holter, Ø.G., Kolga, V., Novikova, I., Ventimiglia, C. and Olsvik, E. (2002d) 'Critical Studies on Men in Ten European Countries (3): The State of Law and Policy', *Men and Masculinities*, 5(2), 199–217.

Hearn, J., Pringle, K., Müller, U., Oleksy, E., Lattu, E., Tallberg, T., Chernova, J., Ferguson, H., Holter, Ø.G., Kolga, V., Novikova, I., Ventimiglia, C., Olsvik, E. (2003b) *Final Report to the Research Directorate of the European Commission for Project Number EU FPV Thematic Network: The Social Problem and Societal Problematisation of Men and Masculinities*, Brussels: Research Directorate, European Commission.

Hearn, J., Pringle, K., Müller, U., Oleksy, E., Lattu, E., Tallberg, T., Ferguson, H., Holter, Ø.G., Kolga, V., Novikova, I. and Raynor, A. (2003c) 'Critical Studies on Men in Ten European Countries (4): Newspapers and Media Representations', *Men and Masculinities*, 6(2), 173–201.

Hearn, J. and Wessels, H. (2006) 'Men's Violence to Women: An Urgent Issue for Education', in Davison, K. and Frank, B. (eds) *Masculinities and Schooling: International Practices and Perspectives*, Althouse Press, Western Ontario, Canada.

Heckert, D.A. and Gondolf, E.W. (2000a) 'Assessing Assault Self-reports by Batterer Program Participants and their Partners', *Journal of Family Violence*, 15, 181–97.

Heckert, D.A. and Gondolf, E.W. (2000b) 'Predictors of Male Violence by Batterer Program Participants', *Journal of Family Violence*, 15, 423–43.

Heikell, T. and Riska, E. (2004) 'Men's Emotional Inexpressivity', *Nordisk Alkohol- & Narkotikatidskrift*, 21, English supplement, 53–62.

Heiskanen, M. and Piispa, M. (1998) *Usko, toivo, hakkaus. Kyselytutkimus miesten naisille tekemästä väkivallasta*, Helsinki: Tilastokeskus. English edn, *Faith, Hope, Battering.*

A Survey of Men's Violence against Women in Finland, Helsinki: Statistics Finland/ Council for Equality between Women and Men.

Helweg-Larsen, K. and Kruse, M. (2004) *Men's Violence against Women: The Extent, Characteristics and Measures to Eliminate Violence. English Summary*, Copenhagen: The National Observatory on Violence Against Women under The Women's Council in Denmark, The National Institute of Public Health, The Minister for Gender Equality.

Helweg-Larsen, K. and Larsen, H.B. (2002) *Unges trivsel år 2002. En undersøgelse med fokus på seksuelle overgreb in barndommen* [The well-being of youth in year 2002. A study focusing on child sexual assault], Copenhagen: National Institute of Public Health.

Hemminki, K. and Li, X.J. (2003) 'Lifestyle and Cancer: Effect of Widowhood and Divorce', *Cancer Epidemiology Biomarkers & Prevention*, 12(9), 899–904.

Hester, M. (2000) 'Child Protection and Domestic Violence: Findings from a Rowntree/NSPCC Study', in Hanmer, J. and Itzin, C. (eds) *Home Truths about Domestic Violence*, London: Routledge, 96–112.

Hester, M. (2005) 'Children, Abuse and Parental Contact in Denmark', in Eriksson, M., Hester, M., Keskinen, S. and Pringle, K. (eds) *Tackling Men's Violence in Families – Nordic Issues and Dilemmas*, Bristol: Policy Press.

Hester, M., Pearson, C. and Harwin, N. (eds) (1998) *Making an Impact. Children and Domestic Violence: A Reader*, Barkingside: Barnardo's; 2nd edn (2000) Jessica Kingsley, London.

Higate, P. (ed.) (2002) *Military Masculinities: Identities and the State*, Westport, Conn.: Greenwood.

Hirdman, Y. (1988) 'Genussystemet – reflexioner kring kvinnors sociala underordning', *Kvinnnovetenskaplig Tidskrift*, 3, 49–63.

Hirdman, Y. (1990) *Att Lägga Livet till Rätta: Studier i Svensk Folkhemspolitik*, Stockholm: Carlssons.

Hobsbawm, E. (1998) *On History*, London: Abacus.

Hobson, B. (ed.) (2002) *Making Men into Fathers: Men, Masculinities and the Social Politics of Fatherhood*, Cambridge: Cambridge University Press.

Hofstede, G. (1980) *Culture's Consequences: International differences in work-related values*, London: Sage.

Holst, E. and Spiess, C.K. (2004) 'The Transition into Work – Specialities for the Hidden Labour Force in Comparison with Other Economically Active Persons', EPAG *Working Paper* 2004–49, Colchester: University of Essex. Available at: http://www.iser.essex.ac.uk/epag/pubs/workpaps/pdf/2004-49.pdf

Holter, Ø.G. (1989) *Menn* [Men], Oslo: Aschehoug.

Holter, Ø.G. (1997) *Gender, Patriarchy and Capitalism. A Social Forms Analysis*, Oslo: University of Oslo.

Holter, Ø.G. (2001a) *Norway National Report on Law and Policy Addressing Men's Practices: Workpackage 3*, EU FP5 Thematic Network: The Social Problem and Societal Problematisation of Men and Masculinities. Available at: http://www.cromenet.org

Holter, Ø.G. (2001b) *Norway National Report on Newspaper Representations on Men and Men's Practices. Workpackage 4*, EU FP5 Thematic Network: The Social Problem and Societal Problematisation of Men and Masculinities. Available at: http://www.cromenet.org

Holter, Ø.G. (2001c) *Norway National Report on Statistical Information on Men's Practices. Workpackage 2*, EU FP5 Thematic Network: The Social Problem of Men and Societal Problematisation of Men and Masculinities. Available at: http://www.cromenet.org

Holter, Ø.G. and Aarseth, H. (1993) *Menns Livssammenheng*, Oslo: Ad Notem Gyldendal.

Holter, Ø.G. and Olsvik, E. (2000) *Norway National Report on Research on Men's Practices. Workpackage 1*, EU FP5 Thematic Network: The Social Problem of Men and Societal Problematisation of Men and Masculinities. Available at: http://www.cromenet.org
Hooks, b. (1984) *Feminist Theory: From Margin to Center*, Boston: South End Press.
Hondagneu-Sotelo, P. and Messner, M.A. (1994) 'Gender Displays and Men's Power: The "New Man" and the Mexican Immigrant Man', in Brod, H. and Kaufman, M. (eds) *Theorizing Masculinities*, Thousand Oaks, London, New Delhi: Sage, 200–18.
Höpflinger, F., Charles, M. and Debrunner, M. (1991) *Familienleben und Berufsarbeit*, Zürich: Seismo.
http://europa.eu.int/abc/index_en.htm
http://menshealthnetwork.org/
http://www.bzga.de
http://www.cromenet.org
http://www.emhfdatabase.org/
http://www.gthk.com.hk/eng/resources/misc2/section2/page1.asp
http://www.hda-online.org.uk/downloads/pdfs/boyshealth_lit_prac_review.pdf
http://www.homeoffice.gov.uk/rds/index.htm
http://www.igh.ualberta.ca/RHD/Synthesis/Gender.pdf
http://www.maennerleben.de
http://www.menshealthforum.org.uk/
http://www.norden.org/jaemst/sk/maend.asp?lang=4
http://www.socialsciences.manchester.ac.uk/gipp/events/hmc.htm
http://www.stakes.fi
http://www.sverige.se
http://www.undp.org/gender/programmes/men/men_ge.html#Beijing + 5 Special
http://www.who.int/mental_health/prevention/suicide/suiciderates/en/
http://www.who.int/violence_injury_prevention/vaw/infopack.htm
http://www.who.org
http://www.who.int/mental_health/prevention/suicide/en/Figures_web0604_table.pdf
Hughes, D. (2002) 'The Use of New Communication and Information Technologies for Sexual Exploitation of Women and Children', *Hastings Women's Law Journal*, 13(1), 127–46.
Human Development Report 2000 (2000) New York: UNDP.
Human Development Report 2003 (2003) New York: UNDP.
Human Development Report 2005 (2005) New York: UNDP.
Iovanni, L. and Pringle, K. (2005a) *A Review of Academic Studies Relating to Men's Practices in Denmark*, Critical Research on Men in Europe at: http://www.cromenet.org
Iovanni, L.and Pringle, K. (2005b) *A Review of Governmental and Policy Documentation Relating to Men's Practices in Denmark*, Critical Research on Men in Europe at: http://www.cromenet.org
Iovanni, L. and Pringle, K. (2005c) *A Review of Official Statistical Data Relating to Men's Practices in Denmark*, Critical Research on Men in Europe at: http://www.cromenet.org
Inglis, T. (2002) 'Sexual Transgression and Scapegoats: A Case Study from Modern Ireland', *Sexualities*, 5(1), 5–24.
Insinga, R.P. and Fryback, D.G. (2003) 'Understanding Differences between Self-ratings and Populations' Ratings for Health in the EuroQOL', *Quality of Life Research*, 12(6): 611–19.
Institute of Management (1995) *National Management Salary Survey*, Kingston-on-Thames: Institute of Management.

nstitute of Management/Remuneration Economics (1998) *UK National Management Survey*, London: Institute of Management.

ntegrationsverket (2002) *Rapport Integration 2002*, Norrköping: Integrationsverket. www.integrationsverket.se

nternational Commission on the Balkans [Amato Commission] (2005) *The Balkans in Europe's Future*, Sofia: Centre for Liberal Strategies. Available at: http://www.balkan-commission.org/activities/Report.pdf

LGA [International Lesbian and Gay Association] (2000) 'World Legal Survey: Poland'. Available at: http://www.ilga.info/Information/Legal_survey/europe/poland.htm

ackson, S. (2003) 'Batterer Intervention Programs', in Jackson, S., Feder, L., Forde, D.R., Davis, R.C., Maxwell, C.D. and Taylor, B.G. *Batterer Intervention Programs: Where do we go from here?*, National Institute of Justice, Washington DC. Available at: http://www.ncjrs.org/txtfiles1/nij/195079.txt

ackson, S., Feder, L., Forde, D.R., Davis, R.C., Maxwell, C.D., and Taylor, B.G. *Batterer Intervention Programs: Where do we go from here?*, National Institute of Justice, Washington DC. Available at: http://www.ncjrs.org/txtfiles1/nij/195079.txt

almert, L. (1984) *Den svenske mannen* [The Swedish Male], Stockholm: Tiden.

anzen, B.L. and Muhajarine, N. (2003) 'Social Role Occupancy, Gender, Income Adequacy, Life Stage and Health: A Longitudinal Study of Employed Canadian Men and Women', *Social Science and Medicine*, 57(8), 1491–503.

ardine, L. and Smith, P. (eds) (1987) *Men in Feminism*, New York: Methuen.

ärvinen, M. (2004) *Hjemløse flygtninger og indvandrere* [Homeless refugees and immigrants]. Copenhagen: Hans Reitzel.

effries, S. (2005) 'Workers of the World', *G2 (Guardian)*, 9 March, 2–3.

ensen, S.O. (2002) *De vilde unge i Aalborg Øst* [The wild youth of East Aalborg], Aalborg: Aalborg University Press.

ohansson, T. (1998) 'Pappor och deras pappor', in Ekenstam, C., Frykman, J., Johansson, T., Kuosmanen, J., Ljunggren, J. and Nilsson, A. (eds) *Rädd att falla. Studier i manlighet*, Hedemora: Gidlund.

ohansson, T. and Kuosmanen, J. (2003) *Manlighetens många ansikten*, Malmö: Liber.

okinen, A. (2000) *Panssaroitu maskuliinisus: mies, väkivalta ja kulttuuri* [Armoured masculinity: man, violence and culture], Tampere: Tampere University Press.

ungnitz, L., Lenz, H.-J., Puchert, R. Puhe, H. and Walter, W. (2004) *Violence against Men. Men's Experiences of Interpersonal Violence in Germany – Results of a Pilot Study*, Berlin: Federal Ministry for Family Affairs, Senior Citizens, Women and Youth.

urczyk, K. and Rerrich, M.S. (1993) *Die Arbeit des Alltags*, München: Lambertus.

ustice for All (2002) White Paper, Cm. 5563, July. Available at: http://www.cjsonline.org

yrkinen, M. (2005) *The Organisation of Policy Meets the Commercialisation of Sex: Global Linkages, Policies, Technologies*, Helsinki: Swedish School of Economics and Business Administration.

Kambourov, D. (2003) 'The Balkan as the Black Male of Europe', in Novikova, I. and Kambourov, D. (eds) *Men and Masculinities in the Global World: Integrating Post-Socialist Perspectives*, Helsinki: Kikimora Press, Alexanteeri University Press, 139–58.

Kamborouv, D. (2006) 'Bulgaria: Men and Balkan Modernity?' in Pringle, K., Hearn, J. Ferguson, H., Kambourov, D., Kolga, V., Lattu, E., Müller, U., Nordberg, M., Novikova, I., Oleksy, E., Rydzewska, J., Šmídová, I., Tallberg, T. and Niemi, N. *Men and Masculinities in Europe*, London: Whiting & Birch.

Kearney, J., Mansson, S.A., Plantin, L., Pringle, K. and Quaid, S. (2000) *Fatherhood and Masculinities*, Sunderland: University of Sunderland.

Kelly, L., Regan, L. and Burton, S. (1991) *An Exploratory Study of the Prevalence of Sexual Abuse in a Sample of 16–21 Year Olds*, London: Polytechnic of North London.

Kempe, J. (ed.) (2000) *Miesnäkökulmia tasa-arvoon* [Male Views on Equality], Equality Publications 2000:5. Helsinki: Council for Equality, Ministry of Social Affairs and Health.

Kerfoot, D. and Knights, D. (1993) 'Management Masculinity and Manipulation: From Paternalism to Corporate Strategy in Financial Services in Britain', *Journal of Management Studies*, 30(4): 659–79.

Ketterer, M.W., Denollet, J., Chapp, J., Thayer, B., Keteyian, S., Clark, V., John, S., Farha, A.J. and Deveshwar, S. (2004) 'Men Deny and Women Cry, but who Dies? Do the Wages of "Denial" include Early Ischemic Coronary Heart Disease?', *Journal of Psychosomatic Research*, 56(1), 119–23.

Kiely, G. (1995) 'Fathers in Families', in McCarthy, I.C. (ed.) *Irish Family Studies: Selected Papers*, Dublin: University College Dublin, 147–58.

Kimmel, M. (ed.) (1987) *Changing Men: New Directions in Research on Men and Masculinity*, Newbury Park, Ca: Sage.

Kimmel, M. (2001) 'Global Masculinities: Restoration and Resistance', in Pease, B. and Pringle, K. (eds) *A Man's World? Changing Men's Practices in a Globalized World*, London: Zed, 21–37.

Kite, C. (2004) 'The Stability of the Globalized Welfare State', in B. Södersten (ed.) *Globalization and the Welfare State*, Basingstoke: Palgrave Macmillan, 213–38.

Kivimaki, M., Vahtera, J., Pentti, J. and Ferrie, J.E. (2000) 'Factors Underlying the Effect of Organisational Downsizing on Health of Employees: Longitudinal Cohort Study', *British Medical Journal*, 320(7240), 971–75.

Kivivuori, J. (1999) *Suomalainen henkirikos. Teonpiirteet ja tekojen olosuhteet vuosina 1988 ja 1996* [Homicide in Finland. Patterns of criminal homicide in Finland in 1988 and 1999], Helsinki: Oikeuspoliittisen tutkimuslaitoksen julkaisuja 159.

Kjøller, M. and Rasmussen, N.K. (2002) *Sundhed og sygelighed i Danmark 2000: og udviklingen siden 1987* [Health and morbidity in Denmark 2000: and development since 1987], Copenhagen: National Institute of Public Health.

Klinth, R. (2002) *Göra pappa med barn. Den svenska pappapolitiken 1960–1995*, Umeå: Boréa.

Kmiecik-Baran, K. (1999) *Mlodiez i przemoc*. Mechanismy socjologiczno-psychologiczne. Warsaw: Wydawnictwo Naukowe PWN [Chief Statistical Office].

Kolga, V. (2000) *Estonia National Report on Research on Men's Practices: Workpackage 1*, EU FP5 Thematic Network: The Social Problem and Societal Problematisation of Men and Masculinities. Available at: http://www.cromenet.org

Kolga, V. (2001a) *Estonia National Report on Law and Policy Addressing Men's Practices: Workpackage 3*, EU FP5 Thematic Network: The Social Problem and Societal Problematisation of Men and Masculinities. Available at: http://www.cromenet.org

Kolga, V. (2001b) *Estonia National Report on Newspaper Representations on Men and Men's Practices. Workpackage 4*, EU FP5 Thematic Network: The Social Problem and Societal Problematisation of Men and Masculinities. Available at: http://www.cromenet.org

Kolga, V. (2001c) *Estonia National Report on Statistical Information on Men's Practices. Workpackage 2*, EU FP5 Thematic Network: The Social Problem of Men and Societal Problematisation of Men and Masculinities. Available at: http://www.cromenet.org

Kolga, V. (2006) 'Estonia: Societal Context and Transitions', in Pringle, K., Hearn, J. Ferguson, H., Kambourov, D., Kolga, V., Lattu, E., Müller, U., Nordberg, M., Novikova, I., Oleksy, E., Rydzewska, J., Šmídová, I., Tallberg, T. and Niemi, N. *Men and Masculinities in Europe*, London: Whiting & Birch.

Koncepcija dzimumu līdz tiesības īstenošanai (2000) [The Gender Equality Initiative. Draft Document], The Ministry of Welfare. Latvia.

Kortteinen, M. (1982) *Lähiö. Tutkimus elämäntapojen muutoksesta*, Helsinki: Otava.

Kristenson, M., Eriksen, H.R., Sluiter, J.K. and Ursin, H. (2004) 'Psychobiological Mechanisms of Socioeconomic Differences in Health', *Social Science and Medicine*, 58(8), 1511–22.

Kristenson, M., Kucinskiene, Z., Bergdahl, B., Calkauskas, H., Urmonas, V. and Orth-Gomer, K. (2003) 'Increased Psychological Strain in Lithuanian versus Swedish men: The LiVicordia Study: Erratum', *Psychosomatic Medicine*, 65(3), 346.

Kruse, M. and Helweg-Larsen, K. (2004) *Kønsforskelle i sygdom og sundhed* [Gender differences in sickness and health], Copenhagen: Minister for Gender Equality.

Kukhterin, S. (2000) 'Fathers and Patriarchs in Communist and Post-communist Russia', in Ashwin, S. (ed.) *Gender, State and Society in Soviet and Post-Soviet Russia*, London and New York: Routledge, 71–89.

Kvande, E. and Brandth, B. (2003) *Fleksible fedre*, Oslo: Universitetsforlaget.

Lahelma, E., Kivelä, K., Roos, E., Tuominen, T., Dahl, E., Diderichsen, F., Elstad, J., Lundberg, O., Rahkonen O., Rasmussen, and Åberg, Y.M. (2002) 'Analysing Changes of Health Inequalities in the Nordic Welfare States', *Social Science and Medicine*, 55, 609–25.

Lahelma, E. Manderbacka, K., Martikainen, P. and Rahkonen, O. (2003) 'Miesten ja naisten väliset sairastavuuserot', in Luoto, R., Viisainen, K. and Kulmala, I. (eds) *Sukupuoli ja terveys*, Jyväskylä: Vastapaino, 21–32.

Lahelma, E., Martikainen, P., Rahkonen, O. and Silventoinen (1999) 'Gender Differences in Illhealth in Finland: Patterns, Magnitude and Change', *Social Science and Medicine*, 48, 7–19.

Lammi-Taskula, J. (1998) *Miesten perhevapaat. Työ ja perhe – kyselyaineiston tuloksia*, Working Papers. 3/1998. Helsinki: STAKES.

Lammi-Taskula, J. (2000) 'Combining Work and Fatherhood in Finland', in Harvey, C.D.H. (ed.) *Walking a Tightrope: Balancing Work and Family*, Aldershot: Ashgate, 1–24.

Langan, M. and Ostner, I. (1991) 'Gender and Welfare: Towards a Comparative Framework', in Room, G. (ed.) *Towards a European Welfare State*, Bristol: SAUS, 127–50.

Larsen, H.B. and Helweg-Larsen, K. (2003) 'Psykiske problemer hos unge, der har været udsat for seksuelle overgreb' [Psychological problems in youth exposed to sexual abuse], *Nordisk Psykologi*, 55(2), 79–93.

Lee, C. and Owens, R.G. (2002) *The Psychology of Men's Health*, Buckingham and Philadelphia: Open University Press.

Leibfried, S. (1993) 'Towards a European Welfare State', in Jones, C. (ed.) *New Perspectives on the Welfare State in Europe*, London: Routledge, 133–56.

Leira, A. (1992) *Welfare States and Working Mothers: The Scandinavian Experience*, Cambridge: Cambridge University Press.

Leira, A. (1994) 'Combining Work and Family: Working Mothers in Scandinavia and the European Community', in Brown, P. and Crompton, R. (eds) *Economic Restructuring and Social Exclusion*, London: UCL Press, 86–107.

Lempert, J. and Ölemann, B. (1995/1998) '. . . *dann habe ich zugeschlagen'. Gewalt gegen Frauen. Auswege aus einem fatalen Kreislauf* ['. . . and then I hit her'. Violence against women. Ways to escape a fatal circle], Hamburg and Munich: Deutscher Taschenbuch Verlag.

Levi, F., Lucchini, F., Negri, E., Boyle, P. and La Vecchia, C. (2004) 'Cancer Mortality in Europe, 1995–1999, and an Overview of Trends since 1960', *International Journal of Cancer*, 110(2), 155–69.

Lewis, J. (1992) 'Gender and the Development of Welfare Regimes', *Journal of European Social Policy*, 2(3), 159–73.

Lewis, J. (ed.) (1993) *Women and Social Policies in Europe: Work, Family and the State*, Aldershot: Edward Elgar.

Lewis, J. and Ostner, I. (1991) 'Gender and the evolution of European social policies', paper at CES Workshop on Emergent Supranational Social Policy: The EC's Social Dimension in Comparative Perspective. Center for European Studies: Harvard University.

Liberty (ed.) (1999) *Liberating Cyberspace: Civil Liberties, Human Rights and the Internet*, London: Pluto/Liberty.

Liebert, U. (1999) 'Gender Politics in the European Union', *European Societies*, 1(2), 197–239.

Lithuanian Human Development Report 2000 (2000) Available at: http://www.un.lt/HDR2000

Loader, B.D. (ed.) (1997) *The Governance of Cyberspace*, London: Routledge.

Loewenthal, K.M., Macleod, A.K., Lee, M., Cook, S. and Goldblatt, V. (2002) 'Tolerance for Depression: Are there Cultural and Gender Differences?', *Journal of Psychiatric & Mental Health Nursing*, 9(6), 681–8.

Long, S. (1999) 'Gay and lesbian movements in Eastern Europe: Romania, Hungary, and the Czech Republic', in Adam, B.D., Duyvendak, J.W. and Krouwel, A. (eds) *The Global Emergence of Gay and Lesbian Politics*, Philadelphia: Temple University Press, 142–65.

LO-notat (2000) A-typiske trek på arbeidsmarkedet (AKU), Samfunnsnotat 13/00.

Lopez-Claros, A. and Zahidi, S. (2005) *Women's Empowerment: Measuring the Global Gender Gap*, Geneva: World Economic Forum. Available at: http://www.weforum.org/pdf/Global_Competitiveness_Reports/Reports/gender_gap.pdf

Lucht, M., Schaub, R.T., Meyer, C., Hapke, U., Rumpf, H.J., Bartels, T., von Houwald, J., Barnow, S., Freyberger, H.J., Dilling, H., John, U. (2003) 'Gender Differences in Unipolar Depression: A General Population Survey of Adults between Age 18 to 64 of German Nationality', *Journal of Affective Disorder*, 77(3), 202–11.

Luck, M., Bamford, M. and Williamson, P. (2000) *Men's Health: Perspectives, Diversity and Paradox*, Oxford: Blackwell Science.

Lundgren, E., Heimer, G., Westerstrand, J. and Kalliokoski, A-M. (2001) *Slagen Dam: Mans Vald mot Kvinnor I Jamstallda Sverige – en Omfangsundersokning* [also in English: *Captured Queen: Men's Violence against Women in 'Equal' Sweden – A Prevalence Study*], Stockholm and Umeå: Fritzes Offentliga Publikationer and Brottsoffermyndigheten.

Lykke, N. (2003) 'Intersektionalitet – ett Användbart Begrepp för Genusforskningen', *Kvinnovetenskaplig Tidskrift*, 24(1), 47–56.

Mackay, J. (2000) *The Penguin Atlas of Human Sexual Behavior, Sexuality and Sexual Practice Around the World*, New York: Penguin.

Mackenbach, J., Kunst, A.E., Groenhof, F., Borgan, J.K., Costa, G., Faggiano, F., Józan, P., Leinsalu, M., Martikainen, P., Rychtarikova, J. and Valkonen, T. (1999) 'Socioeconomic Inequalities in Mortality among Women and among Men: An International Study', *American Journal of Public Health*, 89(12), 1800–06.

Madsen, S.A., Lind, D. and Munck, H. (2002) *Fædres tilknytning til spædbørn* [Fathers' bonding to infants], Copenhagen: Hans Reitzel.

Madsen, S.A., Munck, H. and Tolstrup, M. (1999) *Fædre og fødsler* [Fathers and childbirth], Copenhagen: Frydenlund.

Mangan, J. and Walvin, J. (eds) (1987) *Manliness and Morality*, Manchester: Manchester University Press.

Mansfield, A.K., Addis, M.E. and Mahalik, J.R. (2003) '"Why Won't He Go to the Doctor?": The Psychology of Men's Help Seeking', *International Journal of Men's Health*. Available at: http://www.findarticles.com/p/articles/mi_m0PAU/is_2_2/ai_107836730

Månsson, S.-A. (2001) 'Men's Practices in Prostitution: The Case of Sweden', in Pease, B. and Pringle, K. (eds) *A Man's World: Changing Men and Masculinities in a Globalized World*, London: Zed Books, 191–204.

Månsson, S.-A. and Söderlind, P. (2004) *Sexindustrin på nätet. Aktörer, innehåll, relationer och ekonomiska flöden*, Stockholm: Égalité.

Marikova, H. (1999) *Muz v rodine: Demokratizace sfery soukrome* [A man in the family: democratisation of the private sphere], Praha: Sociologicky ustav – Czech Academy of Sciences.

Marikova, H. (ed.) (2000) *Promeny soucasne ceske rodiny* [Transformations of contemporary Czech family], Praha: SLON.

Mathers, C.D., Sadana, R., Salomon, J., Murray, C. J. and Lopez, A.D. (2001) 'Healthy Life Expectancy in 191 countries, 1999', *The Lancet*, 357, 1685–97.

Mayer, O., Simon, J., Heidrich, J., Cokkinos, D.V. and De Bacquers, D. (2004) 'Educational Level and Risk Profile of Cardiac Patients in the EUROASPIRE II Substudy', *Journal of Epidemiology and Community Health*, 58(1), 47–52.

McKeown, K., Ferguson, H. and Rooney, D. (1998) *Changing Fathers? Fatherhood and Family Life in Modern Ireland*, Cork: Collins Press.

McMahon, A. (1993) 'Male Readings of Feminist Theory: the Psychologization of Sexual Politics in the Masculinity Literature', *Theory and Society*, 22(5), 675–96.

Melkas, T. (1998) *The Gender Barometer. Equality between Men and Women in Finland*, Helsinki: Statistics Finland.

Melkas, T. (2001) *The Gender Barometer. Living Conditions 2002:2*, Helsinki: Statistics Finland/Council for Equality. TANE Publications 2002:2.

Melkas, T. (2004) *Tasa-arvobarometri 2004*. Helsinki: STM. Julkaisuja 2004:20. Available at: http://www.stm.fi/Resource.phx/publishing/store/2004/11/hu1100588891119/passthru.pdf

Meryn, S. and Jadad, A. J. (2001) 'The Future of Men and their Health', *British Medical Journal*, 323, 1013–14.

Meshcherkina, E. (2000) 'New Russian Men. Masculinity Regained?', in Ashwin, S. (ed.) *Gender, State and Society in Soviet and Post-Soviet Russia*, London and New York: Routledge, 105–17.

Messner, M. (1997) *The Politics of Masculinities: Men in Movements*, Thousand Oaks, Ca.: Sage.

Metz-Göckel, S. and Müller, U. (1986) *Der Mann*, Weinheim and Basel: Die Birgitte Studie.

Middleton, P. (1992) *The Inward Gaze*. London: Routledge.

Mies, M. (1986) *Patriarchy and Accumulation on a World Scale: Women in the International Division of Labour*, London: Zed.

Mills, A. and Tancred, P. (eds) (1992) *Gendering Organizational Analysis*, Newbury Park, Ca.: Sage.

Ministry of Social Affairs and Health (1996) *Equality: a Habit to Aim For*, Helsinki: Ministry of Social Affairs and Health Publications on Equality.

Ministry of Social Affairs and Health (1997) *From Beijing to Finland: the Plan of Action for the Promotion of Gender Equality of the Government of Finland*, Helsinki: Publications of the Ministry of Social Affairs and Health 1997: 20.

Mintel (1994) *Men 2000*, London: Mintel.

Mirrlees-Black, C. (1994) *Estimating the Extent of Domestic Violence: Findings from the 1992 BCS*. Home Office Research Bulletin No. 37, London: Home Office Research and Statistics Department.

Modood, T., and Werbner, P. (eds) (1997) *The Politics of Multiculturalism in the New Europe: Racism, Identity and Community*, London: Zed Books.

Moller-Leimkuhler, A.M. (2002) 'Barriers to Help-seeking by Men: A Review of Socio-cultural and Clinical Literature with Particular Reference to Depression', *Journal of Affective Disorders*, 71(1–3), 1–9.

Moller-Leimkuhler, A.M, Bottlender, R., Strauss, A. and Rutz, W. (2004) 'Is there Evidence for a Male Depressive Syndrome in Inpatients with Major Depression?', *Journal of Affective Disorders*, 80(1), 87–93.

Mooney, J. (1993) *The Hidden Figure: Domestic Violence in North London*, London: Centre for Criminology, Middlesex University; Islington, London: Islington Borough Council.

Mooney, J. (1994) *The Prevalence and Social Distribution of Domestic Violence: An Analysis of Theory and Method*, Unpublished Ph.D., Middlesex University.

Mooney, J. (1999) *The North London Domestic Violence Survey: Final Report*, London: Middlesex University.

Morley, R. and Mullender, A. (1994) 'Domestic violence and children: what do we know from research?' in Mullender, A. and Morley, R. (eds) *Children Living with Domestic Violence*, Whiting & Birch, London, 24–42.

Morrell, R. (ed.) (2001) *Changing Men in Southern Africa*, London: Zed.

Morrell, R. and Swart, S. (2005) 'Men in the Third World: Postcolonial perspectives on masculinity', in Kimmel, M., Hearn, J. and Connell, R.W. (eds) *Handbook of Studies on Men and Masculinities*, Thousand Oaks, Ca.: Sage, 90–113.

Mozny, I. (1991) *Proc tak snadno . . .* [Why so easy . . .], Praha: SLON.

Mullender, A. (1997) *Rethinking Domestic Violence: the Social Work and Probation Response*, London: Routledge.

Mullender, A. and Burton, S. (2001) 'Dealing with perpetrators' in Taylor-Browne, J. (ed.) *What Works in Reducing Domestic Violence?*, London: Whiting and Birch.

Müller, U. (2000) *Germany National Report on Research on Men's Practices. Workpackage 1*, EU FP5 Thematic Network: The Social Problem of Men and Societal Problematisation of Men and Masculinities. Available at: http://www.cromenet.org

Müller, U. (2001a) *UK National Report on Law and Policy Addressing Men's Practices: Workpackage 3*, EU FP5 Thematic Network: The Social Problem and Societal Problematisation of Men and Masculinities. Available at: http://www.cromenet.org

Müller, U. (2001b) *Germany National Report on Statistical Information on Men's Practices. Workpackage 2*, EU FP5 Thematic Network: The Social Problem of Men and Societal Problematisation of Men and Masculinities. Available at: http://www.cromenet.org

Müller, U. (2006) 'Germany: Traditionalism and Difference, Unification and Diversification', in Pringle, K., Hearn, J., Ferguson, H., Kambourov, D., Kolga, V., Lattu, E., Müller, U., Nordberg, M., Novikova, I., Oleksy, E., Rydzewska, J., Šmídová, I., Tallberg, T. and Niemi, N. *Men and Masculinities in Europe*, London: Whiting & Birch.

Müller, U. and Jacobsen, A. (2001) *Germany National Report on Newspaper Representations on Men and Men's Practices. Workpackage 4*, EU FP5 Thematic Network: The Social Problem and Societal Problematisation of Men and Masculinities. Available at: http://www.cromenet.org

Müller, U. and Schröttle, M. (2004) *Health, Well-being and Personal Safety of Women in Germany. A Representative Study of Violence against Women in Germany*, Berlin: Federal Ministry for Family Affairs, Senior Citizens, Women and Youth.

Munday, B. (1996) 'Introduction: Definitions and Comparisons in Europe', in Munday, B. and Ely, P. (eds) *Social Care in Europe*, Hemel Hempstead: Prentice Hall Europe, 1–20.

Murphy, J.M., Horton, N.J., Laird, N.M., Monson, R.R., Sobol, A.M. and Leighton, A.H. (2004) 'Anxiety and Depression: A 40-year Perspective on Relationships regarding Prevalence, Distribution, and Comorbidity', *Acta Psychiatrica Scandinavica*, 109(5), 355–75.

Mustard, C.A, Vermeulen, M. and Lavis, J.N. (2003) 'Is Position in the Occupational Hierarchy a Determinant of Decline in Perceived Health Status?', *Social Science and Medicine*, 57(12), 2291–303.

The National Health Promotion Strategy 2000–2005 (2001) Dublin: Department of Health and Children.

Neale, S. (1983) 'Masculinity as Spectacle', *Screen*, 24(6), 2–16.

Nehls, E. (2003) *Vägvalet. Lastbilsförare i fjärrtrafik. Perspektiv på yrkeskultur och genus*, Göteborg: Etnologiska Föreningen i Västsverige, no. 41.

The Network Newsletter (2000) Special issue 'Gender and Masculinities' (British Council), 21.

Niedhammer, I. and Chea, M. (2003) 'Psychosocial Factors at Work and Self Reported Health: Comparative Results of Cross Sectional and Prospective Analyses of the French GAZEL Cohort', *Occupational and Environmental Medicine*, 60(7), 509–15.

Niemi, I., Eglite, P., Mitrikas, A., Patrushev, V. and Paakonen, H. (1991) *Time Use in Finland, Latvia, Lithuania and Russia*. Helsinki: Central Statistical Office in Finland.

Nielsen, S.B. (2003) 'Mænd søges! – om de herskende forståelser af behovet for mænd i dagsinstitutioner' [Men wanted! – on the prevailing understandings of the need for men in daycare institutions], in Hjort, K. and Nielsen, S.B. *Mænd og omsorg* [Men and care], Copenhagen: Hans Reitzel, 27–47.

Nikander, T. (1995) *Suomalaismiehen perheellistyminen*, Helsinki: Statistics Finland.

Nixon, S. (1997) 'Exhibiting Masculinity', in Hall, S. (ed.) *Representation. Cultural Representations and Signifying Practices*, London: Sage/Open University Press, 291–330.

Nordberg, M. (2000) 'Hegemonibegreppet och hegemonier i mansforskningsfältet', in Folkesson, P., Nordberg, M. and Smirthwaite, G. (eds) *Hegemoni och mansforskning. Rapport från Nordiska workshopen i Karlstad 19–21 mars 1999*. Karlstads universitet: Institutionen för samhällsvetenskap & Jämställdhetscentrum, 37–66.

Nordberg, M. (2001) 'Teori som importvara "hegemonisk maskulinitet" – teoretiskt axiom i svensk genusforskning med fokus på män?', in Johansson, A. (ed.) *Svensk genusforskning i världen*, Göteborg: Nationella sekretariatet för genusforskning, 124–42.

Nordberg, M. (2002) 'Constructing Masculinity in Women's Worlds. Men working as Pre-school Teachers and Hairdressers', *NORA (Nordic Journal of Women's Studies)*, 10(1), 26–37.

Nordberg, M. (2005) *Jämställdhetens spjutspets? Män i kvinnoyrken, maskulinitet, femininitet och heteronormer*, Göteborg: Mara.

Nordberg, M. (2006) 'Sweden: the Gender Equality Paradise?', in Pringle, K., Hearn, J. Ferguson, H., Kambourov, D., Kolga, V., Lattu, E., Müller, U., Nordberg, M., Novikova, I., Oleksy, E., Rydzewska, J., Šmídová, I., Tallberg, T. and Niemi, N. *Men and Masculinities in Europe*, London: Whiting & Birch.

Notz, G. (1991) *'Du bist als Frau um einiges mehr gebunden als der Mann'. Die Auswirkungen der Geburt des ersten Kindes auf die Lebens- und Arbeitsplanung von Muettern und Vätern*, Bonn: Dietz.

Novikova, I. (2000a) *Latvia National Report on Research on Men's Practices. Workpackage 1*, EU FPV Thematic Network: The Social Problem of Men and Societal Problematisation of Men and Masculinities. Available at: http://www.cromenet.org

Novikova, I. (2000b) 'Soviet and Post-Soviet Masculinities: After Men's Wars in Women's Memories', in Breines, I., Connell, R. and Eide, I. (eds) *Male Roles, Masculinities and Violence. A Culture of Peace Perspective.* Paris: UNESCO, 117–29.

Novikova, I. (2001a) *Latvia National Report on Law and Policy Addressing Men's Practices. Workpackage 3,* EU FP5 Thematic Network: The Social Problem and Societal Problematisation of Men and Masculinities. Available at: http://www.cromenet.org

Novikova, I. (2001b) *Latvia National Report on Newspaper Representations on Men and Men's Practices. Workpackage 4,* EU FP5 Thematic Network: The Social Problem and Societal Problematisation of Men and Masculinities. Available at: http://www.cromenet.org

Novikova, I. (2001c) *Latvia National Report on Statistical Information on Men's Practices. Workpackage 2,* EU FP5 Thematic Network: The Social Problem of Men and Societal Problematisation of Men and Masculinities. Available at: http://www.cromenet.org

Novikova, I. (2006) 'Latvia and the (Re)Creation of Nationhood', in Pringle, K., Hearn, J., Ferguson, H., Kambourov, D., Kolga, V., Lattu, E., Müller, U., Nordberg, M., Novikova, I., Oleksy, E., Rydzewska, J., Šmídová, I., Tallberg, T. and Niemi, N. *Men and Masculinities in Europe,* London: Whiting & Birch.

O'Brien, M. (1981) *The Politics of Reproduction,* London: Routledge & Kegan Paul.

O'Brien, M. (1986) *Reproducing the World,* Boulder, Col: Westview.

O'Connor, J.S. (1993) 'Gender, Class and Citizenship in the Comparative Analysis of Welfare State Regimes: Theoretical and Methodological Issues', *British Journal of Sociology,* 44, 501–18.

Oakley, A. (1985) *Sex, Gender and Society,* Aldershot: Gower.

Oakley, A. and Rigby, A.S. (1998) 'Are Men Good for the Welfare of Women and Children?', in *Men, Gender Divisions and Welfare,* Popay, J., Hearn, J. and Edwards, J. (eds), London: Routledge, 101–27.

OECD Employment Outlook (2002) Paris: OECD. Available at: http://www1.oecd.org/publications/e-book/8102081E.PDF

Ohlsson, L. and Sundgren Grinups, B. (1994) *Jämställdhetskunskap,* Karlstad: Högskolan i Karlstad: Jämställdhetscentrum.

Oleksy, E. (2000) *Poland National Report on Research on Men's Practices. Workpackage 1,* EU FPV Thematic Network: The Social Problem of Men and Societal Problematisation of Men and Masculinities. Available at: http://www.cromenet.org

Oleksy, E. (2001a) *Poland National Report on Law and Policy Addressing Men's Practices: Workpackage 3,* EU FP5 Thematic Network: The Social Problem and Societal Problematisation of Men and Masculinities. Available at: http://www.cromenet.org

Oleksy, E. (2001b) *Poland National Report on Newspaper Representations on Men and Men's Practices. Workpackage 4,* EU FP5 Thematic Network: The Social Problem and Societal Problematisation of Men and Masculinities. Available at: http://www.cromenet.org

Oleksy, E. (2001c) *Poland National Report on Statistical Information on Men's Practices. Workpackage 2,* EU FP5 Thematic Network: The Social Problem of Men and Societal Problematisation of Men and Masculinities. Available at: http://www.cromenet.org

Oleksy, E. and Rydzewska, J. (2006) 'Poland: Gender Relations in the "New Europe"' in Pringle, K., Hearn, J., Ferguson, H., Kambourov, D., Kolga, V., Lattu, E., Müller, U., Nordberg, M., Novikova, I., Oleksy, E., Rydzewska, J., Šmídová, I., Tallberg, T. and Niemi, N. *Men and Masculinities in Europe,* London: Whiting & Birch.

Olsen, B.M. (2000) *'Nye fædre på orlov – en analyse af de kønsmæssige aspekter ved forældreorlovsordninger'* [New fathers on leave – an analysis of the gender aspects of parental leave schemes], Ph.D. Series Nr. 14, Department of Sociology, Copenhagen: Copenhagen University.

Olsen, L.R., Mortensen, E.L. and Bech, P. (2004) 'Prevalence of Major Depression and Stress Indicators in the Danish General Population', *Acta Psychiatrica Scandinavica*, 109(2), 96–103.

Orloff, A.S. (1993) 'Gender and the Social Rights of Citizenship: State Policies and Gender Relations in Comparative Research', *American Sociological Review*, 58, 303–28.

Ostner, I. (1994) 'The Women and Welfare Debate', in Hantrais, L. and Mangan, S. (eds) *Family Policy and the Welfare of Women. Cross-National Research Papers*, Third Series, 3. Loughborough: European Research Centre, University of Loughborough.

Oushakine, S. (ed.) (2002) *On Masculinity*, Moscow: Novoe Literaturnoe Obozrenie.

Ouzgane, L. and Coleman, D. (1998) Postcolonial Masculinities: Introduction. *Jouvert: A Journal of Postcolonial Studies*, 2(1). Available at: http://social.chass.ncsu.edu/jouvert/v2i1/con21.htm

Ouzgane, L. and Morrell, R. (eds) (2005) *African Masculinities: Men in Africa from the Late Nineteenth Century to the Present*, Basingstoke: Palgrave Macmillan.

På tal om kvinnor och män [On Men and Women] Stockholm: SCB.

Papic, Z. (2003) Violence: Eastern Europe. In Helsinki Forum. Available at: http://www.mv.helsinki.fi/helsinkiforum/english/text/papic.html

Pease, B. and Pringle, K. (eds) (2001) *A Man's World? Changing Men's Practices in a Globalized World*, London: Zed.

Pedersen, T.B. et al. (1996) *Kjønn i media* [gender in the media], Conference report. Oslo: The Women's Studies Secretariat, Research Council of Norway.

Pence, E. and M. Paymar, M. (1990) *Power and Control Tactics of Men who Batter*, Duluth: Minnesota Program Development.

Pence, E. and M. Paymar, M. (1993) *Power and Control: Tactics of Men Who Batter: An Educational Curriculum*, Duluth, Mn.: Minnesota Program Development.

Penttilä, M. (1999) 'Paperiin piirretty mies: *Cosmoksen, Men's Healthin ja Miehen Glorian mieskuva'* [Sketches of a man: the images of men in *Cosmos, Men's Health* and *Men's Gloria*], *Tiedotustutkimus*, 22(2), 22–9.

Perlman, F., Bobak, M., Steptoe, A., Rose, R. and Marmot, M. (2003) 'Do Health Control Beliefs Predict Behaviour in Russians?', *Preventive Medicine*, 37(2), 73–81.

Peterson, V. and Runyan, A. (1999) *Global Gender Issues*, Boulder, Co: Westview Press.

Pielkowa, A. (1997) 'Postrzeganie przez meza bezrobotnego wlasnej pozycji w obrebie rodziny', *Roczniki Socjologii Rodziny*, 9, 233–41.

Pirog-Good, M.A. and Stets-Kealey, J. (1985) 'Male Batterers and Battering Prevention Programs: A National Survey', *Response*, 8, 8–12.

Plantin, L. (2001) *Män, familjeliv & föräldraskap*, Umeå: Borea.

Plummer, K. (ed.) (1981) *The Making of the Modern Homosexual*, London: Hutchinson.

Plummer, K. (ed.) (1992) *Modern Homosexualities*, London: Routledge.

Popay, J., Hearn, J. and Edwards, J. (eds) (1998) *Men, Gender Divisions and Welfare*, London: Routledge.

Powell, Gary (1988) *Women and Men in Management*, Newbury Park, Ca.: Sage.

Power, A. and Tunstall, R. (1997) *Dangerous Disorder: Riots and Violent Disturbances in thirteen areas of Britain 1991–1992*, York: York Publishing Services.

Price, R.H., Friedland, D.S. and Vinokur, A.D. (1998) 'Job Loss: Hard Times and Eroded Identity', in Harvey, J.H. (ed.) *Perspectives on Loss: A Sourcebook*, Philadelphia, Pa.: Brunner/Mazel, 303–16.

Pringle, K. (1995) *Men, Masculinities and Social Welfare*, London: UCL Press.

Pringle, K. (1998a) *Children and Social Welfare in Europe*, Buckingham: Open University Press.

Pringle, K. (1998b) 'Men as Carers', in Popay, J., Hearn, J. and Edwards, J. (eds) *Men, Gender Divisions and Welfare*, London: Routledge, 312–36.

Pringle, K. (1998c) 'Men as Workers in Professional Child Care Settings', in Owen, C., Cameron, C. and Moss, P. (eds) *Men as Workers in Services for Young Children. Issues of a Mixed Gender Workforce*, London: Institute of Education, University of London, 163–81.

Pringle, K. (1998d) 'Profeminist Debates on Men's Practices and Social Welfare', *British Journal of Social Work*, 28: 623–33.

Pringle, K. (2000) *UK National Report on Research on Men's Practices. Workpackage 1*, EU FPV Thematic Network: The Social Problem of Men and Societal Problematisation of Men and Masculinities. Available at: http://www.cromenet.org

Pringle, K. with the assistance of Raynor, A. and Millett, J. (2001) *UK National Report on Law and Policy Addressing Men's Practices. Workpackage 3*, EU FPV Thematic Network: The Social Problem and Societal Problematisation of Men and Masculinities. Available at: http://www.cromenet.org

Pringle, K. (2002) *Final Report to the ESRC on Project R000223551*, on REGARD DATABASE website at: http://www.esrcsocietytoday.ac.uk

Pringle, K. (2003) 'Paradise Never Attained Rather than Paradise Lost? – Some Nordic Welfare Systems in a Comparative Perspective', Inaugural Lecture for the Chair in Social Work, Aalborg University, 12 December. Published 2005 as FoSo Research Paper, no. 1, Aalborg: FoSo, Aalborg University.

Pringle, K. (2004) 'Maends Vold – en enormt globalt problem' [Men's violence – an enormous global problem], *NIKK magazine*, 1/2004, 23–5.

Pringle, K. (2005) 'Neglected Issues in Swedish Child Protection Policy and Practice: Age, Ethnicity and Gender', in Eriksson, M., Hester, M., Keskinen, S. and Pringle, K. (eds) *Tackling Men's Violences in Families – Nordic Issues and Dilemmas*, Bristol: Policy Press.

Pringle, K. (2006) 'United Kingdom: the Problems that Men Create and the Problems that Men Experience', in Pringle, K., Hearn, J., Ferguson, H., Kambourov, D., Kolga, V., Lattu, E., Müller, U., Nordberg, M., Novikova, I., Oleksy, E., Rydzewska, J., Šmídová, I., Tallberg, T. and Niemi, N. *Men and Masculinities in Europe*, London: Whiting & Birch.

Pringle, K. and Harder, M. (1999) *Through Two Pairs of Eyes: A Comparative Study of Danish Social Policy and Child Welfare Practice*, Aalborg: Aalborg University Press.

Pringle, K., Hearn, J., Ferguson, H., Kambourov, D., Kolga, V., Lattu, E., Müller, U., Nordberg, M., Novikova, I., Oleksy, E., Rydzewska, J., Šmídová, I., Tallberg, T. and Niemi, H. (2006) *Men and Masculinities in Europe*, London: Whiting and Birch.

Pringle, K., Raynor, A. and Millett, J. (2001) *UK National Report on Statistical Information on Men's Practices. Workpackage 2*. EU FPV Thematic Network: The Social Problem of Men and Societal Problematisation of Men and Masculinities. Available at: http://www.cromenet.org

The Protection of Women against Violence (2002), Recommendation Rec/(2002)5, Strasbourg: Council of Europe.

Rai, S., Pilkington, H. and Phizaclea, A. (eds) (1992) *Women in the Face of Change: The Soviet Union, Eastern Europe and China*, London: Routledge.

Råkil, M. (ed.) (2002) *Menns vold mot kvinner. Behandlingserfaringer og kunnskapsstatus*, Oslo: Universitetsforlaget (Aschehoug).

Ramberg, I. (2001a) *Seminar. 'A New Social Contract between Women and Men: The Role of Education'. Proceedings*, 7–8 December 2000, EG/ED (2000) 13, Strasbourg: Council of Europe.

Ramberg, I. (2001b) *Violence against Young Women in Europe: Seminar Report*, Strasbourg: Human Rights Education Programme/Council of Europe Publishing.

Raynor, A., Pringle, K. and Millett, J. (2001) *UK National Report on Newspaper Representations on Men and Men's Practices. Workpackage 4*, EU FPV Thematic Network: The Social Problem and Societal Problematisation of Men and Masculinities. Available at: http://www.cromenet.org

Reinicke, K. (2002) *Den hele mand – manderollen i forandring* [The whole man: masculinity in transition], Copenhagen: Schønberg.

Reinicke, K. (2004) *Mænd i lyst og nød* [Men for better or for worse], Copenhagen: Schønberg.

Reis, C. (2004) *The Private and Public Lives of Men Managers in a European Transnational Company*, Mering and München: Rainer Humpp Verlag.

Research and Development Statistics of British Home Office: http://www.homeoffice.gov.uk/rds/index.htm

Respect (2000) *Statement of Principles and Minimum Standards of Practice*, London.

Ribet, C., Zins, M., Gueguen, A., Bingham, A., Goldberg, M., Ducimetiere, P. and Lang T. (2003) 'Occupational Mobility and Risk Factors in Working Men: Selection, Causality or Both? Results from the GAZEL Study', *Journal of Epidemiology and Community Health*, 57(11), 901–06.

Rieder, A. and Meryn, S. (2001) 'Sex and Gender Matter', *The Lancet*, 358(9284), 8 September.

Rigspolitichefen [National Police Commissioner] (1998) *Vold på gaden, i hjemmet og på arbejdet – oversigt over resultater fra voldsofferundersøgelsen 1995/1996* [Violence on the street, in the home and at work: an overview of the results from a violence victimisation study 1995/1996], Copenhagen: Rigspolitichefens Trykkeri.

Rikollisuus ja seuraamusjärjestelmä tilastojen valossa [Crime and Criminal Justice in Finland] (1997) Helsinki: Oikeuspoliittinen tutkimuslaitos.

Riska, E. (2004) *Masculinity and Men's Health: Coronary Heart Disease in Medical and Public Discourse*, Lanham, Md.: Rowman & Littlefield.

Robertsson, H. (2002) *Maskulinitetskonstruktioner och könssegregering i sjukvård. Manliga sjuksköterskor och hegemonisk maskulinitet.* Arbetsliv i omvandling, Stockholm: Arbetslivsinstitutet.

Roche, M. and van Berkel, R. (eds) (1997) *European Citizenship and Social Exclusion*, Aldershot: Ashgate.

Romanov, K., Hatakka, M., Keskinen, E., Laaksonen, H., Kaprio, J., Rose, R.J. and Koskenvuo, M. (1994) 'Self-Reported Hostility and Suicidal Acts, Accidents, and Accidental Deaths: A Prospective Study of 21,443 Adults Aged 25 to 59', *Psychosomatic Medicine*, 56, 328–36.

Room, G. (1992) 'Social Exclusion, Solidarity and the Challenge of Globalization', *International Journal of Social Welfare*, 8, 166–74.

Roper, M.R. (1994) *Masculinity and the British Organization Man since 1945*, Oxford: Oxford University Press.

Rowbotham, S. (1979) 'The Trouble with Patriarchy', *New Statesman*, 98, 970–1.

Roxburgh, S. (2004) ' "There Just aren't Enough Hours in the Day": The Mental Health Consequences of Time Pressure', *Journal of Health and Social Behaviour*, 45, 115–31.

Russian Federation National Report on Newspaper Representations on Men and Men's Practices. Workpackage 4 (2001) EU FPV Thematic Network: The Social Problem of

Men and Societal Problematisation of Men and Masculinities. Available at: http://www.cromenet.org

Ruxton, S. (ed.) *Gender Equality and Men*, Oxford: Oxfam.

Sabo, D. (2005) 'The Study of Masculinities and Men's Health: An overview', in Kimmel, M., Hearn, J. and Connell, R.W. (eds) *Handbook of Studies on Men and Masculinities*, Thousand Oaks, Ca.: Sage, 326–52.

Sabo, D. and Gordon, D.F. (eds) (1995) *Men's Health and Illness*, Thousand Oaks, Ca.: Sage.

Said, E. (1979) *Orientalism*, New York: Vintage.

Sainsbury, D. (1996) *Gender, Equality and Welfare States*, Cambridge: Cambridge University Press.

Sainsbury, D. (ed.) (1994) *Gendering Welfare States*, London: Sage.

Sainsbury, D. (ed.) (1999) *Gender and Welfare State Regimes*, Oxford: Oxford University Press.

Salisbury, J. and Jackson, D. (1995) *Challenging Macho Values*, London: Falmer.

Sanne, B., Mykletun, A., Dahl, A., Moen, B.E., Tell, Grethe, S. (2003) 'Occupational Differences in Levels of Anxiety and Depression: The Hordaland Health Study', *Journal of Occupational and Environmental Medicine*, 45(6), 628–38.

Sattel, Jack, W. (1976) 'The Inexpressive Male: Tragedy or Sexual Politics?', *Social Problems*, 23, 469–77.

SCB (2002) *OM kvinnor och män. Liten lathund om Jämställdhet*, Statistiska Centralbyrån.

Schacht, S.P. and Ewing, D. (eds) (1998) *Feminism and Men: Reconstructing Gender Relations*, New York: New York University Press.

Schmeiser-Rieder, A., Kiefer, I. and Panuschka, C., Hartl, H., Leitner, B., Schmeiser, M., Csitkovics, M., Schmidl, H. and Kunze, M. (1999) 'The Men's Health Report of Vienna 1999', *Aging Male*, 2, 166–79.

Seager, A. (2005) 'No Vote Hurts Euro with Consumer and Company Confidence on the Ropes', *Guardian*, 1 June: 14.

Segal, L. (1990) *Slow Motion: Changing Masculinities, Changing Men*, London: Virago.

Sennett, R. (1998) *The Corrosion of Character: the Personal Consequences of Work in the New Capitalism*, London: W.W. Norton.

Shephard, M.F. and Pence, E.L. (eds) (1999) *Coordinating Community Responses to Domestic Violence: Lessons from Duluth and Beyond*, Thousand Oaks, Ca.: Sage.

Šiklová, J. (1996) 'Jiný kraj, jiné ženy' [Different country, Different women], *Respekt*, 13/1996, 17.

Smart, C. (1999) 'The "New" Parenthood: Fathers and Mothers after Divorce', in Silva, E.B. and Smart, C. (eds) *The New Family*, London: Sage, 100–14.

Smejklová, J. (1996) 'On the road: Smuggling feminism across the post-Iron Curtain', *Replika*, Special Issue 'Feminism': 97–102. Available at: http://www.c3.hu/scripta/scripta0/replika/honlap/english/01/10fsmej.htm

Šmídová, I. (2002) 'Muži v České republice podle Jiných mužů', *Sociální studia*, 7, 89–117.

Šmídová, I. (2003) 'Matkové', in *Modernizace a česká rodina*. Brno: Barrister & Principal, 157–76.

Šmídová, I. (2006) 'Czech Republic: Domination and Silences', in Pringle, K., Hearn, J., Ferguson, H., Kambourov, D., Kolga, V., Lattu, E., Müller, U., Nordberg, M., Novikova, I., Oleksy, E., Rydzewska, J., Šmídová, I., Tallberg, T. and Niemi, N. *Men and Masculinities in Europe*, London: Whiting & Birch.

Smith, L. (1989) *Domestic Violence: an Overview of the Literature*, Home Office Research Study 107, London: HMSO.

Sørensen, B.W. (2001) 'Men in transition: the representations of men's violence against women in Greenland', *Violence Against Women*, 7(7), 826–47.

Stanko, E., Crisp, D., Hale, C. and Lucraft, H. (1998) *Counting the Costs: Estimating the Impact of Domestic Violence in the London Borough of Hackney*, Swindon: Crime Concern.

Stanley, L. and Wise, S. (1983) *Breaking Out: Feminist Consciousness and Feminist Research*, London: Routledge & Kegan Paul.

The Statistical Yearbook of Latvia, Riga: State Committee for Statistics of the Republic of Latvia.

Steinert, H. and Pilgram, A. (eds) (2002) *Welfare Policy from Below: Struggles against Social Exclusion in Europe. Towards a Dynamic Understanding of Participation*, Aldershot: Ashgate.

Sterr, L. (1997) *Frauen und Männer auf der Titelseite. Strukturen und Muster der Berichterstattung am Beispiel einer Tageszeitung*, Pfaffenweiler: Centaurus.

Stychin, C.F. (2003) *Governing Sexuality: The Changing Politics of Citizenship and Law Reform*, Oxford: Hart Publishing.

Sulkunen, P., Alasuutari, P., Nätkin, R. and Kinnunen, M. (1985) *Lähiöravintola* [The local restaurant], Helsinki: Otava.

The Swedish Institute (2001) *Dear Child – on Men, Children and Gender Equality in Sweden*, Stockholm: The Swedish Institute.

Sweetman, C. (1997) 'Introduction', *Gender and Development*, 5(2), 2–7.

Sweetman, C. (ed.) (2001) *Men's Involvement in Gender and Development Policy and Practice: Beyond Rhetoric*, Oxford: Oxfam.

Szaflarski, M. and Cubbins, L.A. (2004) 'Self-reported Health in Poland and the United States: A Comparative Analysis of Demographic, Family and Socioeconomic Influences', *Health*, 8(1), 5–31.

Taniguchi, K., Akechi, T., Suzuki, S., Mihara, M. and Uchitomi, Y. (2003) 'Lack of Marital Support and Poor Psychological Responses in Male Cancer Patients', *Supportive Care in Cancer*, 11(9), 604–10.

Tarkowska, E. (1992) *Czas w zyciu Polakow*. Warszawa: Polaska Akademia nauk.

Tartakovskaya, I. (2000) 'The Changing Representation of Gender Roles in the Soviet and Post-Soviet Press', in Ashwin, S. (ed.) *Gender, State and Society in Soviet and Post-Soviet Russia*, London and New York: Routledge, 118–36.

Thayer, J.F., Rossi, L.A., Ruiz-Padial, E. and Johnsen, B.H. (2003) 'Gender Differences in the Relationship between Emotional Regulation and Depressive Symptoms', *Cognitive Therapy and Research*, 27(3), 349–64.

Tigerstedt, C. (1994) 'Kotityö ja isyys uusina projekteina?', in Roos, J.P. and Peltonen, E. (eds) *Miehen elämää*, Helsinki: Tietolipas, 68–85.

Time Use Survey 1996 (1998) Warsaw: Chief Statistical Office.

Tjeder, D. (2003) *The Power of Character: Middle-class Masculinities, 1800–1900*, Stockholm University.

Todaro, J.F., Shen, B.J., Niaura, R., Spiro, A. and Ward, K.D. (2003) 'Effect of Negative Emotions on Frequency of Coronary Heart Disease (The Normative Aging Study)', *American Journal of Cardiology*, 92(8), 901–06.

Tolman, R.M. and Bennett, L.W. (1990) 'A Review of Quantitative Research on Men who Batter', *Journal of Interpersonal Violence*, 5, 87–118.

Travis, A. (2004) 'Britain's Family Revolution: Poll Shows Parents Reject "Workaholic" Life', *Guardian*, 17 August. Available at: http://www.guardian.co.uk/guardianpolitics/story/0,,1284591,00.html

Treaty establishing a Constitution for Europe (2004) *Official Journal of the European Union*, C 310, Volume 47, 16.12.2004. Available at: http://www.unizar.es/euroconstitucion/Treaties/Treaty_Const.htm

Trifiletti, R. (1999) 'Southern European Welfare Regimes and the Worsening Position of Women', *Journal of European Social Policy*, 9, 49–64.
Tuchman, G. (1973) 'The Technology of Objectivity: Doing "Objective" T.V. News Film', *Urban Life and Culture*, 2, 3–26.
Tyyskä, V. (1995) *The Politics of Caring and the Welfare State: the Impact of the Women's Movement on Child Care Policy in Canada and Finland, 1960–1990*, Helsinki: Suomalainen Tiedeakatemia, ser B, tom 277.
UNICEF (1999) *Women in Transition*, Regional Monitoring Reports, No. 6. Florence: UNICEF International Child Development Centre.
Urlanis, B. (1978) 'And Over Again – Take Care of Men', *Literaturnaya gaseta*, 7 June.
Vahtera, J., Kivimaki, M., and Pentti, J. (1997) 'Effect of Organizational Downsizing on Health Employees', *The Lancet*, 350, 1124–8.
Veikkola, E.-S. (2002) 'Sukupuolten asema tilastoissa' [Gender in statistics] in Holli, A.M., Saarikoski, T. and Sana, E. (eds) *Tasa-arvopolitiikan haasteet* [Challenges of gender equality policies], Helsinki: WSOY, 50–69.
Veikkola, E.-S., Hänninen-Salmelin, E. and Sinkkonen, S. (1997) 'Is the Forecast for Wind or Calm?', in Veikkola, E.-S. (ed.) *Women and Men at the Top: A Study of Women and Men at the Top*, Helsinki: Gender Statistics 1997:1. Statistics Finland, 82–7.
Ventimiglia, C. (1987) *La Differenza Negata. Ricerca sulla Violenza Sessuale in Italia.* Milano: Angeli.
Ventimiglia, C. (2001a) *Italy National Report on Law and Policy Addressing Men's Practices. Workpackage 3*, EU FP5 Thematic Network: The Social Problem and Societal Problematisation of Men and Masculinities. Available at: http:// www.cromenet.org
Ventimiglia, C. (2001b) *Italy National Report on Newspaper Representations on Men and Men's Practices. Workpackage 4*, EU FP5 Thematic Network: The Social Problem and Societal Problematisation of Men and Masculinities. Available at: http:// www.cromenet.org
Ventimiglia, C. and Pitch, T. (2000) *Italy National Report on Research on Men's Practices. Workpackage 1*, EU FPV Thematic Network: The Social Problem of Men and Societal Problematisation of Men and Masculinities. Available at: http://www.cromenet.org
Ventimiglia, C. and Pitch, T. (2001) *Italy National Report on Statistical Information on Men's Practices. Workpackage 2*, EU FPV Thematic Network: The Social Problem of Men and Societal Problematisation of Men and Masculinities. Available at: http:// www.cromenet.org
Vinnicombe, S. (2000) 'The position of women in management in Europe', in Davidson, M.J. and Burke, R.J. (eds), *Women in Management: Current Research Issues: Volume II*, London: Sage, 9–25.
Waddington, D., Critcher, C. and Dicks, B. (1998) '"All Jumbled Up": Employed Women and Unemployed Husbands', in Popay, J., Hearn, J. and Edwards, J. (eds) *Men, Gender Divisions and Welfare*, London: Routledge, 231–56.
Waddington, J. (ed.) (1999) *Globalization and Patterns of Labour Resistance*, London: Mansell.
Wagstyl, S. (2005) 'Accession States Reap Rewards of EU Membership', *Financial Times*, 27 April, 3.
Wahl, A. (ed.) (1995) *Men's Perception of Women and Management*, Stockholm: Fritzes.
Wahl, A. and Holgersson, C. (2003) 'Male Managers' Reactions to Gender Diversity Activities in Organisations', in Davidson, M. and Fielden, S. (eds) *Individual Diversity in Organisations*, London: John Wiley, 313–30.
Walby, S. (1986) *Patriarchy at Work: Patriarchal and Capitalist Relations in Employment*, Cambridge: Polity.

Walby, S. (1990) *Theorizing Patriarchy*, Oxford: Blackwell.

Walby, S. (1997) *Gender Transformations*, London: Routledge.

Walby, S. (1999) 'The European Union and Equal Opportunities Policies', *European Societies*, 1(1), 59–80.

Waldron, I. (2001) 'Trends in Gender Differences in Mortality: Relationships to Changing Gender Differences in Behaviour and Other Causal Factors', in Annandale, E. and Hunt, K. (eds) *Gender Inequalities in Health*, Buckingham and Philadelphia: Open University Press, 150–81.

Waters, M. (1990) 'Patriarchy and Viriarchy', *Sociology*, 23(2), 193–211.

Watson, P. (1996) 'The Rise of Masculinism in Eastern Europe', in Threlfall, M. (ed.) *Mapping the Women's Movement: Feminist Politics and Social Transformations in the North*, London, New York: Verso, 216–31.

Watson, J. (2000) *Male Bodies*, Buckingham: Open University Press.

Weeks, J. (1977/1990) *Coming Out: Homosexual Politics in Britain, From the Nineteenth Century to the Present*, 2nd edn, 1990, London: Quartet.

Weeks, J., Heaphy, B. and Donovan, C. (2001) *Same Sex Intimacies: Families of Choice and other Life Experiments*, London: Routledge.

West, C. and Fenstermaker, S. (1995) 'Doing Difference', *Gender and Society*, 9(1), 8–37.

Westwood, S. (1990) 'Racism, Masculinity and the Politics of Space', in Hearn, J. and Morgan, D. (eds) *Men, Masculinities and Social Theory*, London and New York: Unwin Hyman/Routledge.

Wetherell, M. and Edley, N. (1999) 'Negotiating Hegemonic Masculinity: Imaginary Positions and Psycho-discursive Practices', *Feminism & Psychology*, 9(3), 335–56.

Wheller, C. (2004) 'Russia's Poor Cut Adrift by Putin's Revolution', *Guardian*, 12 August, 10.

White, A. and Cash, K. (2003) *A Report on the State of Men's Health across European Countries*, Brussels: The European Men's Health Forum.

White, A.K. and Banks, I. (2004) 'Help Seeking in Men and the Problems of Late Diagnosis', in Kirby, R.S., Culley, C.C., Kirby, M.G. and Farah, R.N. (eds) *Men's Health*, 2nd edn, London: Taylor & Francis/Martin Dunitz, 1–17.

Whitehead, S.M. (2002) *Men and Masculinities: Key themes and new directions*, Cambridge: Polity.

Willitts, M., Benzeval, M. and Stansfeld, S. (2004) 'Partnership History and Mental Health over Time', *Journal of Epidemiology and Community Health*, 58(1), 53–8.

WHO (2000) 'Men, Ageing and Health', *Aging Male*, 3, 3–36.

Yuval-Davis, N. (1997) *Gender and Nation*, London: Sage.

Zalewski, M. and Palpart, J. (eds) (1998) *The 'Man' Question in International Relations*, Boulder, Col.: Westview.

Zamarripa, M.X., Wampold, B.E. and Gregory, E. (2003) 'Male Gender Role Conflict, Depression and Anxiety: Clarification and Generalizability to Women', *Journal of Counseling Psychology*, 50, 167–74.

Zavadskaya, L. (ed.) (2001) *Gender Examination of Russian Legislation Moscow. Constitution of Russian Federation* (1993). Moscow.

Zeny a muzi v cislech [Women and men in figures] (2000) Praha: CSU and MPSV [Czech Statistical Office and Ministry of Work and Social Affairs].

Zeny a muzi v datech 2003 [Women and men in data 2003] (2003) Praha: CSU and MPSV (Czech Statistical Office and Ministry of Work and Social Affairs).

Index